KT-567-557

Online Searching
An Introduction

Online Searching
An Introduction

W.M. HENRY, PhD, MRIC, MIInfSci
Unilever Research Laboratory,
Port Sunlight, Merseyside

J.A. LEIGH, BSc
British Library, Science Reference Library, London

L.A. TEDD, BSc, MIInfSci, AMBCS
Consultant in Computer Systems in Libraries

P.W. WILLIAMS, BA, BSc, PhD, FBCS, FIMA, MIInfSci
Computation Department, University of Manchester
Institute of Science and Technology

UNIVERSITY OF STRATHCLYDE
Architecture & Building Science
Information Room

BUTTERWORTHS
LONDON – BOSTON
Sydney – Wellington – Durban – Toronto

United Kingdom	**Butterworth & Co (Publishers) Ltd** London: 88 Kingsway, WC2B 6AB
Australia	**Butterworths Pty Ltd** Sydney: 586 Pacific Highway, Chatswood, NSW 2067 Also at Melbourne, Brisbane, Adelaide and Perth
Canada	**Butterworth & Co (Canada) Ltd** Toronto: 2265 Midland Avenue, Scarborough, Ontario, M1P 4S1
New Zealand	**Butterworths of New Zealand Ltd** Wellington: T & W Young Building, 77–85 Customhouse Quay, 1, CPO Box 472
South Africa	**Butterworth & Co (South Africa) (Pty) Ltd** Durban: 152–154 Gale Street
USA	**Butterworth (Publishers) Inc** Boston: 10 Tower Office Park, Woburn, Mass. 01801

All rights reserved. No part of this publication may be reproduced or transmitted in any form or by any means, including photocopying and recording, without the written permission of the copyright holder, application for which should be addressed to the Publishers. Such written permission must also be obtained before any part of this publication is stored in a retrieval system of any nature.

This book is sold subject to the Standard Conditions of Sale of Net Books and may not be re-sold in the UK below the net price given by the Publishers in their current price list.

First published 1980

© Butterworth & Co. (Publishers) Ltd., 1980

ISBN 0 408 106 964

British Library Cataloguing in Publication Data

Online searching.
   1. On-line bibliographic searching
I. Henry, W M
029.7   Z699.3   80–40242

   ISBN 0–408–10696–4

D
025 · 04
ONL

Typeset by Scribe Design, Gillingham, Kent
Printed & bound in England by Redwood Burn Ltd,
Trowbridge & Esher

Preface

UNIVERSITY OF STRATHCLYDE

Architecture & Building Science

Information Room

In library and information work the 1970s were a time of rapid change and development. Technology at last began to make big inroads into areas where customs and techniques had scarcely altered for decades, and provided the means to transform some long-cherished ideas into working realities. One innovation in particular, online searching, has made a tremendous impact; and for anyone of serious intent entering the library or information profession in the 1980s, a sound knowledge of this technique will be essential. The continuing growth in demand for education and training in the use of online searching is a sign that its importance and potential are now widely accepted.

Although some specific examples from real systems have been given in this book, it is not directed towards any particular system. Most of the search facilities available have been described in a general fashion, so that readers may acquire an overall view of the range available to them. This approach is vindicated by the manner in which desirable features on one system are, whenever possible, adopted by other systems. The first three chapters provide a general overview of online searching, including the scope of the services and databases, and the equipment that is required. Chapters 4–7 give a detailed description of search facilities and techniques, including information about database structure. The last three chapters include a discussion on the role of the intermediary, details of the management aspects, and a description of aids and methods for the task of education and training.

The field of online bibliographic searching is still rapidly developing, with new systems operators, databases, search facilities and communication networks becoming available. It is inevitable, therefore, that part of the material presented here will soon become outdated, although much of it will remain valid for a considerable time. In view of this, it cannot be emphasised too often that the best sources of current information, particularly with regard to the appendices, are the user manuals and newsletters issued by the systems operators. The authors felt that some indication of the features of the different systems was essential to appreciate the variety of systems and the differences from one to another. Therefore a series of appendices have been included giving some details of a number of systems operators.

The authors have a wide experience of online searching, and have been active in its development in the UK. Their range of interests covers education, industry, research and management, and this variety is reflected by their different styles and approaches to the subject. The book evolved from a seminar at which the authors gave an introduction to online searching for bibliographic references, and it is designed for an audience including both managers and would-be practitioners. No attempt has been made to cover the retrieval of information from videotex systems such as Prestel, or the retrieval of statistical or other non-bibliographic information, since it was felt that these areas require a quite separate treatment.

Malcolm Henry
John Leigh
Lucy Tedd
Philip Williams

Contents

Chapter 1   General Introduction   1

Chapter 2   Origin and Scope of the Services and Databases   6

2.1   How the industry came into being   6
2.2   The suppliers of online services   7
2.3   Subject coverage   9
2.4   Size of databases   12
2.5   Document descriptions   13
2.6   Databases — some points to watch   18

Chapter 3   The Hardware   20

3.1   Introduction   20
3.2   The network   21
3.3   The telephone   22
3.4   Computer terminals and their selection   23
3.5   Modems   26

Chapter 4   How to Search   28

4.1   The main operations   28
4.2   Connecting to the online system   29
4.3   Selecting the file to be searched   31
4.4   The search proper: selecting and combining search terms   31
4.5   Printing the results   34
4.6   Some further system features   36
4.7   Getting information about online searching   41

Chapter 5   The Structuring of Information within a Database   43

5.1   General   43
5.2   Record structure   45
5.3   File structure   45
5.4   Adding a record to the database   47
5.5   Dictionaries   47

5.6	Treatment of phrases	54
5.7	Inversion of the document record	55

Chapter 6 The Search Facilities Available — 57

6.1	Introduction	57
6.2	Single term	57
6.3	Term truncation	58
6.4	Displaying dictionaries	60
6.5	Field searching	61
6.6	Phrase searching	65
6.7	Combining terms and search statements	65
6.8	Proximity operators	67
6.9	String searching	68
6.10	Limiting searches	69
6.11	The save search facility	70
6.12	Multifile searching	71
6.13	Search history	71
6.14	A common (all-purpose) command language	71
6.15	Conclusion	72

Chapter 7 Search Preparation and Strategy — 75

7.1	The typical online search	75
7.2	Being prepared	78
7.3	Receiving the search request	78
7.4	Deciding whether enquiry is suitable for online	79
7.5	Choosing which files to search	79
7.6	Which systems to use	80
7.7	Analysing the search topic	80
7.8	The selection of search terms	82
7.9	Preparing a plan	89
7.10	The terminal	90
7.11	Obtaining the results	92
7.12	Searching for chemicals	92

Chapter 8 The Role of the Intermediary — 95

8.1	Introduction	95
8.2	Comparisons of searcher alternatives	96
8.3	The functions of an intermediary	98
8.4	The qualities required to be an intermediary	99
8.5	Conclusions	99

Chapter 9 Management of Aspects of Online Searching — 101

9.1	The role of management	101
9.2	Persuading higher management	101
9.3	Publicising the service	102
9.4	Training the staff	103

9.5	Setting up a service	104
9.6	Running the service	105
9.7	Running costs	105
9.8	Charging for the service	106
9.9	The impact of staff	107
9.10	The development function	108

Chapter 10 Education and Training — 109

10.1	Introduction	109
10.2	Who is involved in education and training?	110
10.3	Aspects in the design of courses	112
10.4	Aids in teaching	115
10.5	Conclusions	119

Note to the Appendices — 121

Appendix 1 A Check List for Search Preparation and Search Strategy — 123

Appendix 2 Blaise — 128

Appendix 3 ESA–IRS — 138

Appendix 4 Infoline — 145

Appendix 5 Lockheed — 151

Appendix 6 SDC — 173

Appendix 7 Euronet — 188

Chapter 1

General Introduction

It is now possible by means of a simple telephone call to gain access to hundreds of information collections containing a total of tens of millions of document abstracts. Information equal in extent to a million books or more can be searched to find the items which are relevant to a specific query. All that is needed, in addition to the telephone, is a teletypewriter and a device to connect this to the telephone. A teletypewriter is very like a typewriter but there are additional keys for communicating with a computer. The connection box, which can be about the size of this book, converts the electrical signals from the teletypewriter to audible signals which are sent down the telephone line, and reverses the process for the return messages. Because of the simplicity of these systems and the large amount of information which has now been made available, there has been a dramatic effect on the way information is accessed.

For some years technical information has been expanding too fast for most people to keep pace, even with the knowledge in their own specialist area. The number of journals has grown dramatically, and this has accelerated the growth of secondary abstracting services which direct users to the source journals containing articles relevant to a particular topic. It is the high volume of material covered by these abstracting journals that has indirectly produced the development that will alleviate the literature-searching problem, at least for a time.

The problem of printing accurately, in the shortest possible time, the lists of references in a collection of abstracts is particularly suitable for a computer solution. The correction and editing process is straightforward when the information is in electronic form; the information is held on the computer and can be verified from a keyboard connected to the computer and modified when necessary. Also, the sorting and re-formatting which is necessary to give the different forms of the abstract collection, such as alphabetical author list, inverted file in alphabetical order of keywords, lists in classification order, and other lists, are much simpler when the information is moved round in electronic form. Furthermore, the magnetic tape holding the information can be delivered to the printer and used to produce the printed output directly. The various type sizes and founts, the layout and the text justification can all be produced by signals inserted by a computer program. Thus, the commercial economics of efficient publication give, as a by-product, complete data on the journal references in a computer-readable form. This makes them available for computer searching or for distribution to individual organisations.

One of the first organisations to make use of this technique was the US National Library of Medicine in the mid-1960s in the production of the printed *Index Medicus* and the related MEDLARS (Medical Literature Analysis and Retrieval System) files. Since then many organisations have made use of a computer in the production of their abstract journals and have thus generated files of machine-readable bibliographic descriptions; these files are usually called databases. The range of databases available at the present time includes reference collections in most scientific and technical disciplines and also, increasingly, in the educational, sociological, economic, business and humanities areas. In addition, there are now many machine-readable files of numerical information; these are known as databanks. There are also some information systems containing the full text of documents for retrieval.

These databases were initially made available in the late 1960s to users as a batch search service — that is, queries were submitted to a central organisation and these queries were then gathered together. This made a cost-effective way of searching the computer files, but the searcher received the results some time later. However, the public impact of this method of information supply was small, and the recent explosive development of computerised information services was dependent on the extent and reliability of communication networks for the interchange of computer messages. These were first developed by large organisations such as banks, building societies and big corporations, where it was important for many units to have access to accurate current data. The technology developed in this way led to networks of communications through which any member of the public could access computers via the normal public telephone network.

Networks such as Tymnet and Telenet became available in North America in the early 1970s and were soon accessible from Europe as well as other countries in the world. Euronet provides a European network for the transmission of digital information.

Another important development was the setting up of organisations providing the necessary computing facilities to store these databases and to enable the searchers to communicate directly with the databases in an 'online' manner. Examples of such organisations include Lockheed and SDC (System Development Corporation) and BRS (Bibliographic Retrieval Service) in the USA, Blaise (British Library Automated Information Service) and Infoline in the UK, and DIMDI (Deutsches Institut für Medizinische Dokumentation und Information) and ESA (European Space Agency) in Europe. Thus, it is the conjunction of simple access through the public telephone network with large reference collections available in computer-readable form that has created the present easy access to information.

The growth resulting from these developments has been dramatic. Williams[1] estimates that there were 700 000 searches in 1974, 1 000 000 in 1975, 1 200 000 in 1976 and 2 000 000 in 1977. The number of searches in the UK has been increasing rapidly and was in excess of 100 000 in 1978.

The major users of the service are in industry and commerce, with academic institutions next. The public libraries use the services less but their usage is growing.

Searching is performed by looking for a match between search terms and terms stored in the description of the journal article. These terms may be phrases such as *information retrieval* or *library management systems*, or words such as *information, retrieval*, etc. There are also methods to allow for uncertainty. For example, COMPUT? will give a match with all phrases beginning with these six letters, such as *computer, computing, computable, compute, computation, computer-aided design, computer systems,* etc. Also, ON*LINE will match with *online, on-line* and *on line*. In some systems there are methods to allow for matching a fragment of a word, which is particularly useful for chemical names. These searches may be restricted to terms from an approved thesaurus of controlled-language terms which indexers and searchers must use, or alternatively a free-language system may be used where a searcher can use any words that seem descriptive of the search topic. Matches may be sought with terms from many sections – for example, the title, the abstract, the indexing field – or a search may be made for a particular author name or journal name, or the name of the sponsoring institution of the author. In some subjects there are also standard classification codes which can be used for searches. These possibilities give very flexible search systems, and individual search terms can be combined by specifying either that any of a number of terms must be present or that all of a number of terms must be present.

The searching process typically starts with a searcher choosing search terms either by consulting printed dictionaries of approved terms or by inspecting the dictionaries stored in the computer by printing out sections at the terminal. The selected terms are then fed into the computer. At each stage the number of items referenced under a selected search description is printed, so that the user can modify the search by combining terms, or by trying new terms, until a reasonable number of items has been selected from the database. The selected items can then be printed either online at the terminal, when there is a small volume of printed material, or offline at the site of the computer, from where they are despatched by post to the user. The selected items can usually be printed in a variety of ways: in a short format, such as an abstract number; or as abstract number and title; or as full bibliographic reference – that is, author, title, journal reference, classification codes, indexing terms; or as full bibliographic reference plus an abstract of perhaps 600 words. The systems at present available do not normally provide access to the full text of a reference, although there are some systems which enable a photocopy or microfiche to be ordered from the terminal.

The newcomer to online searching will want to know how these computer systems relate to normal manual methods of searching the literature. The most obvious feature of the computer systems is that each search can be costed, so that the cost of information becomes highlighted. If a research assistant spends a few days in the library pursuing references, the cost to an organisation is hidden. There is a strong tendency to accept hidden costs but not overt ones, so the cost of online searching may be an important factor determining the usage of the systems. The power of these systems will quickly become evident to the new user. An extensive list of synonyms can easily be used combined with other similar sets to provide a search that would be very tedious to perform manually. The immediate notification of the number of references for a chosen search definition gives the opportunity for repeated refinement until satisfactory results are achieved. The convenience of having finally a printed list of the references will not be underestimated by anyone who has painstakingly copied a few dozen references from the abstract journals. Online searching typically enables the searcher to access directly different parts of the record as well as the individual words in the title or abstract, thus alleviating much of the serial searching necessary when a printed index is used. Speed is another advantage of online searching. An online search is many times faster than a search of the printed version of the same database. In one study Johnston found that an online search took on average one-sixth of the time of a manual search[2].

There are, of course, some drawbacks to online searching. One problem is the need for special equipment; another is the need for a suitable person to carry out the search. This is discussed further in Chapter 8. There are also occasional problems with equipment which may mean a delay before a search can be carried out. At present most of the databases only cover literature published since about 1970, and in most subjects online searches for earlier material cannot be made. There are occasions when a manual search would be as effective (for example, consulting the papers by a known author or obtaining a sample of the references under a specific subject heading), but, in general, the main deterrent to using the systems will be whether the value of the information exceeds the cost of obtaining it.

In the remaining chapters the searching process will be discussed in detail and the implications of online searching will be explored. It is clear from the reactions of the users that these new systems encourage access to the literature for many who would otherwise have been badly informed. The case for online systems is not primarily that they are a more cost-effective way of carrying out our present activities; it is, rather, that a new expense will give the average user a completely new level of contact with information in his subject area. In the past access to abundant energy produced dramatic changes in our capability, as did the advent of computer power. Perhaps easy access to accumulated information will lead to another radical increase in our achievements.

REFERENCES

1. Williams, M.E. 'Database and online statistics', *Bulletin of American Society of Information Scientists*, **4**, No. 2, 21–23 (1977)
2. Johnston, S.M. 'Choosing between manual and online searching – practical experience in the Ministry of Agriculture, Fisheries and Foods', *Aslib Proceedings*, **30**, Nos 10, 11, 383–393 (1978)

FURTHER READING

Atherton, P. and Christian, R.W. *Librarians and Online Services*, Knowledge Industry Publications, White Plains, N.Y. (1977). ISBN 0-914236-13-X
Cuadra, C. 'Commercially funded online retrieval services – past, present, and future', *Aslib Proceedings*, **30**, No. 1, 2–15 (1978)
Hall, J.L. *Online Information Retrieval Sourcebook*, Aslib, London (1977). ISBN 0-85142-106-7
Hawkins, D.T. 'Online information retrieval bibliography'. Second update, *Online Review*, **3**, No. 1, 37–73 (1979)
Houghton, B. and Convey, J. *Online Information Retrieval Systems*, Bingley, London (1977). ISBN 0-208-01660-0

First International Online Information Meeting, London 13–15th December 1977. Learned Information, Oxford (1978). ISBN 0-904933-10-5

Second International Online Information Meeting, London 5–7th December 1978. Learned Information, Oxford (1978). ISBN 0-904933-15-6

Third International Online Information Meeting, London 4–6th December 1979. Learned Information, Oxford (1978). ISBN 0-904933-21-0

Kent, A. and Galvin, T.J. (Eds). *The Online Revolution in Libraries*, Marcel Dekker, New York (1978). ISBN 0-8247-6754-3

Lancaster, F.W. and Fayen, E.G. *Information Retrieval Online*, Melville Publishing, Los Angeles (1973). ISBN 0-471-51235-4

McCarn, D.B. 'Online systems – techniques and services', in Williams, M.E. (Ed.), *Annual Review of Information Science and Technology*, Vol. 13. Knowledge Industry Publications, White Plains, N.Y. (1978). ISBN 0-914236-21-0

Watson, P.G. (Ed.). *Online Bibliographic Services – Where We are, Where We're Going*, American Library Association, Chicago (1977)

Williams, M.E. 'Online retrieval – today and tomorrow', *Online Review*, 2, No. 4, 353–366 (1978)

Chapter 2

Origin and Scope of the Services and Databases

2.1 BIRTH OF AN INDUSTRY

Three main factors have made possible the online services as we see them today.

First, there are the organisations, companies, societies, etc., which compile and collate large collections of bibliographic material. Although most of these collections were originally intended for the production of printed indexes, an increasing number of them in recent years have been prepared in machine-readable form; this enabled producers to take advantage of index generation by computer. Once in this form, the information is of course highly amenable to much more extensive processing by computer, and had these collections of data not been available at the right time, then there is little doubt that online services would have got off to a much slower start. Even now, the retrospective conversion of data into machine-readable form is expensive, and difficult to justify.

The second factor relates to the recent advances in communications and computing technology. This has allowed the setting up of reliable, long-distance communication networks, linked to computers with powerful data handling facilities and large online storage capacities. So effective is this combination that there is now scarcely any noticeable difference when a machine is being interrogated, whether it is on the other side of the room or the other side of the world.

The third factor concerns the expertise and enterprise that has welded together the information resources and new technology, and nursed the product from an idea to a reality. A major task was the writing of programs (software), which – starting from relatively raw information – were able to build and manage the highly structured databases which made online searching possible. These programs must also shield users from the complexities of the computer operations, allowing them to 'converse' with the system in a relatively simple manner. This concept of 'user friendliness' – as it has become known – is very important, as it can strongly influence a user's attitude to a system.

The organisations that have brought together the ingredients of information resources and new technology are known variously as hosts, host operators, host systems and here systems operators. They are slowly increasing in number, although the present economics of the 'hosting' operation suggest that not all will survive. An intriguing question is posed by the fact that online systems are utilising the by-products of the printed indexes industry. While the latter remains healthy this is of little consequence, but if subscribers continue to switch to systems operators for the provision of their information online, there will have to be some skilful adjustments to the price equations if dislocations in either service are to be avoided.

It is ironic that the library and information world, renowned for its conservatism and tradition, should have had unleashed upon it the product of such advanced technology. Computer applications generally, and online searching in particular, have not been without their critics, but few now would disagree that the past decade has witnessed a renaissance in the information world, with online searching acting as a potent force for change. Communications and computing technologies continue their rapid advance, and there can be little doubt that even the present capabilities, impressive though they are, will pale into insignificance before another decade has passed.

2.2 THE SUPPLIERS OF ONLINE SERVICES

In the provision of commercially accessible online databases, Lockheed[1] and System Development Corporation (SDC)[2] may be regarded as pioneers of the art. Both of these systems operators are based in California, but a vigorous campaign in Europe has resulted in a steady penetration by their services since about 1974–75, just a few years behind a similar pattern in the USA. Present-day users in Europe have reason to be grateful for the entrepreneurial activities of these two organisations, which have contributed significantly to the spread of online searching. In terms of subject coverage, both Lockheed and SDC offer an enormous range of material, spread over a large number of databases. The search languages of the two systems, Dialog (Lockheed) and ORBIT (SDC), display some interesting differences in the ways in which searches can be developed. Users of both systems will recognise these differences and the relative merits of each – depending on the requirements of a particular search. In pursuit of convenience and flexibility for the user, continual modifications to the search languages of both systems have – not surprisingly – tended to narrow the differences between them.

Lockheed's present software (Dialog) evolved from the Recon software developed by Lockheed themselves for the US National Aeronautics and Space Agency. Recon was also used by the European Space Agency (ESA) for its Information Retrieval Service (ESA-IRS), although the latest version of their software is known as Quest. The ESA-IRS system provides access to some 20 databases (mainly scientific) from its computer at Frascati, near Rome[3].

The US National Library of Medicine (NLM) has been involved for a considerable time in supplying online bibliographic search services. The database MEDLARS (Medical Literature Analysis and Retrieval System), which corresponded roughly to the printed *Index Medicus,* was used in offering a batch retrospective search service – in the USA from 1964 and in the UK from 1966[4].

After running an experimental online service using software written for the National Library of Medicine by SDC, the online search service based on MEDLARS, and thus known as Medline, was set up in 1973. The software is known as Elhill (after the Lister Hill National Centre for Biomedical Communications), and is similar to ORBIT.

Searching most of NLM's databases is now possible in Britain via Blaise (British Library Automated Information Service)[5]. Blaise, which also uses the Elhill software, was established in 1977, and is the name applied to all computer-based services of the British Library Bibliographic Services Division. The Marc (machine-readable cataloguing) files, which cover bibliographic details of all books published in the UK (since 1950) and the USA (since 1968), are also available for searching. Blaise is unusual in that it offers a cataloguing service as well as an online information retrieval service. Using specially written software known as Editor, it is possible to edit retrieved Marc records, create catalogue records for items not covered by the Blaise files and then use Locas (Local Cataloguing Service) to produce a local (in-house) catalogue.

Another relative newcomer to the online business is Bibliographic Retrieval Services (BRS). It evolved in 1976 from a system operated at the State University of New York, and uses a modified version of IBM's STAIRS (Storage and Information Retrieval System) software to provide search services to a collection of about 25 of the most widely used bibliographic databases. BRS adopted a novel approach to pricing strategy, in that the more search time a customer agreed to purchase — in advance — the cheaper the rate. It has reduced storage overheads for the larger databases, by holding online some two to three years of the most recent data only. The remainder of the data are accessible via an automatic overnight search process, the results of which are available for online inspection the following day. For heavy users of the larger databases, this approach has its attractions, and it was noticeable that the advent of BRS heralded a decrease in charges by some other suppliers. From the searcher's viewpoint, the slight delay in completing a search of a large database is usually of little consequence, provided that most other benefits of online searching are preserved. A comparison of BRS, Lockheed and SDC is given by Hoover[6].

A second system, also based on the US East Coast, is the New York Times Information Bank; it is unusual in several respects. For one thing, it is an example of a combined database compiler and online systems operator. For another, it uses a unique command language based on a strictly controlled vocabulary[7], although it has been announced that the more usual full text searching facilities are to be made available.

In late 1979 a new British system, Infoline, became operational. Infoline was formed by a consortium of interested parties: The British Library, The Chemical Society, The Department of Industry, The Institute of Electrical Engineers (producers of the INSPEC database on physics, electrotechnology, computers and control) and Derwent Publications Limited (producer of patents information, including the WPI database). The system uses an enhanced version of the BASIS (Battelle Automated Search Information System) software to manage and search its databases. Initially, Infoline will offer databases containing information relating to chemistry, patents and physics[8].

There are many other suppliers of online services, although the main ones are among those mentioned above. In Canada the Can/Ole (Canadian Online Enquiry) service run by the National Library forms part of the scientific and technical

Table 2.1 Brief details of some of the major suppliers of online search services

Supplier	Location	Command language	Subject coverage	Approx. No. of databases (1979)
Blaise	London	Elhill	Medical/Books	6
BRS	New York State	STAIRS	Wide	20
ESA-IRS	Rome	Quest	Mainly scientific	20
Infoline	London	BASIS	Scientific	3
Lockheed	Palo Alto, California	Dialog	Very wide	100
NLM	Washington, DC	Elhill	Medical	8
SDC	Santa Monica, California	ORBIT	Very wide	50

information service. The National Library of Australia has set up Ausinet to provide for online searching of several databases.

More details about the major systems operators are given in Appendices 2–6. *Table 2.1* summarises this information. With regard to accessing these various databases, the setting up of the Euronet communications network may bring European systems and users closer together. Unfortunately, negotiations for access to the US systems via Euronet could be protracted.

2.3 SUBJECT COVERAGE

The enormous range of information available from a terminal is one of the great strengths of online searching. References to much of the world's recently published literature, particularly in the various areas of science and technology, have been brought to within an arm's length of the searcher, and the remaining gaps are being steadily filled. However, while the subject scope exceeds that of most of the world's libraries, it should be borne in mind that the extent of retrospective coverage is so far fairly limited.

It was mentioned in Chapter 1 that almost all material currently prepared for index and abstract publications is available in machine-readable form, so it is scarcely surprising if the present online databases, by and large, mirror the existing hard-copy reference material. (Nevertheless there are some databases, such as the international textile information database, TITUS, which have no equivalent printed index.) Clearly, any machine-readable data of this type, because they are so amenable to computer processing, are ripe for assimilation by an online system. The rapid initial growth in the number of bibliographic online databases has been a consequence of this, but now that most of the major and widely used reference sources have been absorbed, future expansion is likely to proceed at a steadier pace. In a competitive world duplication of services, especially for the more popular and widely used databases, is bound to occur. Within limits, this multiplicity of services is not undesirable from the users' viewpoint, not least because of the occasional lack of computer availability, planned or otherwise, and the fact that the search and print facilities of various systems often vary in suitability, depending upon the nature of the question. Healthy though this competition may be, the long-term viability of some of the growing number of systems operators who are competing for a limited number of databases and customers must be called into question.

Traditionally, most areas of science and technology have been well furnished with abstract and reference publications. Not only is the systematic recording of results and observations a prerequisite for orderly progression, but also there is the added spur that scientific laws and principles, being universally valid, merit the widest possible publication. This last point has not been so true for information relating to areas such as commerce and legislation, where until recently most activities have been a fairly parochial affair. Now, as the world shrinks, the relevance of other subjects becomes increasingly widespread and there is a need for the wider accessibility of all types of information.

Not surprisingly, current online services tend to reflect this state of affairs. For example, the biological, chemical, physical and medical sciences are all strongly in evidence; so too are engineering and agriculture, and a number of subjects such as energy and environmental studies, which impinge on a variety of disciplines. But there is a host of other databases, covering such areas as linguistics, history, education, literature and philosophy, and strenuous efforts are being made to increase the coverage of business and commercial activities. A guide to databases and databanks available to the public in Europe – including those from non-European operations such as Lockheed and SDC – was first published in 1975; it has been updated regularly since[9]. It is interesting to note the growth in the number of databases and, more spectacularly, the number of databanks (*Table 2.2*). The journal *Online Review* regularly publishes details,

Table 2.2 Details of growth of available databases and databanks in Europe

	1975	1976	1977	1978
Number of databases available	335	337	422	533
Number of databanks available	51	149	268	568

including costs, of databases and databanks available through the major services. The December 1978 issue lists 136 databases and databanks available on Blaise, BRS, ESA-IRS, Lockheed, NLM and SDC; of these, the following databases were available on no fewer than four separate services:

Biosis Previews – biology
Chemical Abstracts Condensates (CACON) – chemistry
INSPEC – physics, electrotechnology, computers and control
NTIS (National Technical Information Service) – US government reports
Pollution Abstracts

The Eusidic guide[9] is arranged by subject and includes 37 subsections, with some entries appearing in more than one subsection. The numbers of databases and databanks in each subject are given in *Table 2.3*.

Most of the databases currently available from the major online service suppliers are in English, although they may describe documents not originally

Table 2.3 Numbers of databases and databanks available in Europe

Subject	No. of databases	No. of databanks
Aerospace	4	2
Agriculture	55	30
Armed Forces	1	–
Art, Literature, Music	5	1
Biology	11	6
Business and Economics	23	194
Chemistry	42	54
Civil Engineering	16	4
Demography and Geography	11	20
Earth and Space	12	21
Education	12	9
Electrical Engineering	23	11
Energy	12	13
Environment	41	32
History	10	1
Information and Documentation	8	1
Law	21	29
Linguistics	4	21
Marine	7	8
Mathematics	5	1
Mechanical Engineering	25	8
Medicine	35	48
Metals, Ceramics, Glass	16	10
Nucleonics	13	13
Paper, Printing, Packaging	7	–
Patents and Trade Marks	17	4
Petroleum	5	17
Philosophy	3	–
Physics	17	3
Public Administration	40	15
Religion	3	–
Social Sciences	22	8
Sport	3	2
Telecommunications	8	6
Textiles	3	–
Timber	3	2
Transport	16	10

written in English. The databases given by Eusidic[9] are in a variety of languages, including French, German, Italian and Norwegian. McCarn[10] estimates that the most frequently searched databases (not including catalogue record information) in the USA are:

Medline – medical
ERIC – educational
Chemical Abstracts
Psychological Abstracts
Biosis Previews
NTIS
New York Times Information Bank

Some databases are document-specific rather than subject-specific. This is a useful point to remember when one is planning a search, since a single relevant thesis or patent, for example, may be more useful than several widely scattered papers. Document specificity of this type includes books, patents, theses, etc., which are represented by databases such as:

Derwent World Patent Index
CLAIMS – chemical patents
Apipat – petroleum patents
Marc – books
CDI (Comprehensive Dissertation Index) – theses
Avline – audiovisual materials
Serline – periodicals

Many databases are multidisciplinary, some by design (Scisearch), some because they are document-specific (Comprehensive Dissertation Index) and some because over the years they have grown to embrace an ever-widening area. Chemical Abstracts, for example, covers an enormous area of the published literature, and draws also on a wide range of document types, including patents. It would be difficult to single out any topic for which no relevant material could be located online, since, even where there is no relevant subject-specific database, there are always the multidisciplinary files to fall back on. (This is not to imply that all queries are best handled by online techniques.)

2.4 SIZE OF DATABASES

To emphasise once more the potential of online services, it is useful to examine a few of the quantitative aspects. Williams[11] states that there were 33 million bibliographic references available for online searching in 1976, and by 1977 this had grown to 55 million. Many of the databases contain around one million references (Biosis Previews, Agricola, Derwent WPI), and a few are well in excess of this (Excerpta Medica, Chemical Abstracts, Medline). These are all enormous collections of data, containing the co-ordinates to a vast storehouse of information. Most of the databases are rapidly expanding, and individual growth rates of hundreds of thousands of document records per year are not unusual. Whether the amount of material online will be allowed to grow indefinitely or whether it will be periodically relegated to less frequently accessible files (batch mode searching, for example), will depend on the demand – and, hence, the economics. For this reason, it will be interesting to see whether the BRS approach (holding only recent data online), mentioned earlier, is a foretaste of things to come or whether it will remain a unique type of service.

As well as the very large databases, there are small ones covering specialised subjects. For example, the Child Abuse and Neglect Database has about 800 new records each year. The retrospective coverage of databases varies, and though many go back to the late 1960s or early 1970s, there are a few extreme examples. The CDI database covers material produced since 1861, whereas at the other end of the spectrum SSIE (research in progress) for obvious reasons carries only very recent data. SDILINE contains references for the last month only.

The total charge for online searching is sensitive to a number of factors, and varying the amount of information held online at any given time is just one of several ways in which costs may be altered. But it is in areas such as data storage technology and communications charges where breakthroughs and changes could have the most effect. For example, the appearance of very cheap mass storage devices and/or a more imaginative approach to communications charges — especially for the North Atlantic links — could cause a dramatic upsurge in demand. This in turn would probably help to sustain more and bigger databases.

2.5 DOCUMENT DESCRIPTIONS

2.5.1 The Document Record

The size of the document records that the user can access varies from little more than a title and source, right through to a lengthy abstract and complete biblio-graphic information, including details such as source, author, organisation, language, publisher, document type, funding body, etc. Within a given database, the structure and content of the records are usually standardised, and the user can discover what to expect either by consulting the relevant database guide or by examining a full record while online. The size of records, and, hence, the amount of information carried in them, has an important bearing on the choice of target database(s) for searching. The user with poor back-up resources (no easily available library or loan facilities) or the user who is urgently seeking directly usable information (as opposed to references to information) may decide to limit searches whenever possible to those databases containing an abstract. *Figure 2.1* shows document records from databases on BRS, ESA-IRS, Blaise, SDC and Lockheed. The size of a record is no reflection on the systems operator; it is simply that some databases include abstracts with the records, while others do not. An important point to notice is the structuring which occurs in all records. This influences the formatting of search questions and illustrates the point that a knowledge of the target databases — as well as search language — is necessary for successful searching.

```
AN 77-15726.
AU ROBERTS, EDWARD B.
TI GENERATING EFFECTIVE CORPORATE INNOVATION.
SO PUB: TECHNOLOGY REVIEW. V80 N1. PAG: P26-33. OCT./NOV. 1977.
PT 02.
CD TEREA.
YR 77.
DE AREAS, COMMERCIAL, COMPANIES, CORPORATIONS, CREATIVE, ENTREPRENEURS,
   FUNCTIONS, GRAPHS, INFORMATION, INNOVATIONS, MANAGERS, MARKETING,
   PROJECTS, ROLES, SCIENTISTS, SMALL, SOCIAL, STRATEGY, STRESS,
   TECHNICAL, TECHNICAL-INFORMATION.
AB THERE ARE 4 CRITICAL AREAS IN SUCCESSFUL CORPORATE INNOVATION -
   STAFFING OF KEY FUNCTIONS, ORGANIZATIONAL-STRUCTURING TO IMPROVE THE
   FLOW OF INFORMATION TO R&D, MARKETING TO MAKE INNOVATIONS
   COMMERCIALLY SUCCESSFUL, AND STRATEGIC PLANNING TO INTEGRATE
   TECHNICAL PLANS WITH CORPORATE STRATEGY. KEY STAFFING ROLES INCLUDE A
   CREATIVE SCIENTIST, THE ENTREPRENEUR THAT PUSHES THE COMMERCIAL IDEA,
   THE PROJECT MANAGER THAT COORDINATES THE EFFORT, THE SPONSOR WHO ACTS
   AS AN ADVOCATE, AND THE GATE-KEEPER WHO BRINGS CRITICAL TECHNICAL OR
   MARKETING INFORMATION INTO THE ORGANIZATION. THE ORGANIZATION'S
   STRUCTURE SHOULD EMPHASIZE THE FLOW OF TECHNICAL INFORMATION, AND
   CLOSE PHYSICAL PROXIMITY AND SOCIAL RELATIONSHIPS FOSTER THIS FLOW.
   MARKETING MUST STRESS VENTURE STRATEGIES. LONG-TERM PERSISTENCE AND
   THE DUPLICATION OF SMALL COMPANY ENTREPRENEURSHIP ARE USUALLY
   ASSOCIATED WITH VENTURE STRATEGY. PLANNING IS ALSO NEEDED. GRAPH.
JC CD-TCR.
IS 0040-1692.
```

Figure 2.1 Some document records: (a) ABI/Inform on BRS

```
PB-207 763/7SL  NTIS  1905601
Monograph on Enzyme-Modified Milk Fat
Fld: 6H, 6T, 98H*, 57Y*
 Controlled terms: *Food additives / Fats / Dietary fats / Milk /
Enzymes / Chemical properties / Toxicology / Pharmacology /
Nutrition / Food consumption / Bioassay / Laboratory animals /
Tables (Data) / Experimental data / Lipase / Esterases
 Uncontrolled terms: *GRAS food ingredients / Generally recognized
as safe food ingredients / NTISFDAHFF
```

(b) NTIS on ESA-IRIS

```
AU - Epstein MH
AU - Wieland WF
TI - Prevalence survey of inhalant abuse.
AB - Although there is a paucity of hard epidemiologic data on the
     prevalence of inhalant abuse, there is considerable anecdotal
     evidence that such abuse is continuing. Recently, we received
     repeated reports that one particularly public housing project in
     Atlanta had high rates on inhalant abuse, and to assess the
     prevalence of such abuse in children 4 to 20 years old, we
     conducted a random household survey in 400 of the project's 1,140
     units. In an attempt to get complete and reliable data, we  chose
     and trained 10 residents as interviewers. Fifty youngsters were
     identified as ever having used inhalants, representing a sample
     prevalence of approximately 4%. The typical sniffer was a male,
     age 15, in the 9th grade or currently out of school. Some
     sniffers, though, continued to use inhalants into the 20s. Not
     unexpectedly, sniffers were found to use alcohol and other drugs
     at greater rates than other children. Although the parents of
     sniffers often said that they recognised drug-related problems in
     their children, the seldom sought help. Nevertheless, most
     residents felt that a drug-counseling program should be
     established in the project to provide alternative recreational
     activities.
SO - Int J Addict 13(2):271-84, 1973
```

(c) Medline database on Blaise

```
-1-
AN - ABD01-26430
TI - PEACE, LEGITIMACY, AND THE EQUILIBRIUM (A STUDY OF THE STATESMANSHIP OF
     CASTLEREAGH AND METERNICH)
AU - KISSINGER, HENRY A.
SO - HARVARD UNIVERSITY (MASSACHUSETTS), PH.D., 1954.
IS - DOCUMENT NOT AVAIL. FROM UMI.
CC - 616 (POLITICAL SCIENCE, INTERNATIONAL LAW AND RELATIONS)
```

(d) CDI/Dissertation Abstracts on SDC

```
CA005520199049B
  The design and operation of a cryomagnetic system for Faraday
rotators used in high-power laser induced fusion research
   Author: Ackermann, R. A., Rhodenizer, R. L., Ward, C. O., Morrow, G.
R., Wilcox, R. E.
   Location: Intermagn. Gen. Corp., Guilderland, N. Y.
   Section: CA071001, CA073000   Publ Class: J
   Journal:  Proc. Symp. Eng. Probl. Fusion Res.    Coden: PSERDR
Publ: 75    Series: (,    Pages: 601-5    meeting Date: 75
   Identifiers: Cryomagnetic system laser fusion,  Faraday rotator
cryomagnetic system

CA005261996649B
   Descriptors: Nuclear fusion;Laser radiation,chemical and physical
effects;Cryostats
   Identifiers:  Induced  design operation cryomagnetic system Faraday
rotators
```

(e) Chemical Abstracts Condensates on Lockheed

Figure 2.1 (continued)

Figure 2.2 shows the same document described by three separate database producers (the organisations that compile the data, not the system operator making it available online). The Social Science Citation Index (SSCI) record contains no assigned codes or terms to describe the document, so subject searching must rely on words from the title. Details are given, however, of references

```
/5/5
708855   ARTICLE   CATS ORDER✱: CW061   4 REFS
    SELECTING A COMPUTER TERMINAL FOR LIBRARY   (EN)
    KAZLAUSKAS EJ
    UNIV SO CALIF,SCH LIB SCI/LOS ANGELES//CA/90007
    SPECIAL LIBRARIES, V6 , N1, P24-27, 1977

    MEADOW CT (MAN MACHINE COMMUNIC, 1970)
    OBRIEN BV (COMPUTER DECISIONS, V5, P37, 1973)
    STERNIC BR (ON LINE COMMUNICATIO)
    ZAIS H (COMPARISON 3 ONLINE, 1974)
```

(a) Social Science Citation Index

```
5/5/1
EJ162644   IR504609
    Selecting a Computer Terminal for the Library
    Kazlauskas, Edward John
    Special Libraries, 68, 1, 24-27    Jan 77
    Descriptors: *Selection/ Libraries
    Identifiers: *Computer Terminals
```

(b) ERIC

```
-1-
AN - 77-3246
TI - Selecting a computer terminal for the library
AU - Kazlauskas, Edward John
SO - Spec. Libr., 68 (1) Jan 77, 24-27, 4 refs
LA - English
CC - ZkjVrsOwj
IT - Computerised Subject Indexing-Information Storage and Retrieval Systems
     by Subject Specification: On-line information retrieval; Computer
     terminals; Evaluation
ST - Terminals; Searching; Computerised subject indexing
AB - Paper presented at a joint meeting on computer terminals, held by the Los
     Angeles Chapters of the Special Libraries Association and the American
     Society for Information Science, Jan 76. With the increased use of
     on-line systems in libraries, the problem arises as to which computer
     terminal to select. Such topics as hardcopy versus CRT terminal, type of
     character font and format, size of screen display, system compatibility,
     storage and editing capability and cost are presented as points to be
     considered in any terminal selection process.
```

(c) LISA
Figure 2.2 Same item on different databases

cited at the end of the article, and these can be used in searching (this technique is also useful for retrieving reviews of a particular book). The ERIC record contains subject terms and phrases taken from the published Thesaurus of ERIC Descriptors. The LISA (Library and Information Science Abstracts) record also includes subject terms and phrases used in the chain indexing for the printed publication and a classification code used in the production of the associated printed publication.

77C020374 INSPEC Journal Paper
Selecting a computer terminal for the library
Kazlauskas, E.J.
Univ. of Southern California, School of Library Sci., Los Angeles,
CA, USA
Spec. Libr. (USA), vol.68, no.1 1086686 splba, Jan. 1977, 24-7,
4 Refs Treatment Practical

With the increased use of on-line systems in libraries the problem
arises as to which computer terminal to select. Such topics as
hardcopy versus CRT terminal, type of character font and format,
size of screen display, system compatibility, storage and editing
capability and costs are presented as points to be considered in any
terminal selection process.

Classification Codes: C7210, C5540
Controlled Terms: Library mechanisation / computer selection and
evaluation
Uncontrolled Terms: libraries / computer **terminal** / display /
system compatibility / storage / editing capability / costs /
terminal selection process

(a) ESA-IRS

-1-
AN - C77020374
TI - SELECTING A COMPUTER TERMINAL FOR THE LIBRARY
AU - KAZLAUSKAS, E.J.
OS - UNIV. OF SOUTHERN CALIFORNIA, SCHOOL OF LIBRARY SCI., LOS ANGELES, CA,
     USA
SO - SPEC. LIBR. (USA) (SPLBAN), VOL.68 NO.1, PP,24-7, JAN. 1977, 4 REF.
DT - J (JOURNAL): PR (PRACTICAL)
LA - ENGLISH
CC - *3C7210; 3C5540
IT - LIBRARY MECHANISATION: COMPUTER SELECTION AND EVALUATION
ST - LIBRARIES; COMPUTER TERMINAL; DISPLAY; SYSTEM COMPATIBILITY; STORAGE;
     EDITING CAPABILITY; COSTS; TERMINAL SELECTION PROCESS
AB - WITH THE INCREASED USE OF ON-LINE SYSTEMS IN LIBRARIES THE PROBLEM ARISES
     AS TO WHICH COMPUTER TERMINAL TO SELECT. SUCH TOPICS AS HARDCOPY VERSUS
     CRT TERMINAL, TYPE OF CHARACTER FONT AND FORMAT, SIZE OF SCREEN DISPLAY,
     SYSTEM COMPATIBILITY, STORAGE AND EDITING CAPABILITY AND COSTS ARE
     PRESENTED AS POINTS TO BE CONSIDERED IN ANY TERMINAL SELECTION PROCESS.

(b) SDC

1086686 C77020374
SELECTING A COMPUTER TERMINAL FOR THE LIBRARY
KAZLAUSKAS, E.J.
UNIV. OF SOUTHERN CALIFORNIA, SCHOOL OF LIBRARY SCI., LOS ANGELES,
CA, USA
SPEC. LIBR. (USA) VOL.68, NO.1 24-7 JAN. 1977 Coden: SPLBAN
Treatment: P
02
WITH THE INCREASED USE OF ON-LINE SYSTEMS IN LIBRARIES THE PROBLEM
ARISES AS TO WHICH COMPUTER TERMINAL TO SELECT. SUCH TOPICS AS
HARDCOPY VERSUS CRT TERMINAL, TYPE OF CHARACTER FONT AND FORMAT, SIZE
OF SCREEN DISPLAY, SYSTEM COMPATIBILITY, STORAGE AND EDITING
CAPABILITY AND COSTS ARE PRESENTED AS POINTS TO BE CONSIDERED IN ANY
TERMINAL SELECTION PROCESS (4 Refs).
Descriptors; LIBRARY MECHANISATION; COMPUTER SELECTION AND
EVALUATION
Identifiers; LIBRARIES; COMPUTER TERMINAL; DISPLAY; SYSTEM
COMPATIBILITY; STORAGE; EDITING CAPABILITY; COSTS; TERMINAL SELECTION
PROCESS.

(c) Lockheed

Figure 2.3 Same record, same database, different search services

Figure 2.3 shows the same document as that in *Figure 2.2*, but this time from the INSPEC database and retrieved from three different systems operators — ESA-IRS, SDC and Lockheed.

2.5.2 Print formats

Some systems offer a choice from a range of fixed-print formats and others allow the user to specify the desired combination of fields in the print commands. There is also a user option within some systems for permanently assigning the most useful print field specifications for each file; these become the default mode for that particular database, unless specifically overridden.

System-defined fixed formats

Print formats pre-defined by the system are usually referred to by number. For example, PRINT 10 FORMAT 4 could be a command to print ten records in format number four. Typical formats are:

1. 75:026,793   (the briefest of all possible formats; this is an abstract number referring to a print equivalent index)

2. 75:026,793
   Sleep Patterns of Tasmanian Toads

3. 75:026,793
   Sleep Patterns of Tasmanian Toads
   Jenkins P.L., Mole B.
   Journal of Antipodean Behavioural Biology, 74:A126–131

4. 75:026,793
   Sleep Patterns of Tasmanian Toads
   Insomnia; Hibernation; REM; Dreaming
   Jenkins P.L., Mole B.
   Amphibian Research Institute, Wigan
   Journal of Antipodean Behavioural Biology, 74:A126–131
   Arabic
   A colony of toads was studied over a period . . ., etc.

User-defined variable formats

With variable formats, the record fields are specified by the user, to build up the required format. For example, PRINT 15 TI, AN could be a command to print the accession number and title for the first fifteen records. Some typical user-defined formats might be:

A.   AN 75:026,793

B.   JR Journal of Antipodean Behavioural Biology, 74:A126–131
     AU Jenkins P.L., Mole B.

C.   TI Sleep Patterns of Tasmanian Toads
     AN 75: 026,793

D.   TI Sleep Patterns of Tasmanian Toads
     JR Journal of Antipodean Behavioural Biology, 74:A126–131

E.   AU Jenkins P.L., Mole B.
     TI Sleep Patterns of Tasmanian Toads
     SO Amphibian Research Institute, Wigan
     AN 75:026,793

F.   AN 75:026,793
     TI Sleep Patterns of Tasmanian Toads
     AU Jenkins P.L., Mole B.
     JR Journal of Antipodean Behavioural Biology, 74: A126–131
     LA Arabic
     KW Insomnia; Hibernation; REM; Dreaming
     SO Amphibian Research Institute, Wigan
     AB A colony of toads was studied over a period . . ., etc.

If users are searching a database for which the printed equivalent is available locally, then titles and abstract numbers (e.g. format 2 or C) will probably be sufficient for their needs (titles to assess the relevance, and abstract numbers to locate the full record in the hard-copy form). Under these circumstances, if the number of retrieved references is high and initial online sampling suggests that their relevance is acceptable, then it is often sufficient to print the abstract numbers only. Format 1 or A, for example, can be delivered online on a 30 characters per second (30 cps) terminal at a rate of somewhere between 50 and 150 references per minute, depending on the precise format and presentation of the records. Format 2 or 3, or the user-specified formats B–E, all of which offer a reasonable chance of containing sufficient information for a relevance judgement, inevitably slow the delivery rate to about 7 to 12 records per minute (on a 30 cps terminal). However, they are extremely useful for sampling from a large number of retrieved documents, before deciding on the next course of action, which might be (a) printing all results offline in a fuller format or (b) printing online in fuller format (e.g. 4 or F) the few references which appear to be relevant.

There can be no hard and fast rules about printing, the facilities are extremely flexible, and the user, having regard for such factors as local library resources, cost and urgency, is free to select the most appropriate course of action.

2.6 DATABASES – SOME POINTS TO WATCH

One of the difficulties experienced by new searchers is in trying to assess those databases which are on the fringe of their main interests. Fortunately, the subject guides – both online and printed – can help considerably with the problem of choosing suitable target files. In the case of databases derived from the print-equivalent indexes with which the searcher is already familiar, there is usually little difficulty in adjusting to the new search techniques.

The cost of interrogating a database depends very much on the systems operator, the type of contract which the user enters into, the amount of search time (for possible discount) and, in some cases, whether or not the user subscribes to the print-equivalent material produced by the database suppliers. The present range is somewhere between about $20 and $150 per hour*, although

* Charges are given in the currency quoted by the systems operators.

most of the major, wide-interest files are in the $40–$60 range. It should be remembered that these costs are quite separate from the communications charges, which can sometimes be higher than the rate for searching.

Not all systems operators keep the same amount of material online for a given database. In some instances databases have been split into two or even three sections, so that a search strategy may have to be matched against more than one file. There is also the arrangement whereby older material is stored offline and made available for automatic overnight searches using a strategy developed online against the most recent data. Some databases are interrelated in such a way that searches can be usefully switched across files in order to maximise exploitation of the available information. The Predicasts group of files falls into this category.

Most databases are updated at least monthly, and weekly or fortnightly updating is fairly common. Continual improvements made by both the systems operators and the database suppliers can lead to structural and/or content changes to files. For example, subject classifications may change, abstracts may be introduced or additional key-words/descriptors may be added to document records. Such changes are rarely retrospective, and can introduce inhomogeneities into a database.

Appendices 2–6 give detailed information about databases available on a number of systems at January 1979. Any list such as this inevitably becomes outdated, but it will usefully serve for some time to come as a guide to much of the world's online bibliographic information.

REFERENCES

1. Summit, R.K. 'DIALOG interactive information retrieval system', in Kent, Allen, Lancour, Harold (Eds), *Encyclopedia of Library and Information Science*, Vol. 7, pp. 161–169, Marcel Dekker, New York, 1972. ISBN 0-8247-2107-1
2. Cuadra, C.A. 'SDC experiences with large databases', *Journal of Chemical Information and Computer Sciences*, 15, No. 1, 48–51 (1975)
3. 'EURONET hosts – the space documentation service, Frascati, Italy', *Online Review*, 2, No. 2, 149–150 (1978)
4. Harley, A.J. 'An introduction to mechanized information retrieval', *Aslib Proceedings*, 30, No. 12, 420–425 (1978)
5. Collinge, B. 'BLAISE – the British Library Automated Information Service', *Aslib Proceedings*, 30, Nos 10, 11, 394–402 (1978)
6. Hoover, R.E. 'A comparison of three commercial online vendors', *Online*, 3, No. 1, 12–21 (1979)
7. Senlowitz. L. 'All the news that's fit to print', *Online*, 1, No. 1, 57–60 (1977)
8. 'Infoline – a new European online service', *Online Review*, 2, No. 4, 325–327 (1978)
9. Tomberg, A. (Ed.). *Eusidic Database Guide*, Learned Information, Oxford (1978). ISBN 0-904933-13-X
10. McCarn, D.B. 'Online systems – techniques and services', in Williams M.E. (Ed.), *Annual Review of Information Science and Technology*, Vol. 13, pp. 85–124, Knowledge Industry Publications, White Plains, N.Y. (1978). ISBN 0-914236-21-0
11. Williams, M.E. 'Database and online statistics – 1977', *Bulletin of the American Society for Information Science*, 4, No. 2, 21–23 (1977)
12. Hall, J.L. *Online Bibliographic Databases – 1979 Directory*, Aslib, London (1979). 01-85142-115-6

Chapter 3
The Hardware

3.1 INTRODUCTION

The overall process of online searching is illustrated in *Figure 3.1*. It involves a terminal connected via a modem to the telephone which is used to access the required computer system. The telephone may be linked either directly to the computer centre or to the node of a telecommunications network which can be

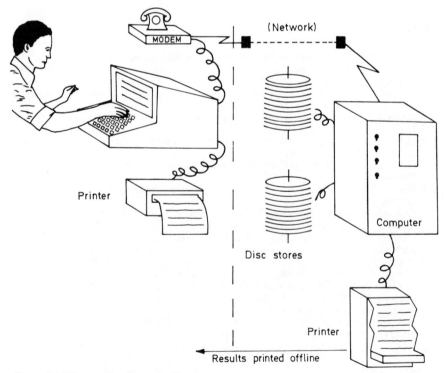

Figure 3.1 The overall online searching process

connected to the computer centre. The computer is typically a large timesharing installation which might enable access by tens or even hundreds of terminals at the same time. The files available for searching are stored on magnetic discs — direct-access storage devices which allow almost instant access to their contents. A search takes a similar form to a telephone call asking for information. A request is typed at the terminal and transmitted to the computer. The computer responds with a preliminary answer which is displayed at the terminal. In the light of this and further responses, the enquiry is developed until the searcher feels that there is a clear enough picture of the information available on the topic to ask for the full details to be displayed at the terminal, or, if there is too much for this to be an economical proposition, printed offline at the computer centre and posted to him. The conversational nature of online operation is its main strength and the feature which provides it with a great advantage over the alternative form of computer searching by batch processing, which it has to a large extent replaced.

3.2 THE NETWORK

One of the most valuable features of online information retrieval is accessibility: the fact that, having little more than a telephone and a terminal, it is possible to link into a range of computer systems spanning half the world and covering nearly all the major bibliographic databases. The searcher need not be in a library or information centre to do this, but could be in an office or laboratory or even at home. This high degree of accessibility is owed to the development of international telecommunications networks. These networks have been designed for transmitting information to and from computers rather than to and from people. One technique used by many of these networks is that of packet switching. Packet switching entails the splitting up of messages to be sent through the network into short fixed-length packets. Each packet includes the address of the final destination, and the packets travel separately, perhaps taking different paths through the network. This means that a large number of messages can be combined together along the same line, which gives useful economies of scale. The searcher of online databases does not need to become involved with the technicalities of packet switching; however, if interested, further details are available in Bunch and Alsberg[1].

Notable among telecommunications networks are Tymnet and Telenet. These are predominantly North American networks (having over 200 nodes between them), although there are nodes in Europe (for example, Brussels, Frankfurt, Geneva, The Hague, London, Paris, Rome, Vienna), as well as in other parts of the world (for example, Hong Kong, Manila, San Juan, Singapore). These nodes, into which the searcher can dial, thus provide access to nearly all the major American online services.

Access to Tymnet and Telenet from Europe is possible via agreements with the national Post, Telephone and Telegraph (PTT) authorities, who then charge the searcher for using the network. In the UK the Post Office has set up the International Packet Switching Service (IPSS), which, as well as enabling British searchers to access computers in North America, enables North American searchers to access computers in Britain. The charge for using IPSS consists of a fixed rate of £6 per hour plus a variable rate which depends on the number of packets sent and received (roughly £4 per hour).

The network node is a minicomputer which is able to handle communications traffic. It carries out preliminary checks and organises the sending of messages between the searcher and the computer. An example of a searcher using IPSS and Tymnet to access the Lockheed computer is given in Chapter 4.

In Europe the main fully operational network is that of the European Space Agency's Information Retrieval Service (ESA-IRS). Esanet, as it is called, provides access to the ESA computer in Frascati near Rome from points in most west European countries. This is not a general-purpose network but one specific to a particular computer system. Details of other networks in Europe are given by Tomberg[2]. Attention for the future is drawn to the Euronet project, which has the object of providing ready and equal access to scientific and technical information for all member countries of the European Community[3]. The basis of this is an international telecommunications network to be used for general data traffic between computers. By encouraging the establishment of information systems and research into factors such as the language problem, the European Commission hopes that this will lead to efficient and co-ordinated information management within the Community. Euronet will link a wide range of existing European systems, including ESA-IRS, Blaise, Infoline, DIMDI (the West German medical information service), ARIANE (a French service in civil engineering) and ITF (an international textile information service based in Paris), and will link to other networks such as Scannet (a packet-switched network operated by Nordfosk, the Scandinavian Council for Applied Research). See Appendix 7 for details of services planned to be available through Euronet.

3.3 THE TELEPHONE

Although networks take care of the long-distance communications, they are dependent on the telephone system to provide the final link to the searcher's terminal, just as airlines depend on local taxi or bus services. When the computer centre is close at hand, there is no need for a network; it can be dialled directly. The telephone arrangements desirable for online work are a standard telephone hand-set linked to a direct outside line. The hand-set should be of standard design, because you may want to use an acoustic coupler to link the telephone to the terminal. This means fitting the hand-piece into a pair of padded cups in the coupler to allow the signal to be transmitted. Imitation 1920s styles or the modern featureless hand-pieces are not suited to this purpose. The telephone line should preferably be a direct outside line, for several reasons. You inevitably get more possibilities of interruption when going through a switchboard. You may be occupying an outside line for lengthy periods and this would not be popular with those trying to make ordinary telephone calls through the switchboard. If you do need to go through the switchboard, it is worth advising the operator of the peculiar noises that will be heard on that line while the call is in operation; otherwise, a conscientious operator, not hearing speech, may cut you off. It is also a great convenience in online searching to be sure of getting a telephone line when you need one. The telephone is an essential link in the chain, and adequate arrangements are as important for this as for any other part of the process.

Rather than an acoustic coupler, a permanently wired modem may be used to link to the terminal. In this case there is no need to use the hand-piece of the telephone to transmit the signal. There will be a switch on the telephone or the terminal to switch the signal through once a connection has been made.

Using the public switched telephone network to call up computers (either directly or via networks) is often referred to as dial-up access. An alternative for the heavy user is a leased-line telephone connection directly to the computer. This makes possible much higher speeds of transmission (240 characters per second or even higher), and so introduces many interesting possibilities in the use of intelligent terminals and local storage devices. The capability of service suppliers to handle this alternative, however, is limited at present and there must be heavy use to justify the cost of the line, which is generally rented by the telephone company according to distance. Sample annual charges in the UK (excluding rental of modems) for 240 characters per second lines are £610 (20 miles), £1295 (50 miles) and £2055 (100 miles).

3.4 COMPUTER TERMINALS AND THEIR SELECTION

The terminal illustrated in *Figure 3.1* is one with a screen and an attached printer which enables a record of the search to be produced. There are many different models of terminal on the market, and selecting one for online searching can be a difficult problem for the complete newcomer to the field. Rather than making a decision in isolation, it is a good idea to seek the advice of a nearby library or information centre which has substantial searching experience. There are also some published surveys of the models available, a particularly excellent one being that of Radwin[4]. In Britain the UK On-line Information Centre has also produced a good guide.

There are basically two types: printing terminals, which are more or less like electric typewriters, and visual display units, which have a cathode ray tube (CRT) display. CRT terminals give the impression of being more modern but in fact, since it is almost a necessity to have a continuous printed record of searches, printing terminals are the more obvious choice. If a CRT model is used, it must have an attached printer (which is a 'receive only' printing terminal with no keyboard), and this generally makes it the more expensive alternative. Another possibility is to link an ordinary printing terminal to the CRT terminal, The printer, incidentally, must be capable of working in parallel with the CRT. Having to copy from the screen, which is a common alternative facility, is very unsatisfactory. It requires that the same data be printed twice, once on to the screen and then on to the printer, which adds to the search time. It means that you have to keep stopping the output as soon as the screen or the memory of the CRT is full, and this is a tricky matter to judge. Having a complete record of the search interaction is almost impossible with this arrangement.

There are some applications for which a CRT terminal is better. If more than two people need to be able to see the search going on, the CRT screen provides a much better view than is obtained from a printing terminal. It is usually possible to link television monitors to a CRT terminal to provide a display for a large group. For display purposes a cassette tape recorder can be linked to the terminal which can be used both to record and to play back searches, and this is a very useful educational aid. More details on this are given in Chapter 10 CRT terminals are also usually capable of operating up to very high speeds although a leased-line connection is required for this to be taken advantage of

The speeds commonly supported for online searching are 10, 30 and 120 characters per second (cps). The last of these, at the time of writing, is still relatively restricted in availability. Ten cps is really too slow; 30 cps is quite fast enough unless you need to do a lot of online printing for references, and there are many good printing terminals which operate at this speed and are modestly priced at about £1000. The obvious choice of terminal for general searching is therefore a 30 cps printing terminal. In the future 120 cps printing terminals will become cheaper and more widely supported. They may then replace 30 cps terminals as the standard choice, although in fact, printing of references apart, this does not speed up the searching process a great deal.

Another common and economical arrangement is to have a very cheap visual display unit (they can cost as little as £500) with an attached printer. This is a good arrangement for when quieter operation is required or just to save on paper.

Printing terminals use two alternative types of printing mechanism — impact and thermal. Thermal printers produce an image by a heat process, as the name suggests, and require a special heat-sensitive paper. They are often extremely quiet and may be very lightweight, but they do have some disadvantages for online searching. The process does not permit the production of multiple copies, and the nature of the printed image does not always lend itself to photocopying. Also, the special paper required is an additional expense and keeps less well than plain paper. Impact printers do not have these disadvantages (although they do need to have ink ribbons replaced), and, particularly if more than one copy of searches is required, should be the first choice.

However, it may be that a portable terminal is needed, and then weight becomes the dominant requirement. Portable terminals are available weighing less than 20 lb. They come complete with a handled carrying case and have a built-in acoustic coupler. In general, they cost somewhat more than a stationary model, but for carrying out or demonstrating searches at different sites they are indispensable.

The above are the main types of standard terminal, but increasingly terminals are becoming available with extra facilities and with built-in intelligence. The possibility of linking a cassette tape to a CRT terminal for educational purposes has been mentioned. Cassette tape-recorders, or terminals with their own built-in cassette devices, can be used in practical searching also. Their main value at present is to prerecord search terms so that they can be fed into the computer straight from the tape. This means that time can be saved online by carrying out offline the tedious job of typing a large number of search terms. As higher transmission speeds become available, recording the search results straight from the terminal on to tape will also become a useful possibility. Some tape machines have features for searching by character strings, so providing further retrieval possibilities. Other storage devices use floppy discs rather than cassettes. Floppy discs are direct-access stores which allow quite sophisticated searching, editing and even sorting operations. With local storage and local intelligence it is possible to build up a file of references retrieved from various sources, and develop your own local information system. Not surprisingly, many database producers are against the creation of secondary files in this way, and recording search results in machine-readable form is forbidden by their agreements. If these difficulties can be sorted out, however, this will be an important technique in the future.

Maintenance and repairs are extremely important factors. Most suppliers are prepared to provide or arrange a service contract which entitles you to a breakdown service and regular maintenance visits. Roughly speaking, the annual charge for this service is about 10 per cent of the purchase price of the terminal. Whether you have such a contract or not, it is essential to know how long the suppliers would take to answer a breakdown call. Ideally they should be prepared to arrive the same day, which would make it possible to allow for being without a terminal for no more than a day or two. However, if the suppliers are at all hesitant about their capacity to service the machine, there must be very strong advantages for it to be chosen.

The noise of most modern terminals, 10 cps teletypes apart, is not excessive, and unless particularly subdued operation is required, does not weigh heavily in the choice. Rather than the volume, the kind of sound made may irritate some people. If there is a special requirement for silent or near-silent operation, a CRT terminal with a linked thermal printer is probably the best alternative.

The print quality of most printing terminals of 30 cps or above is adequate but not good. The characters are usually made up from a dot matrix and do not have the sharpness and density of ordinary printing. Some seem to have problems with lower case characters that extend below the line and adopt rather squashed-up alternatives. Others have no proper lower case at all but use a reduced-size upper case. There are terminals which will produce good-quality print, but these are somewhat more expensive. Daisy-wheel printers are an example; these cost between £2000 and £5000.

There is usually some element of choice in the set of keys provided. It is important for the legibility of the output to have upper and lower case. If you are likely to need any other characters such as £ or $, check whether they are present or can be supplied. An escape key is more or less essential for using some services, but may need to be specified as an option.

In addition to keys, terminals are also fitted with various switches, and when first looking over a terminal, these are a guide as to what it can and cannot do. There is a speed, or baud rate, switch which will indicate the alternative transmission speeds. (The baud, bits per second, rate is about ten times the figure for characters per second.) Prominent also should be a DUPLEX/HALF DUPLEX switch. This refers to the mode of transmission of messages down the telephone line. DUPLEX transmission involves data going in opposite directions down the line at the same time; HALF DUPLEX, only in one direction at a time. In HALF DUPLEX mode the terminal prints locally at the same time that characters are transmitted to the computer, whereas in FULL DUPLEX characters transmitted from the terminal are echoed back rather than being typed locally. FULL DUPLEX operation gives rise to a woolliness of operation, caused by the delay required for the key depression to take effect, which may disconcert someone used to a typewriter. Some terminals only operate in HALF DUPLEX, and although networks may support such terminals, they are less convenient to use.

Another switchable alternative on some terminals is parity. Parity is a device for checking whether data have been corrupted in transit. An extra bit (binary digit) is added to each character before it is transmitted. If the parity is set to be odd, the terminal arranges (by adding an extra bit if necessary) that there is always an odd number of bits in the character; similarly, if set to be even parity, an even number of bits in each character is generated. This is checked at the other end of the line. If the parity bit is not used for checking, it may be set to be always 1 or always 0. There is a possibility for incompatibility here between terminals and the systems. A terminal which has a switch to alter or stop the parity check or setting will be more versatile. The compatibility of the terminal with the system it is intended to use should always be checked by trial use.

In making a selection in the light of the factors discussed above, the more chance you get to try the terminal in operational use and the more terminals you try, the more satisfactory a decision will be made. Many sales representatives are only too willing to demonstrate their wares, and in spite of the feeling of obligation this engenders, it is an opportunity worth taking. Trade exhibitions of computer peripherals provide good opportunities to see what is on the market.

3.5 MODEMS

Modem stands for MODulator DEModulator, and its function is to convert the digital messages which the terminal and the computer understand to analogue messages which are capable of being transmitted down telephone lines. There is a similar device at the computer's end of the connection. There are two main kinds: hard-wired modems, which are permanently wired to the telephone handset; and acoustic couplers, which make use of audible signals and have rubber cups to take the hand-piece of the telephone.

The standard modem is a fairly large and heavy (13½ kg) box which is permanently connected to the telephone wiring system, and this is not at all portable. Miniaturised modems are also available which are much more compact and fit underneath a standard telephone. The British Post Office's miniaturised modem can only be used for speeds up to 30 cps. If telephone sockets, of the sort that are used for an extension telephone, are available, then this type of modem can be used in different locations. In the UK hand-wired modems that are likely to be required by searchers (that is, operating at 30 cps) cannot be bought but are rented from the Post Office for about £100 per year.

Acoustic couplers are cheap to buy (from about £200) and are very flexible in operation, since they can be used with any standard telephone. However, at 30 cps they tend to result in a 'noisier' signal with more transmission errors. They cannot be recommended for use at higher speeds than 30 cps. Hard-wired modems are therefore the better alternative unless you need to keep moving the terminal, but it is often useful to have an acoustic coupler as a stand-by.

Portable terminals usually have an acoustic coupler built into them, and this is clearly a highly convenient arrangement.

For 120 cps operation or higher, special modems are required. Advice about the type of modem to get for these higher speeds should be obtained from the service supplier or telephone company.

REFERENCES

1. Bunch, S.R. and Alsberg, P.A. 'Computer communications networks', in Williams, M.E. (Ed.), *Annual Review of Information Science and Technology*, Vol. 12, pp. 183–216, Knowledge Industry Publications, New York (1977). ISBN 0-914236-11-3
2. Tomberg, A. 'European information networks', in Williams, M.E. (Ed.), op. cit., pp. 219–246
3. Dunning, A.J. 'The origins, development and future of EURONET', *Program*, 11, No. 4, 145–155 (1977)

4. Radwin, Mark S. 'The intelligent person's guide to choosing a terminal for online inter-active use', *Online,* 1, No. 1, 11–19, 64–66; 1, No. 2, 61–73 (1977)

FURTHER READING

Lancaster, F.W. *Information Retrieval On-line*, Melville, Los Angeles (1973) (particularly Chapter 2)
Stewart, Alan. 'The 120 baud experience', *Online,* 2, No. 3, 13–18 (1978)

Chapter 4

How to Search

4.1 THE MAIN OPERATIONS

As was explained earlier, the databases available online in many cases correspond to abstracting and indexing journals. The file of references to be searched is the same in each. Not surprisingly, therefore, there are many similarities between online searching and the manual searching of the conventional printed tools. Both processes involve the matching of words which describe the subject of the search (search terms in online searching) against descriptors used to index the collection of references. For an abstracting journal the descriptors are the entries in the indexes. In an online search they can be any part of the document description present in the file being searched, including author names, assigned index terms and words in titles or abstracts. Selecting terms is an exploratory process, whether it involves flipping through pages or using a terminal. This is a key process which has retained its importance in the transition to online searching. The main difference is that scanning through and cross-matching descriptors, which even when it is carried out mentally can be said to be a mechanical process, is indeed carried out by machine.

The computer, of course, has to be instructed as to what to do, and this is the purpose of the system's command language. Important command languages are Dialog, ORBIT, Elhill, Quest and STAIRS. They are usually specific to a particular online service (for example, Dialog is the command language of the Lockheed Information Retrieval Service), but the Euronet common command language is likely to be adopted widely in Europe and others, such as the National Library of Medicine's Elhill language, have been leased by other service centres and are already in fairly wide use. There is also, as was explained in Chapter 2, a similarity between Elhill and ORBIT and between Dialog and Quest. Even command languages which appear to be distinct, such as ORBIT and Dialog, show a great deal of similarity in the range of operations which they permit. It is the range of operations which we are concerned with here rather than the detailed grammar of the particular command languages, for which the system manuals must be consulted, but real examples will be chosen to illustrate how they are carried out. The main operations are:

Connecting to the computer and logging on to the online system.
Selecting the file to be searched.
Entering and combining search terms.
Printing results.
Logging off and disconnecting.

There is an equally important preparation stage which comes before the use of the terminal. Much of the selection of search terms and thinking about the strategy to adopt usually takes place prior to linking up to the computer. The preparation of a search is described fully in Chapter 7, and the selection and combination of terms is covered in more detail in Chapter 6.

4.2 CONNECTING TO THE ONLINE SYSTEM

Connecting to the online system consists, first of all, of establishing a physical link between your computer terminal and the computer installation or, if the link is to be via a telecommunications network, the nearest node of the network. This is simply a matter of dialling up the node or the computer installation. If there is a leased line link, the connection is already made and all you have to do is switch on the equipment. The next step is to enter various passwords to identify your organisation and, if going via a network, the system you wish to use. A typical procedure is as follows:

(1) Switch on the equipment and make sure that the necessary connections are made between the terminal and the modem or coupler, and the terminal and printer if there is a separate one. Check that the DUPLEX, PARITY, SPEED and LOCAL/ONLINE switches are in the correct positions.

(2) Dial the appropriate telephone number. A successful call is indicated by a continuous high-pitched tone. An engaged tone or continuous ringing means either that the node or computer is not working or that you have a wrong number.

(3) Switch the signal through to the terminal by placing the hand-set in the acoustic coupler or, if using a hard-wired modem, by pressing the connecting button on the telephone or terminal.

(4) Type the terminal identifier. This enables the computer or the network to adjust the information it sends to suit the characteristics of your particular terminal.

(5) Enter the password required by the network. This will include a section which identifies the system or host computer you wish to link up to.

(6) Enter the password required by the online system.

The example in *Figure 4.1* shows what happens when logging in to the Lockheed system through the British Post Office's International Packet Switching Service and Tymnet. Note that input, that typed by the searcher, is underlined to distinguish it from the output of the system.

The terminal identifier in this example is A2, which is for a 30 characters per second terminal having 80 characters per line. It is in this case preceded by two and succeeded by one press of the CARRIAGE RETURN KEY indicated by [R]. In online searching the depression of the return key is the usual trigger for sending messages to the computer, so that the [R] symbol should be presumed to end every line typed by the searcher, although it is not shown in the following examples.

Once it has received the terminal identifier, the node replies by a message which identifies itself and gives a port number (201). The next step is to enter the user identifier (prmntm, etc.). Then the part of the password which specifies

```
[R] [R] A2 [R]                          - terminal identifier
+LONPSC-201                             - network node response giving port no.
prmntmxxx5822-                          - user identifier for accessing network
ADD?

a31060061*dlrrs;ipsslon                 - network user address-i.e. Lockheed

COM31060061

to⟩ host is online                      - network response


ENTER YOUR DIALOG PASSWORD              - response of host system
XXXXXXXX                                - password (blocked out by system)
▌x▌x▌x▌x▌x▌x▌   LOGON File12 Tue 6mar79 4:27:00


DIALOG IS NOW OPERATING ON EASTERN
STANDARD TIME....
NEW SCHEDULE OF HOURS.  SEE ?NEWS and
?SCHEDULE.
NEW VERSION OF POLLUTION ABSTRACTS,
FILE 41, NOW AVAILABLE.  SEE ?NEWS.
?
```

Figure 4.1 Logging into the Lockheed system through the British Post Office's International Packet Switching Service and Tymnet

the system you wish to use, the network user address, is entered in response to the question ADD? The node acknowledges the receipt of the final section of the password by COM31060061.

The next response is from the Tymnet network, which announces that the required host (that is, Lockheed) is online. Other Tymnet messages which might occur are:

ALL PORTS BUSY – all the host's ports (connecting points) available to Tymnet are busy.

CIRCUITS BUSY – all available paths through the network are busy.

REQUESTED SUBPROCESS IS UNAVAILABLE – the process required on the host computer is not available.

HOST DOWN – host computer not working.

However, if the attempted link-up is successful, we get a message from the host computer asking for our Dialog password. When this has been entered, it is overprinted by the system to render it illegible.

Once through to the system, we are put into a default file, which is file 12 here, and then given the date and time and some system news. Finally, the system leaves us with a prompt – the question mark ? – to the left of the bottom line. Nearly all systems have some sort of prompt which indicates when the computer is ready to receive information.

4.3 SELECTING THE FILE TO BE SEARCHED

You may need to select a file as soon as you are connected to the system or you may be put straight into the file you want. Note that files are discrete parts of the system which must be searched separately. Several systems (such as Lockheed and Blaise) put you initially into a file known as the default file. The user may specify which the default file is to be, and from that can switch to any other file. In the SDC system, which has the command language ORBIT, the user is put first into a file called ORBIT. This is a dummy file with only one record, which, because it is comparatively cheap, is an appropriate place to 'park' while 'exploring' the system by means of the EXPLAIN or NEWS commands (see below). Specifying the file you want from the ORBIT file is done by the file-switch command, which has the form FILE a (*Figure 4.2*).

```
USER:

FILE NTIS
PROG:
ELAPSED TIME ON ORBIT: 0.02 HRS.
YOU ARE NOW CONNECTED TO THE NTIS DATABASE.


SS 1 /C?
USER:
```

Figure 4.2 Selecting the NTIS file on SDC ORBIT

On switching files it is usual to be given details of the time spent in the previous file or further information such as cost. Note that the prompt in the SDC example is a two-line one consisting of SS 1 /C?, which is a request to enter a search statement or a command, and the word USER:, which simply means 'your turn'. Another standard feature of multifile systems is that you can get a list of the files to see what is available. This is accomplished by the FILES command on SDC (*Figure 4.3*).

```
SS 1 /C?
USER:
FILES


PROG:
YOU MAY ACCESS THE CIS INDEX, QUEBEC, SSCI, CHEMCON, CHEM7071, AGRICOLA,
CDI, DEMNTIS, NTIS, ISMEC, SAFETY, COMPENDEX, LIBCON/E, CIN, LISA, INSPEC,
POLLUTION, SSIE, SAE, P/E NEWS, BIOSIS, FSTA, FEDREG, OCEANIC, ASI, ENERGYLINE
PAPERCHEM, MANAGEMENT, CAS77, CRECORD, ACCOUNTANTS, BIO6973, ENVIROLINE,
CHEMDEX, BIOCODES, TITUS, INFORM, CBPI, LABORDOC, CNI, DBI, ERIC, INSP6976,
PSYCHABS, CONF, PROMPT, GEOREF, USPSD AND ORBIT DATABASES.
YOU ARE NOW CONNECTED TO THE ORBIT DATABASE.

SS 1 /C?
USER:
```

Figure 4.3 Listing available files on SDC (March 1979)

4.4 THE SEARCH PROPER: SELECTING AND COMBINING SEARCH TERMS

The search itself, which consists of entering search terms, combining them in various ways and printing results, may be a relatively short business when compared with the preparation stage and the time required to analyse the results. *Figures 4.4–4.7* show a simple illustrative search for references on the subject of *lung cancer and smoking.* The file searched is the Scisearch file of the Institution of Scientific Information, and the system is Lockheed. Records in Scisearch are similar in content to the Social Science Citation Index record shown in Chapter 2. Thus, terms are matched with words in the title.

```
?begin34


        6mar79 4:27:56 UserT77
$0.94 0.017 Hrs File12*
File34:SCISEARCH 79/WKC4
(Copr. ISI Inc.)
SEE FILE 94(74-77)
        Set Items Description (+=OR;*=AND;-=NOT)
        --- ----- ------------------------------
? select cancer

        1   3655 CANCER
? select carcinoma

        2   2597 CARCINOMA
? select lung

        3   2190 LUNG
? select lungs

        4    315 LUNGS
? combine (1 or 2) and (3 or 4)

        5    422 (1 OR 2) AND (3 OR 4)
```

Figure 4.4 Example search, Part 1

In the first part of the search (*Figure 4.4*) the Scisearch file is selected by the BEGIN-FILE CHANGE command. This has the effect of starting afresh by erasing all traces of previous searches and switching from file 12 to file 34, which is Scisearch. The time and date (note that the search was carried out on 6 March 1979) and a certain amount of data about the use of the system in the previous file are printed at this point. There is also a message drawing attention to file 94, which covers the earlier years of the Scisearch database. Scisearch is one of a growing number of files which are segmented by date.

The next operation is the entry of four search terms descriptive of the concept *lung cancer* using the SELECT command. This is a minimal range of terms to use for this topic but adequate to illustrate the point. As each term is selected, a *set* is formed, (1, 2, 3 and 4) and a number of postings given. The number of postings is the number of records in the Scisearch file which contain that particular term. Thus, there are 3655 records in the Scisearch file containing the word *cancer.* The formation of sets, also called search statements, is a characteristic feature of online systems. These are the building-blocks of a search and can be combined together by the local operators AND, OR, NOT with complete freedom to form further sets. The meaning of these operators is probably what most people would guess it to be.

1 AND 2 forms a set of references which match *both* sets 1 *and* 2. AND is used to link different concepts of a search.

1 OR 2 forms a set of references which match *either* 1 *or* 2 or *both.* OR is used to link synonymous concepts of a search.

1 NOT 2 forms a set of references which match 1 but *not* 2. NOT is used to exclude concepts from a search.

Thus, the command COMBINE 3 OR 4 will match with the references that include either the word *lung* or *lungs* or both words.

The last step in this section is to combine the various terms together, using the COMBINE command to give a fifth set of 422 references dealing with *lung cancer*. The combinations of terms specified by this operation are:

LUNG AND CANCER
LUNG AND CARCINOMA
LUNGS AND CANCER
LUNGS AND CARCINOMA

The next part of the search (*Figure 4.5*) involves exploring for further terms descriptive of the concept *smoking*. Although it is possible in many cases to anticipate what terms to use, it is often useful to be able to display listings of terms online. In this example this is accomplished by the EXPAND command.

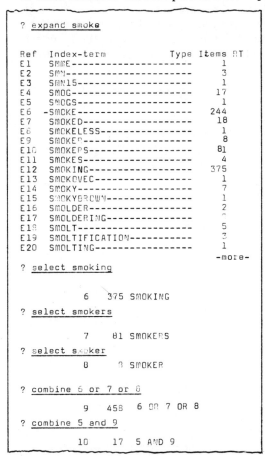

```
? expand smoke

Ref   Index-term              Type Items RT
E1    SMME----------------------    1
E2    SMN-----------------------    3
E3    SMN15---------------------    1
E4    SMOG----------------------   17
E5    SMOGS---------------------    1
E6   -SMOKE---------------------  244
E7    SMOKED--------------------   18
E8    SMOKELESS-----------------    1
E9    SMOKER--------------------    8
E10   SMOKERS-------------------   81
E11   SMOKES--------------------    4
E12   SMOKING-------------------  375
E13   SMOKOVEC------------------    1
E14   SMOKY---------------------    7
E15   SMOKYBROWN----------------    1
E16   SMOLDER-------------------    2
E17   SMOLDERING----------------
E18   SMOLT---------------------    5
E19   SMOLTIFICATION------------    3
E20   SMOLTING------------------    1
                               -more-
? select smoking

       6    375 SMOKING
? select smokers

       7     81 SMOKERS
? select smoker

       8      8 SMOKER

? combine 6 or 7 or 8

       9    458  6 OR 7 OR 8
? combine 5 and 9

      10     17  5 AND 9
```

Figure 4.5 Example search, Part 2

EXPANDing *smoke* produces an alphabetical listing around the term *smoke*. The numbers given are the postings for each term.

There are three terms here which are appropriate to the search – SMOKING, SMOKER and SMOKERS – and these are selected to form *sets* 6, 7 and 8. On the Lockheed system these terms would not normally be selected in this way, because there is a much simpler way of doing it. ?SELECT E10,E11,E17 would have the same result. Not all systems have this time-saving feature. These terms having been selected, they are first of all combined together to give *set* 9, which contains 458 references on *smoking, smoker* or *smokers. Set* 9 is then combined with the earlier references from *set* 5 on *lung cancer* to give *set* 10. Set 10 contains 17 references which should be on the subject *smoking and lung cancer*. Thus, the search has been narrowed down quickly to produce quite a small group of references on the search topic.

4.5 PRINTING THE RESULTS

In the third part of the search (*Figure 4.6*) three references are printed online using the TYPE command. The full command specifies the first 3 references to be typed from *set* 10 using *format* 2 (full bibliographic description). The full 17 references are then printed offline by using the similar PRINT command.

```
? type 10/2/1-3

10/2/1
0497896  ARTICLE  OATS ORDER#: FW240  22 REFS
   SISTER  CHROMATID EXCHANGES IN PERIPHERAL-BLOOD OF CIGARETTE SMOKERS
AND IN LUNG-CANCER PATIENTS - EFFECT OF CHEMOTHERAPY  (ENGLISH)
   HOLLANDER DH; TOCKMAN MS; LIANG YW; BORGAONKAR DS; FROST JK
   HUMAN GENETICS , V44, N2, P165-171, 1978
   JOHNS HOPKINS UNIV,SCH MED,DEPT PATHOL/BALTIMORE//MD/21205;  JOHNS
HOPKINS UNIV,SCH MED,DEPT MED/BALTIMORE//MD21205

10/2/2
0440130  ARTICLE  OATS ORDER#: FR703  0 REFS
   SMOKING-HABITS OF LUNG-CANCER PATIENTS - TIME OF CONSUMPTION AND TAR
CONTENTS OF SMOKED BRANDS  (GERMAN)
   KUNZE M; HERBERG D; VUTUC C
   PRAXIS UND KLINIK DER PNEUMOLOGIE , V32, N10, P655-658, 1978
   UNIV VIENNA,INST HYG,SOCIALMED ARBEITSGRP/A-1095 VIENNA//AUSTRIA/

10/2/3
0396832  ARTICLE  OATS ORDER#: DV131  16 REFS
   RADIOLOGICALLY  OCCULT  INSITU  AND  INCIPIENT  INVASIVE  EPIDERMOID
LUNG-CANCER - DETECTION BY SPUTUM CYTOLOGY IN A SURVEY OF ASYMPTOMATIC
CIGARETTE SMOKERS  (ENGLISH)
   MELAMED MR; ZAMAN MB; FLEHINGER BJ; MARTINI N
   AMERICAN JOURNAL OF SURGICAL PATHOLOGY , V1, N1, P5-16, 1977
   MEM  SLOAN  KETTERING  CANC  CTR,DEPT  PATHOL,CYTOL  SERV/NEW
YORK//NY/10021;  MEM  SLOAN  KETTERING  CANC CTR,THORAC SURG SERV/NEW
YORK//NY/10021; IBM CORP,THOMAS J WATSON RES CTR,DEPT GEN SCI/YORKTOWN
HTS//NY/10598

? print 10/2/1-17

Printed10/2/1-17
?
```

Figure 4.6 Example search, Part 3

The offline prints will be printed later, probably overnight, at the computer installation and posted to you. Some systems allow the address to be specified at this point.

All 17 references could have been printed online, but printing offline is a cheaper method of getting the information. A usual practice is to print online enough references for immediate use or to be sure that the *set* contains the references required, and to print the remainder offline, but obviously this depends on the urgency.

Examining references online may suggest new terms. Here we can see that *cigarette* would be a useful alternative to *smoking*.

```
?  logoff

              6mar79  4:43:38  UserT77
        $1.96   0.028 Hrs File34  7 Descriptors

LOGOFF    4:43:41


CLR DTE  0:17:6 138  62
```

Figure 4.7 Example search, Part 4

The final stage (*Figure 4.7*) is to exit from the system, and on Lockheed this is accomplished by the LOGOFF command, which switches you back to the node of the network. The node provides some control information (CLR DTE) which shows that the session lasted 17 minutes and 6 seconds, and that 138 segments (of 64 characters each) were received during the session and 62 sent. You can now either type another user-identifier and link to another system or switch off the equipment and replace the telephone hand-set.

This search could, in fact, have been carried out in a much brisker fashion by using command abbreviations and by stringing commands together. This would be a more normal method of working (*Figure 4.8*).

```
?  scancer;scarcinoma;slung;slungs;ssmoking;ssmoker;ssmokers


            1    3655 CANCER
            2    2597 CARCINOMA
            3    2190 LUNG
            4     315 LUNGS
            5     375 SMOKING
            6       8 SMOKER
            7      81 SMOKERS
?  c(1or2)and(3or4)and(5or6or7)

            8      17 (1OR2)AND(3OR4)AND(5OR6OR7)
```

Figure 4.8 Example of Dialog's compact notation

The power of online searching depends very much on the possibilities the system provides for specifying and combining search terms. This is discussed in Chapters 5 and 6. Further selection and combination facilities include:

The selection of groups of alphabetically related terms by truncation.

The selection of subject-related terms by means of classification schemes and selecting from online term displays.

Narrowing the search to particular fields of the citation, such as title, index terms, source, abstract, author, etc.

Specifying the proximity of terms to one another and their order.

Searching for strings of characters within a preselected group of citations.

Selecting by very broad characteristics, such as date, type of literature, language, source and country of origin.

Citation searching.

Specifying major or minor terms.

4.6 SOME FURTHER SYSTEM FEATURES

So far we have only dealt with the basic functions required to carry out a simple search. Online systems usually have many other facilities. Some of the important ones are described and illustrated below by Blaise, which uses the Elhill command language. How these are carried out on other major systems can be found from the Appendices.

4.6.1 Correcting errors

Miskeying can be corrected by erasing character by character or by erasing the whole line, provided that the RETURN KEY has not been pressed. The symbols used vary between systems and according to the keyboard of the terminal (*Figure 4.9*).

```
SS 13 /C?
USER:
LIVER DISEESES \\\\ ASES
PROG:
SS (13) PSTG   (1287)

USER:
"PRT 1Ø TITLESØ
USER:
```

Figure 4.9 Example from Blaise of correcting miskeys by erasing individual characters or the full line

The backward slash, \, erases a single character; a $ sign followed by the RETURN deletes a complete line.

Once an operation has been initiated by pressing the RETURN, it can usually be interrupted. The BREAK key is the commonest device for this, but the RETURN and ESCAPE keys are sometimes applicable.

4.6.2 Getting information at the terminal about the system

Most systems have an EXPLAIN or similar command which provides information about commands, files or system messages. The full range of options is obtainable by simply EXPLAINing the EXPLAIN command (*Figure 4.10*). (Note that all commands on Blaise are preceded by a double quote mark, ".)

Blaise also has a desperation command for when you cannot think how to proceed. HELP, appropriately enough, is the command for this function (although HELP on other systems has the same function as EXPLAIN). (See *Figure 4.11.*)

```
"explain explain
PROG:

THE EXPLAIN COMMAND:


THE COMMAND "EXPLAIN" USED ALONE RESULTS IN AN EXPLANATION OF THE
LAST STANDARD PROGRAM MESSAGE THAT HAS COME FROM THE SYSTEM.

THE COMMAND "EXPLAIN----" WITH A TERM OR TERMS REPLACING THE DASHES,
RESULTS IN AN EXPLANATION OF WHATEVER IS NAMED BY THE INSERTED TERM.
INSERTED TERMS MAY BE ANY OF THE FOLLOWING:

1. (STANDARD COMMANDS): VERSION, RENAME, FIND, DIAGRAM, NEIGHBOR,
   NEIGHBORDET, SUBHEADINGS, PRINT, FILE, HELP, EXPLAIN, ERASEBACK,
   ERASEALL, RESTACK, RESTART, AND STOP.

2. (SPECIAL COMMANDS AND ACTIONS): TREE, MESHNO, EXPLODED SEARCH,
   ORDER, COMMENT, NEWS, AND USERS.

3. (PROGRAM MESSAGES): READINESS CUE, LIST SEARCH, CONTINUATION CUE,
   SEARCH SERIES FULL, DESIGNATE ELEMENTS, CONTINUE PRINTING,
   CONFIRM RESTART, CONFIRM STOP, NO POSTINGS, MULTI-MEANING, KEYBOARD
   TERM OVERFLOW, STORED POSTINGS OVERFLOW, POSTINGS, NO MATCH,
   UP N OR DOWN N, GENERATED TERM OVERFLOW, REPLY, CONTINUE COMMENT,
   NEXT ORDER, ALL OR NONE, TIME OVERFLOW, POSTINGS PROCESSOR
   OVERFLOW, AND DYNAMIC REJECT.
   YOU MAY ALSO EXPLAIN ANY PROGRAM MESSAGE BY ENTERING THE FIRST 2
   OR 3 (UP TO 23) CHARACTERS OF THE MESSAGE TEXT ITSELF, E.G.:
CONTINUE PRINTING? (YES/NO)

USER:

y
PROG:
                    "EXPLAIN PSTG"

                    "EXPLAIN DYNAJECT"

4. (OTHER ITEMS): UNIT RECORD, OPERATING SUMMARY, LONG SEARCH
   STATEMENTS, LONG PRINT COMMANDS, VARIABLE CHARACTER KEYS, (AND, OR,
   AND AND NOT), NESTED STATEMENTS, SEARCH TERM QUALIFIERS, DEFAULT
   MODE, TYPING ERRORS, SUBHEADINGS, COMMANDS, TIME SLICING,
   RANGING, SS NUMBERS, PRINT FORMATS, COMPACT, INDENTED, KEYWORDS,
   AND PRINT CATEGORY DESIGNATORS.

SS 1 /C?
USER:
```

Figure 4.10 The EXPLAIN command on Blaise (June 1979)

```
"HELP
PROG:
TYPE NUMBER IDENTIFYING YOUR PROBLEM AND CARRIAGE RETURN.

1. AM GETTING NP OR NONE MESSAGE: NEED NEW TERMS OR THE FORM OF
   SOME TERMS.

2. WANT TO SEE SEARCH RESULTS.

3. THE PROGRAM ASKED A QUESTION.

4. NEED TO REVIEW OPERATING FEATURES.

5. NEED TO REVIEW DATA BASE OR UNIT RECORD.

6. WANT NAMES OF COMMANDS.

USER:
```

Figure 4.11 The Blaise HELP command

A listing of files or display of system news may be an EXPLAIN option or, as on Blaise, there may be separate FILE LIST and NEWS commands. Current news items are usually automatically printed out as you log on.

4.6.3 Sending messages

Most systems incorporate some device which allows you to send a message to the computer system. On some it is possible to send messages to other terminals connected to the system. On Blaise there is a special COMMENT command (see *Figure 4.12*).

```
"explain comment
PROG:
THE COMMENT COMMAND
YOU CAN ISSUE A COMMENT COMMAND WHEN YOU WISH TO INSERT A COMMENT THAT
WILL BE ROUTED TO THE PERSONNEL IN CHARGE OF MAINTAINING THIS SYSTEM.
TO ISSUE A COMMENT COMMAND, TYPE:

     "COMMENT"

THE SYSTEM WILL ASK YOU TO SPECIFY YES OR NO TO THE QUESTION OF WHETHER
YOU WISH A REPLY.  IF YOU DO, IT WILL TAKE YOUR NAME AND MAILING
ADDRESS.  OTHERWISE, THE COMMENT IS ANONYMOUS, AND THE PROGRAM WILL
PROCEED BY PROMPTING YOU TO INSERT EACH LINE OF YOUR COMMENT.  WHEN
YOU ARE FINISHED, INDICATE THIS BY ENTERING A SINGLE LINE CONSISTING
ENTIRELY OF THE WORD FINISHED OR THE WORD DONE, AND A CARRIAGE RETURN.

SS 1 /C?
USER:
```

Figure 4.12 The COMMENT command EXPLAINed on Blaise

4.6.4 Hierarchical listings of terms

We have already seen that producing alphabetical listings of terms at the terminal is a standard feature, but where a hierarchical thesaurus is used it may also be possible to produce a hierarchical listing, or a list of subject-related terms (see *Figure 4.13*). The asterisked terms have further subordinate terms.

```
SS 1/C?
"TREE BRAIN
PROG:

Central Nervous System  A8.186
     Brain  A8.186.211
          Brain Stem  A8.186.211.132 (*)
          Cerebellum  A8.186.211.132 (*)
          Cerebral Ventricles  A8.186.211.276 (*)
          Diencephalon  A8.186.211.305 (*)
          Limbic System  A8.186.211.577 (*)
          Mesencephalon  A8.186.211.659 (*)
          Telencephalon  A8.186.211.985 (*)

SS 1/C?
USER:
```

Figure 4.13 The Blaise–Medline TREE command

4.6.5 Listing details of a search

As a search progresses, it is sometimes useful to be able to recapitulate by listing the sets or search statements which have been formed up to that point (see *Figure 4.14*).

```
SS 5 /C?
USER:
"diagram 4
PROG:


SEARCH FORMULATION BEGINNING AT SS 4 :
  (SS  1:
  (LIVER )
  AND SS  2:
  (LUNG NEOPLASMS )
  AND SS  3:
  (SMOKING )
  )

NO SUBHEADINGS APPLIED TO ANY SEARCH STATEMENT.

SS 5 /C?
USER:
```

Figure 4.14 The DIAGRAM command used on Blaise–Medline to show what search statements have been formed

4.6.6 Deleting sets or search statements

Erroneous term selections and combinations and those no longer needed can be deleted on some systems. This tidies up the search and releases work space in the computer for further searching. On Blaise the RESTACK command may be used. This enables the searcher to specify which search statements should be retained. In *Figure 4.15*, after forming 4 search statements it was decided to

```
SS 5 /C?
USER:
"restack 1,3
PROG:

SS 3 /C?
USER:
```

Figure 4.15 The Blaise RESTACK command

erase numbers 4 and 2, and so 1 and 3 are RESTACKed. After the command, search statement number 1 remains as it is, but search statement number 3 becomes search statement number 2, the others being deleted. The system therefore now responds by asking for search statement number 3 (SS 3 /C?) rather than number 5, since 3 will now be the next search statement number.

4.6.7 File changing

Changing files is obviously an essential feature of multifile systems. It usually employs the same command that is used for selecting the first file to be searched (*see Figure 4.16*).

```
USER:
"file toxline
PROG:
YOU ARE NOW CONNECTED TO THE TOXLINE FILE

SS 1 /C?
USER:
```

Figure 4.16 Changing from Medline to Toxline on Blaise

4.6.8 Saving searches

Since files have to be searched separately, the profile — the combination of terms which describe the subject — has to be run afresh in each file. To avoid having to re-enter the profile each time, it can usually be saved in the system and recalled as required. It may be possible to have the system automatically run the profile when a file is updated, so providing an SDI service. Saving the profile involves its being given a serial number or name by which it can be recalled. In *Figure 4.17* the Blaise STORESEARCH command is used to store a search on *the liver and smoking.* The computer asks for a name to be specified, and in this

```
USER:
"storesearch
PROG:
SEARCHNAME?

USER:
Liver
PROG:
ON-LINE OUTPUT:--NPS/PSTG/NONE?

USER:
pstg
PROG:
ENTER SEARCH-

*STS* SS 1 /C?
USER:
liver
PROG:
SS (1) PSTG (14109)

*STS* SS 2 /C?
USER:
smoking
PROG:
SS (2) PSTG (2300)

*STS* SS 3 /C?
USER:
1 and 2
PROG:
SS (3) PSTG (18)

*STS* SS 4 /C?
USER:
"finished
PROG:
OK? (Y/N/C/ADDRESS)

USER:
y
PROG:
STORESEARCH COMPLETED.

SS 4 /C?
USER:
```

Figure 4.17 The STORESEARCH command on Blaise

case the name was given as 'Liver'. The next question is whether the user wants the postings information to be displayed as the profile is constructed. Then the search terms, *liver* and *smoking*, are entered and combined. The command FINISHED ends the sequence. The profile on liver and smoking is now stored and can be recalled by using the name 'Liver'.

4.6.9 Getting timing details

Since the main cost element in online searching is the time for which you are linked to the system, it is important to know how long the search is taking. Most systems provide regular timing details, but there may also be commands to

```
USER:
"time
TIME   0:12:14          BL TIME  15:40:38
USER:
```

Figure 4.18 The Blaise TIME command

request the time or the elapsed time. The Blaise TIME command gives both elapsed time and the time of day (*Figure 4.18*).

4.6.10 Document ordering

Online systems are increasingly turning their attention to the next stage of the process of information provision – the supply of documents. Blaise-ADRS (Automatic Document Request Service) enables references retrieved online to be used as requests for loans or photocopies from the British Library Lending Division (BLLD). The procedure involves transferring the selected references within the system to the Blaise 'Editor' (a simple matter) and adding BLLD request numbers. Prior arrangement with BLLD is necessary to benefit from ADRS.

4.7 GETTING INFORMATION ABOUT ONLINE SEARCHING

As we have already seen, it is possible to find out about online searching from the systems themselves by using commands such as EXPLAIN and HELP. However, printed publications are the essential sources of information. The basic details of the systems are available in promotional literature put out by the system suppliers. This is distributed liberally at conferences and courses and through the mail. It usually includes a list of the files covered and prices and information on how to begin using the service.

Once you have signed an agreement with a supplier, a useful first step is for the intended searcher to attend a course of instruction run by the service supplier. These courses usually take place regularly at a variety of locations. Courses are also available from database producers and independent organisations such as NASIC (North East Academic Science Information Centre) in the USA and the Central Information Service of London University.

For the established searcher there is a range of search aids, some of which are essential if competent use is to be made of online systems. Search aids are produced by three different sources: the service suppliers, and these are generally the most important to have; database producers; and independent agents.

The principal aid produced by the service suppliers is the system manual, which provides the definitive description of the command language and the system's files. As a rule, these are loose-leaf and updated as new files are added to the system. Sometimes there are two versions of the manual – a long version and a shorter version, which contains the necessary details in a condensed form and which is updated regularly. Since one of the key requirements of a manual is that it be up to date, the shorter alternatives usually turn out to be the more useful. The main vehicles for news about the systems and details of new features are the various newsletters. Examples are *Euronet Diane News, Blaise Newsletter, SDC News, Dialog Chronolog, Medlars Technical Bulletin* and *Dialtech Newsletter.* It is important that these be filed carefully and kept for ready reference. When starting with online searching, it is essential to get all the relevant parts of the manuals and to establish supplies of the newsletters. Back numbers of the newsletters should be obtained, as they often contain information which has not yet reached the manual.

The database suppliers may also produce guides and occasionally newsletters. Most of these, but not all, are system-independent and describe record structures, subject coverage and indexing policy rather than searching options. Some include thesauri or classification schemes, in which case it is essential to get them.

Other important search aids which are produced by some database producers are thesauri, classification schemes and term frequency lists. The published thesaurus is quite essential for searching some files, notably Medline. Term frequency lists, which may be made available on microfiche, are to some extent equivalent to online term displays. They may also be produced by the service supplier. Lists of journals covered by a database often occur at intervals in the corresponding abstract journal, or may be published as a separate list.

Independently published guides, obviously, must lack the currency and authority of guides produced by those directly responsible for the files and the computer system. However, they may have the advantage of covering a range of systems or files. Some of these search aids are published by organisations of national scope, such as NASIC and NFAIS (National Federation of Abstracting and Indexing Services), but there are many also produced for more local distribution by libraries, information centres and university departments.

A useful adjunct to information sources about online searching is journals devoted to the subject. The journals *Online* and *Online Review* are entirely concerned with the practice of online searching and contain immensely useful articles about services, files and techniques of searching. Back numbers of these journals are almost as valuable as current issues, so that the full sets should be obtained. Some of the more general journals, such as *Database, College and Research Libraries, Special Libraries, Information Processing and Management, Journal of Information Science, Bulletin of the American Society for Information Science* and *Aslib Proceedings,* also include articles of high interest from time to time.

Chapter 5

The Structuring of Information within a Database

5.1 GENERAL

Any description of online search languages, and the facilities they provide for obtaining information from a database, would be incomplete in the absence of an explanation about the structure of online databases. Search language and database structure fit together like two halves of a puzzle; considered separately, they yield only a superficial understanding of the total picture. This chapter sets out some of the procedures and decisions involved in creating a database and entering a new document record into that database. The following chapter describes the search 'tools' available for the reverse process — that is, of retrieving a record from the database. Most readers will only ever be concerned with the second operation, the searching side of the business, but for the reason already mentioned a knowledge of database structure is nevertheless important.

At the very least a bibliographic reference contains a title, source details and one or more authors' names. These parts of a bibliographic reference, or record, are known as fields, and so we refer to the title field, author field, and so on. Most document records are a good deal more complex than this simple three-field (title, source, author) type, and it is not unusual to find information relating to many other fields, including language, country, publisher, corporate source, availability of original document, etc. Those faced with the job of making this sort of information retrievable (traditionally via printed indexes) have had to balance accessibility against effort — that is, the chances of a searcher discovering what is required against the effort required to maintain the necessary indexes. At their simplest, these systems may be the 'one-shot' type, providing only one chance of locating a particular document. For example, *Africa* as the sole entry for a paper dealing with 'The pollution of rivers in Africa' does not help the searcher looking for entries under *River pollution*, or simply *Pollution.* In practice, most indexes have several entry points for each document record, but even so, many users would probably be able to cite examples of glaring omissions condemning many documents (short of serendipitous discovery) to irretrievable burial. Systems based on the printed word are very labour-intensive, so that even after making entries under *Pollution, River* and *Africa*, there may

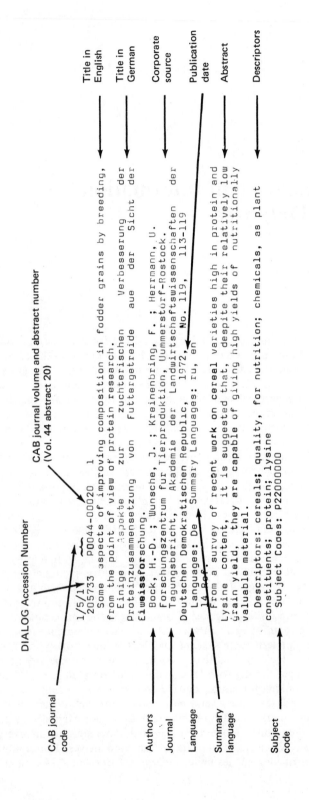

Figure 5.1 Sample record of CAB abstracts on Lockheed

be no attempt to cover other aspects of the document (such as journal title, publisher, language, etc.). What chance then of discovering papers about river pollution in *Journal X* or studies on African rivers in *French*?

The advent of computer processing has simplified these traditional indexing chores, since, once a decision has been taken about the structure and contents of a document record (not necessarily an easy task), the creation of just one machine-readable copy renders it amenable to manipulation in many different ways. This processing allows the creation of a large number of entries – for subsequent search and retrieval – and the sorting of these entries into 'dictionaries', which greatly accelerate that retrieval.

5.2 RECORD STRUCTURE

Let us now examine the structure of a document record:

The transmutation of heavy metals using the deep spin technique
Stone, Phil
Midas, T.
Alchemy in Action, Vol. 10, No. 4, April 1987, pp. 114–122
Rainbow Effects Inc., Liverpool, UK
Frespanian
Lead; Mercury; Nuclear Transformation

This record contains six distinct types of information (title, author, source, company, language, added terms), although both title and added terms could come under the general umbrella of subject field. Codes are often used to refer to the various fields – for example, AU for Author, LA for Language, etc. This record is fairly simple, but a more complex example is given in *Figure 5.1*.

5.3 FILE STRUCTURE

The precise way in which document records are grouped together to form files which allow for online searching is a feature of the software system (Dialog, Elhill, ORBIT, etc.). Usually the full details of each record are stored in one file, sometimes referred to as the bibliographic file. This file is a sequential file, as document records are stored one after another – for example,

Sequential file (bibliographic file):

Record 1   school, library, Britain
Record 2   school, teachers
Record 3   library, public
Record 4   Britain, school

It would be a very time-consuming business for the computer to search through these records sequentially, so to speed up the search process other files are created which contain sorted entries for all the searchable parts of the record:

Inverted file

1, 4	Britain	2
1, 3	Library	2
3	Public	1
1, 2, 4	School	3
2	Teachers	1

Dictionary file

1, 4	Britain	2
1, 3	Library	2
3	Public	1
1, 2, 4	School	3
2	Teachers	1

Provided that the functions of the inverted file and dictionary file are clearly understood, it is irrelevant whether they are considered as one and the same file or as two separate files. For the purposes of the explanation given here, they will be regarded as two distinct files.

The inverted file contains a list of record numbers (later referred to as accession numbers), and the dictionary file contains a total for number of record numbers. For example, if a new document (record number 5) dealing with *library* and *teachers* is added to the database, then the inverted file at Library would show 1, 3, 5 and at Teachers 2, 5; the corresponding dictionary file entries would increase from 2 to 3 and 1 to 2, respectively. If document number 5 had also contained a word which was new to the database (for example, *science*), then a new entry would be generated between *school* and *teachers*, for which the inverted and dictionary files would show 5 and 1, respectively.

The dictionary file may be referred to elsewhere as the index term file, the key term file or even the inverted file; provided that it is clear that the user is describing the alphabetical list of terms, together with the right-hand column of numbers (2,2,1,3,1) shown in the example, the terminology is not too important. Although our 'dictionary' does not contain word meanings, it will be consulted by the online user for much the same reason that people often consult dictionaries — that is, to check for spelling mistakes and variations, and, in the context of online work, the all-important format (for example, PAN, P.T. or PAN, PT or PAN Peter, T., etc.).

Using the files illustrated above, if documents relating to *school* were required, the inverted file shows that records numbered 1,2 and 4 qualified. Similarly, if documents relating to *school* and *Britain* were required, the inverted file shows that the record numbers common to both entries are 1 and 4. Updating these files, as in the example of record number 5 (*Library, Teachers, Science*) given above, is a more complex operation than simply adding the new record to the end of a sequential file. However, it should now be clear that the advantages to be gained when a large database is searched far outweigh the extra processing required to create the sorted files.

The dictionary file contains an entry for each directly searchable term, together with a value for the number of unique document records in which the term occurs. These values – derived from the total number of records in the inverted file – are usually displayed alongside the term, and are commonly referred to as 'postings' or 'hits'.

Term	Postings	
FUNGAL	3544	i.e. the term FUNGAL
FUNGI	5669	occurs in 3544
FUNGIA	19	separate documents;
FUNGICIDAL	185	etc.
FUNGICIDALLY	2	.
FUNGICIDE	2484	.
FUNGICIDES	3005	.
FUNGIFORM	47	
FUNGOID	1	
FUNGOIDES	506	
FUNGUS	6680	
FUNICOLUM	8	
FUNICULAR	23	
.	.	
.	.	
.	.	

5.4 ADDING A RECORD TO THE DATABASE

In the preparation of a record for input to the database, the indexer will pro-bably fill in a prepared form such as that shown in *Figure 5.2* for the Common-wealth Agricultural Bureaux (CAB) database. (The database designers will have decided which fields are to be included in the record.) The indexer may add terms to describe the subject of the document (as in our example of Nuclear Transformation) and might also write an abstract.

On adding a record to the database, the first step is for a unique reference or accession number to be assigned to that record. Thus, if there are already 1 257 288 records in the database, our new record will be number 1 257 289. A copy of the record will be added to the bibliographic (sequential) file, and its accession number is used by the online system whenever it needs to access that record (or to perform logic operations – see next chapter). Access to the full record is usually required for one of two reasons: either to retrieve the record at the display/print stage, or in order to perform a string search (see next chapter). The next step is to generate entries for the inverted and dictionary files.

5.5 DICTIONARIES

It was mentioned earlier that online dictionaries contain entries for all directly searchable parts of the document record; however, the type of dictionary is a feature of the software system (Dialog, Elhill, ORBIT, etc.). Some systems create separate or 'pure' dictionaries for each field, as seen in *Figure 5.3*; others merge all search terms, regardless of field of origin, into one large dictionary, and mark each term with a 'flag' denoting the field type, as seen in *Figure 5.4*

C.A.B. INPUT FORM	Title Sheet	Page of	Temporary Record Number

01 P 11092 X

MET (A.430)   20 Blue

DATE SCANNED			Title Only		JOURNAL	ABSTRACT SEQUENCE No.								TYPE OF ITEM						
Year	Mth.	Day		**04**	a	P	C E	R	G	E	Q	U	A	**05** Numbered N Whole W	Un-numbered U Part P	**06** Linking TRN			Count **07**
73	09	21	**03**		b														

AUTHORS (INCLUDE ROLE, ETC. IN BRACKETS)	Personal	**10**	Bock, H.-D.; Wünsche, J.; Kreinenbring, F.; Herrmann, U.
	Corporate	**11**	

Authors' Variants on names (for inclusion in author index only)	**12**	

ENGLISH TITLE	**20**	Some aspects of improving protein composition in fodder grains by breeding, from the point of view of protein research

Foreign Title	**21**	Einige Aspekte zur züchterischen Verbesserung der Proteinzusammensetzung von Futtergetreide aus der Sicht der Eiweissforschung

Collective Title	**22**	

Serial Name	**30**	Tagungsbericht Akademie der Landwirtschaftswissenschaften der Deutschen Demokratischen Republik

Town and Country of Publication; Publisher Or University.	**31**	

YEAR	**32**	1972	Vol. No. of Serial	**33**	
Bulletin, Issue, Part No. or Edition	**34**	No. 119	PAGES	**35**	113-119
Standard Book No.	**36** SBN ISBN		Order No.	**40**	
LANGUAGE OF TEXT	**41**	De	Language of Summaries	**42**	ru, en
Price	**43**				
Other Information	**44**	14 ref.			
Author's Affiliation	**45**	Forschungszentrum für Tierproduktion, Dummerstorf-Rostock,			
Secondary Journal Source	**46**				

Figure 5.2 Input form for a CAB database record

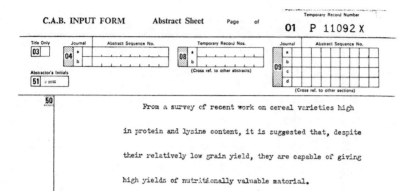

C.A.B. INPUT FORM   **Abstract Sheet**   Page   of

From a survey of recent work on cereal varieties high

in protein and lysine content, it is suggested that, despite

their relatively low grain yield, they are capable of giving

high yields of nutritionally valuable material.

Figure 5.2 (continued)

C.A.B. INPUT FORM	Index Sheet	Page	of	Temporary Record Number

01   P 11032 X

Author Index: Supplementary Entries	60			

		PHRASE LETTER	JOURNAL	
		a	P	cereals; quality, for nutrition
		b	P	cereals; chemicals, as plant constituents ! protein ? lysine
SUBJECT INDEX PHRASES	61			

Other Entries	62			German Democratic Republic

Figure 5.2 (continued)

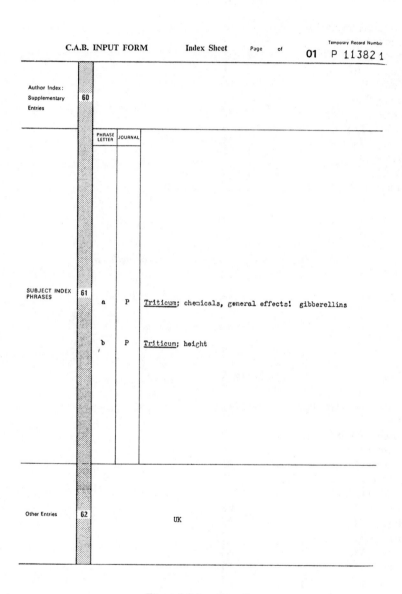

Figure 5.2 (continued)

Term	Postings
Stonaker, Michael R	2
Stone, A L	4
Stone, Andrew L	1
Stone, P John	1
Stone, P	16
Stone, Phil	1
Stone, Philip	2
Storey, T Yvonne	7
Storey, Yvonne	2
Stowey, F M	9
Studd, F G	1
Studdley, Robert Ian	3
etc.	

Figure 5.3 Example of entries in a 'pure' dictionary (author dictionary)

Term	Postings
Healeys Gazette (JO)	341
Healing (AT)	53
Heather (AT)	2
Heather (TI)	4
Heathers (TI)	1
Heathers, Brian D (AU)	5
Heating (AT)	1417
Heating (TI)	1008
Heavily (TI)	26
Heavitrans Ltd (SO)	2
Heavy (TI)	44
Hebrew (LA)	59
Henderson, JK (AU)	14
Henley Univ. (SO)	30
Hetty, Zoe T (AU)	4
etc.	

Figure 5.4 Example of entries in a mixed dictionary

(AU for author, AT for added term, CO for company, JO for journal, LA for language, TI for title).

With non-subject fields it is fairly common practice to preserve the integrity of the field. Thus, for our sample document — shown earlier — the two author entries would be Stone, Phil and Midas, T, both with the same address (1 257 289). Similarly, the journal entry would be Alchemy in Action, and the company entry would be Rainbow Effects Inc., Liverpool, UK.

Another feature of the software system is the way of dealing with subject information. This usually involves a further processing of fields designated as 'subject' fields (typically title, added term, abstract) to generate entries in the dictionary for all 'meaningful' words in these fields. The computer does this by examining each word in the specified field and comparing it with a list of trivial/ non-meaningful (stop) words. The stop list for Dialog, for instance, consists of AN, AND, BY, FOR, FROM, OF, THE, TO, WITH. Thus, the title in our example, 'The transmutation of heavy metals using the deep spin technique', would (under Dialog) cause entries to be generated at: *Transmutation, Heavy, Metals, Using, Deep, Spin, Technique.* This approach is often referred to as full text inversion. For each word from the subject field — or entry from other fields — which is processed, an entry of the accession number (in this case 1 257 289) is made in the inverted file. In a large scientific database, for example, it is likely that the word *spin* would be fairly common, so the accession number 1 257 289 would become just one of the many thousands already listed against *spin* in the inverted file. To complete the update, the dictionary file must also be adjusted (add one), the new total appearing as the 'postings' or the 'hit' number.

Example dictionary entries in region of spin:

Before update			*After* update		
SPILL	407		SPILL	407
SPILT	186		SPILT	186
SPIN	19233		SPIN	19234
SPINACH	406		SPINACH	406
SPINAL	2055		SPINAL	2055

It must be emphasised that users need concern themselves only with the dictionary file and its associated postings. The inverted file — containing actual accession numbers — is a systems device for internal management of database operations.

In some systems additional information pointing to the precise position of a word within its field is given — for example 1 257 289(002) for Transmutation; 1 257 289(004) for Heavy; and so on. The value of this is explained in the following chapter (see Section 6.8). This technique is known as word addressing.

For those fields not subjected to 'full text' treatment, there is a fairly obvious penalty. For example, anyone searching directly for *Liverpool* would not find document number 1 257 289 (although 'string searching' partly overcomes this difficulty).

Decisions taken at the time of loading a database, about which fields are to be full text inverted and which are to be left intact, have a profound effect on the extent to which a database can be probed during subsequent searches.

Typically, online dictionaries contain tens of thousands of terms, and each term may occur in anything from one to many tens of thousands (exceptionally, hundreds of thousands) of document records. Even so, although the document record in the example is just one of an extremely large number of records held in the database, each of its component parts will be identifiable (to the online system) by the unique accession number 1 257 289. Also, as we saw in some instances, this number will even give the position of a word within its original field – 1 257 289 (005) – metals.

At least one of the advantages of the online dictionaries – compared with a printed index – should now be clearer. The ease of machine processing allows a document record to be so finely fragmented that there are many terms (and therefore search approaches) which will lead to its discovery.

5.6 TREATMENT OF PHRASES

Between the two extremes of full text inversion and the insertion, intact, of a complete field into the dictionary, there is also the possibility of preserving phrases and sorting these, intact, into the appropriate dictionary. There are at least two ways of achieving this.

5.6.1 Marked phrases

During the intellectual task of assembling the original document record, the abstracter/indexer may have chosen to designate certain phrases as being worthy of preservation intact – from a retrieval viewpoint. In our example *heavy metals, deep spin* and *nuclear transformation* might well have fitted into this category. Provided that these phrases are marked – at the beginning and end – in such a way that they can be recognised by the computer during database building, there is no reason why they should not be preserved and sorted into the appropriate dictionary entries:

    dealer
    deansgate
    dearnford effect
    deed
    deeds
    deem
    deep
    deep spin
    deep water
    deep waters
    deeps
    deer

Such marking of terms may be undertaken for either of the following reasons. First, to preserve useful phrases which will be dismembered during full text processing (inversion), and second, to designate those phrases (and words) which are of major importance within the context of the document. This second reason requires that the phrases and words carry a special marker (flag) with them, through the dictionary – for example, *mercury*, deep spin*, transmutation** – to differentiate them from ordinary terms.

Sometimes these major terms are the only ones entered in the subject index part of the printed index. The MEDLARS database, for instance, has on average 12 medical subject heading (MESH) terms assigned to each record, of which 3 are major terms and thus used in *Index Medicus*. In our sample record we should expect the occurrence of *mercury** (as opposed to the ordinary indexing of *lead*), to indicate that a major, or very significant, part of the paper dealt with the topic of mercury transmutation. Such a decision can only be made by the abstracter/indexer of the original paper, and not by someone examining the document record alone.

5.6.2 Matched phrases

In the same way that a stop word list can be used to reject terms (in this case trivial), so too can a controlled list of terms — such as in a thesaurus — be used to scan data during input and mark those phrases which are on a 'go' list. Apart from maintenance of the 'go' list, this technique requires no intellectual effort; it has two drawbacks, however. First, it cannot recognise new, significant phrases until they have reached the thesaurus, and second, without very considerable extra machine processing, it cannot even begin to attempt to differentiate between major/non-major terms.

Whatever the methods used to designate special keywords or phrases when online dictionaries are being built, they are usually applied in addition to — and not instead of — the basic job of full text inversion/database building. In the case of our sample document record, this means that although special action may have been taken to preserve, say, *deep spin* as a phrase, it would also be possible to locate document number 1 257 289 at entries for *deep* and *spin* (as a result of full text inversion). The significance of this will become clearer when search facilities are considered.

5.7 INVERSION OF THE DOCUMENT RECORD

Let us re-examine the original document record ready for machine processing. Some phrases have now been specially ear-marked (between % and £) for preservation intact, while other phrases (and words) have been similarly 'flagged' (between @ and *) because they were considered as being of major importance within the context of the original document.

Title	The @transmutation* of %heavy metals£ using the %@deep spin*£ technique
Reference	Alchemy in Action, Vol. 10, No. 4, April 1987, pp 114–122
Author	Stone, Phil
Author	Midas, T
Source	Rainbow Effects Inc., Liverpool, UK
Language	Frespanian
Added Term	Lead
Added Term	@Mercury*
Added Term	%Nuclear Transformation£

Treating subject areas only to full text inversion, and with trivial words 'stopped', the following dictionary entries could be expected:

Alchemy in Action, April 1987	Nuclear
Deep	Nuclear Transformation
Deep Spin*	Rainbow Effects Inc., Liverpool, UK
Frespanian	Spin
Heavy	Stone, Phil
Heavy Metals	Technique
Lead	Transformation
Mercury*	Transmutation*
Metals	Using
Midas, T	

Each of these entries is linked to the document address (1 257 289) and possibly even to a word position (for example, transmutation, 1 257 289(002)). Whether the different categories of key terms (language, author, subject, marked, unmarked, etc.) are to be sorted into a merged dictionary or separate dictionaries is purely a database management decision. If the terms are merged in one dictionary, they will need to carry a field type descriptor (for example, Frespanian – LA). Subject searches usually default to include marked (major) terms, although it is, of course, possible to restrict the search to major terms only, if the original number of hits proves embarrassingly high. It should be noted that although *deep spin* is redundant (in the presence of *deep spin**), there is still good reason to include *deep* and *spin* as *separate* entry points.

Even if a word occurs more than once, it is only counted once per document record in the postings (hits) total when the dictionary is being compiled. A few systems also store an 'occurrence' value; this is the total of all occurrences for a particular term within the database. It bears no relation to the postings value, but by definition can only be equal to, or greater than, the number of postings.

With the exception of the initial intellectual effort required to generate (and specially mark, if required) the original document record, all the processing described in this chapter can be delegated to the computer. Once certain initial database management decisions have been taken, including how to 'structure' the data, and what sort of dictionaries to create, then from one machine-readable document record the computer can generate entry points equivalent to an almost limitless number of printed index or card catalogue search entry points. Furthermore, in this electronic form the data can be manipulated in ways which provide extremely powerful search techniques.

FURTHER READING

Lancaster, F.W. *Information Retrieval Systems,* 2nd edn, Wiley, Chichester (1979). ISBN 0-471-04673-6

Lancaster, F.W. and Fayen, E.G. *Information Retrieval Online,* Melville Publishing, Los Angeles (1973). ISBN 0-471-51235-4

Lynch, M.F. *Computer-based Information Services in Science and Technology – Principles and Techniques,* Peter Peregrinus, Stevenage (1974). ISBN 0-901223-55-7

Chapter 6

The Search Facilities Available

6.1 INTRODUCTION

In the generalised description of search facilities which follows, no attempt has been made to differentiate between the various online systems. Suffice it to say that many search facilities are common to all systems, although the commands and procedures for getting the same end result may be very different.

The suitability and relevance of some search commands can only be assessed in the light of knowledge about structuring within the target database. While many search facilities are available across all databases, there are some which are specific to certain databases only — even within the same systems operator. Used inappropriately, such questions may meet, at best, with no response, and at worst, with an incorrect result.

Assuming that the user has a good knowledge of the target database(s), in terms of both structure and contents, there are two main aspects left to consider when assembling a search strategy; these are the search terms and the co-ordinating logic (AND, OR, NOT). The success of the operation hinges on the appropriate selection of terms and their subsequent arrangement in a logical co-ordinating expression, which properly describes the enquirer's needs.

6.2 SINGLE TERM

The simplest question which may be used is a single word or term. For example:

| USER: | CAT | |
| SYSTEM: | 1 | 587 postings CAT |

This will cause the system to consult the dictionary and thus give the number of document records containing the term. This is often referred to as the number of postings.

The system also assigns a set number to the answer — in this case, 1. This is also sometimes referred to as a question or search statement number.

6.3 TERM TRUNCATION

Truncation of a search term is possible; single-character truncation (here desig-nated by *) is often suitable for simple plurals (though not always — *rat, rats, rate; tub, tubs, tube*) — for example,

USER: CAT*
SYSTEM: 2   901 postings CAT*

The response will now including postings for *cat* and any four-character term beginning *cat*. Naturally, the number of postings will increase as the net widens. Postings are unique: *cat* and *cats* in the same document record will only be counted once. Unlimited truncation (here designated +) opens the net even wider - for example,

USER: CAT+
SYSTEM: 3   75224 postings CAT+

The search statement embraces a whole range of possibilities, including *cat, catalogue, catatonic, catch, cats,* etc. In this particular example the truncation (CAT+) is much too severe and would cover a great deal of irrelevant material. Nevertheless, judiciously applied, truncation facilities are exceedingly useful and save drastically on keying. Entering POLLUT+, for example, will take care of *pollutant(s), pollute(s), polluting, pollution* — anything, in fact, beginning with the character sequence *pollut*.

In some systems it is possible to define the limits of right-hand truncation, either by multiple use of the single-character truncation symbol or by insertion of a limiting numerical value. This feature is of limited use:

CIRC****
OR   For *circle, circlet, circular*, etc., but not
CIRC*4   *circuitry, circulation, circumstance*, etc.

In dealing with search terms which are not truncated, the online system refers to the dictionaries to determine the number of postings:

	Term	*Postings*
cat	CASTLE	28
	CASTLES	63
	CAT	587
	CATAMARAN	1
	CATAPULT	13
	CATAPULTS	22
	CATHOLIC	2
	CATION	104
	CATIONS	209
	CATS	611
	CATTLE	1529
	CAUTION	5

However, although CAT* covers CAT (587 postings) and CATS (611 postings), the result is not necessarily a pure summation of the possibilities (587 + 611), because both terms may sometimes occur in the same document record. With truncated terms, therefore, the system has to check this possibility by comparing the accession numbers for all the terms generated by the truncation. Any kind of truncation implies OR logic (CAT* = CAT OR CATS, etc.), and the more severe the truncation (e.g. CA+, POLY+, etc.) the more 'work' the system has to do in eliminating duplicates from the final posting result. For this reason most systems are programmed to reject truncated terms which generate more than a certain number of dictionary entry points (usually about 800). This may be referred to as a STEM limit, because the truncated term is, in fact, a word stem. It is not a limit on the number of postings. (In the above section of dictionary CAT+ generates 9 search terms because there are 9 relevant stems.)

Truncation may also be used internally, where it can mask alternative spellings and — rather neatly — the user's own uncertainties about spelling:

ALUMIN+M	for *aluminium* or *aluminum*
SUL+UR	for *sulphur* or *sulfur*
MARI*UANA	for *marihuana* or *marijuana*

Many spelling difficulties can be avoided by using this very useful process of 'masking'. For the last example even MAR+ANA would probably give very few irrelevant hits. Other examples of encouragement to laziness include:

AC+M+DAT+	for *accommodate, accommodating, accommodation*
CEL+L+OS+	for *cellulose, celluloses, cellulosic,* etc.
COL+R+	for *colour, color, colours, coloured,* etc.
PROT+N+	for *protein, proteins, proteinaceous, proton,* etc.

An equal balance of adroitness and caution must be exercised when applying truncation. PROT+N (though not PROT**N), for example, would 'hit' *protozoan* as well as *protein*, although in the context of the target database this possibility may be unlikely.

As before, the online system tackles the internal masking by reference first to the dictionary and then — if more than one term qualifies — to the accession numbers in the inverted file.

At the time of writing, left-hand truncation is available for searching only a very limited number of databases. For example,

+PHOSPHATE to match with *diphosphate, dipolyphosphate, orthophosphate, trimetaphosphate,* etc.

Some systems also allow left- and right-hand truncation. For example,

+COGNIT+ to match with *cognition, recognition, cognitive,* etc.

A facility to be described later (string searching: see Section 6.9) enables left- and/ or right-hand truncation to be used against small, preselected parts of a database.

6.4 DISPLAYING DICTIONARIES

At any time during a search the user may choose to display the relevant part of the online dictionary, simply by keying in the correct command (e.g. EX for Expand) together with the term or fragment of interest. If there are several dictionaries available, the system usually displays from the subject dictionary (as opposed to the author or language dictionary). For example,

USER	EX PROT	
SYSTEM:		
Ref. No.	*Term*	*Postings*
1	PROSPECT	16
2	PROSPECTS	20
– 3 –	PROT	
4	PROTAGONIST	7
5	PROTEIN	1638
6	PROTEINACEOUS	259
7	PROTEINS	3554
8	PROTEST	2
9	PROTIENS	5
10	PROTON	862
11	PROTONS	914
12	PROTOTYPE	251

To avoid defaulting to the subject dictionary, the input command for dictionary expansion requires more detailed instructions. For example,

EX BROWN (AU) – to display the author dictionary in the region of *Brown*

Most systems allow the user to PIck directly from the dictionary display those terms which are of interest. The command is addressed to the reference number alongside the terms (see example of EX PROT):

PI 12	for PROTOTYPE
or PI 10, 11 } PI 10– 11	for PROTON(S)
PI 5, 7, 9	for PROTEIN(S), including the incorrect spelling at position 9
PI 5– 9	for all five terms, from positions 5 to 9 inclusive. Note: the irrelevant term at 8 (PROTEST) is scarcely worth the effort of excluding it (by using PI 5, 6, 7, 9)

Again, the PIck command will cause the system to print the number of postings and the set number allocated to this search statement.

Clearly, inspecting the dictionary before selecting terms can be very useful, especially if there are likely to be spelling mistakes. However, spelling errors which occur very early in the stem of a word (for example, PPOTEIN) are likely to be far removed from the relevant portion of dictionary and therefore to remain undetected. Displaying the dictionary is a way of determining the effect of truncating a search term, and it is probably as easy to pick out the possibilities (for example, PI 5–9) as it is to key in the term directly. Notice that PI 5–9, because it is equivalent to truncation, also implies OR logic; once again, the system has to avoid multiple occurrences of accession numbers via reference to the inverted file.

If the dictionary display does not reveal enough terms (systems vary in the number of terms displayed from about 5 to 20), there is usually a command available to continue listing.

Databases which have records indexed using a controlled thesaurus may have another entry in the dictionary display to indicate the number of terms 'related' to the terms displayed. Those related terms can also be displayed and so give the searcher more information about broader terms, narrower terms, and so on. For example,

```
USER:   EX(POLICE)
SYSTEM:
```

Ref. No.	Term		Postings	RT
1	POLICE		285	5
2	LAW ENFORCEMENT OFFICER	U		1
3	TRAFFIC POLICE	N	26	8
4	CIVIL SERVANTS	B	4186	35
5	CRIME	R	5928	14
6	PAROLE OFFICERS	R	416	7

In this example U = *Used for*, N = *Narrower term*, B = *Broader term*, R = *Related term*.

6.5 FIELD SEARCHING

In the absence of a field identifier (AUthor, LAnguage, etc.), search terms are usually matched against the subject dictionary. Alternatives must be specified – for example, MIDAS+/AU to search the author dictionary; FRESPANIAN/LA to search the language dictionary. It may be possible to search more than one field type – for example, BROWN+/TI, AU to search both author and title dictionaries.

The correct format for questions can vary greatly from system to system; so too can the default options (the field or dictionary to which a command refers in the absence of specific instructions). If a system is designed on the mixed dictionary concept, then keying in an unqualified (field not specified) term could provoke a listing of the ambiguities, together with a request for clarification:

```
USER:          BLACK+
SYSTEM:        BLACK           TI
               BLACK           AT
               BLACK D         AU
               BLACKBERRY      TI
               BLACKLEY S      AU
               BLACKSTON INC   CO

               WHICH ?
```

This can be time-consuming and so might be overcome by allowing the term to be preceded by ALL — for example, ALL BLACK+

An important point to remember about fields which are not full-text searchable is that a question such as STONE (AU), which is not truncated, is likely to result in zero postings, since the system rightly interprets it as being an inadequate match for an intact field such as STONE, PHIL. Truncation, as in STONE+ (AU), will overcome this rejection. Format is of critical importance, and even punctuation can lead to difficulties. If, at the database creation stage, for example, STONE, PHIL retains the comma, then STONE P+ (AU), which is clearly designed to catch those occurrences of the author where either the first initial or name have been used, will fail. Once again, inspection of the appropriate dictionary will help to settle this point, although inconsistencies in input are sadly common. (While truncation may be essential for a search term, it is not usually required in dictionary commands.) For example,

USER:	EX STONE+(AU)	
SYSTEM:		
Ref. No.	*Term*	*Postings*
1	Stondin, A K	12
2	Stondy, Albert	1
3	Stone	2
4	Stone, P J	2
5	Stone, P Robert	1
6	Stone, Peter	5
7	Stone, Phil	3
8	Stone, Simon M	4
9	Stone, WM Kenneth	8
10	Stonely, T	16

In this example, if the searcher is uncertain as to the author's full name, apart from 'Stone, Phil', then it would be necessary to pick the authors at 4, 5 and 7 to be on the safe side.

Searching for coded subject information, such as 75100 (BC) for the bio-systematic code in the biology file Biosis Previews, can be achieved using this technique of field searching.

The fields (and their abbreviated codes) available for searching a particular database on a particular system need to be examined when preparing a search. Common fields include:

accession number
title
author
journal name
date of publication
language
added terms
abstract

Figure 6.1 shows the search fields for a Marc record on Blaise; Marc, which gives very detailed bibliographic information about books, therefore has many access points for the searcher, and some 78 fields for printing. Some of these

BLAISE number (BL)
Corporate author (CN)
Control tag (CT)
Corporate word (CW)
Dewey Decimal Classification (DC)
Date of publication (DP)
Entry date (ED)
Corporate name added entry (HC)
Meetings name added entry (HM)
Personal name added entry (HW)
Information codes (IC)
Library of Congress Classification (LC)
Meetings name (MN)
Meetings word (MW)
Précis term (PD)
Personal name (PN)
Subject index number (PS)
Publisher (PU)
Précis word (PW)
Subject heading (SH)
Subject word (SW)
Text word (TW)
Corporate author word added entry (WH)
Meetings name word added entry (WM)

Figure 6.1 Search fields for the Marc databases on Blaise

Accession number (AN)
Descriptor (AN)
Note (NO)
Title (TI)
Author (AU)
Descriptor code (DC)
Document type (DT)
Historical period ending date (HE)
Historical period (HP)
Historical period starting date (HS)
Journal name (JN)
Publisher (PU)
Publication year (PY)
Series (SE)
Subfile (SF)
International Standard Serial Number (SN)
Update (UD)

Figure 6.2 Search fields for Modern Language Association Bibliography database on Lockheed

search fields match with more than one field in the actual record. *Figure 6.2* shows the search fields for the Modern Language Association (MLA) database on Lockheed. The need to be aware of the search field code can be seen in these examples — for example, the search code for year of publication of Marc is DP, whereas on MLA it is PY.

Terms which may have been designated as 'major' terms (as described in Chapter 5), may also be entered as a search statement. For example,

COMPUTERS/MAJ(AT)

If a searcher intends to spend a considerable time searching a field other than the default field, it may be possible to temporarily override the default field. For example,

SET FIELD = AU   (for authors)
SET FIELD = JO   (for journals)

As will be seen later, if one term is to be ANDed with some other aspect of the search, then a more severe form of truncation is usually acceptable — since irrelevant documents are less likely to satisfy the entire logic. For example,

STONE+ (AU) AND TRANSM+

Search terms which might reasonably be expected to retrieve (among others) the sample record in the previous chapter include:

STONE, P+ (AU)
TRANSMUT+
LEAD
RAINBO+ (SO)
MIDAS+ (AU)
ALCHEM+ (RF)
SPIN
DEEP
TRANSF+N

(Here it is assumed that terms not qualified by a field descriptor automatically default to a subject area, consisting of both title terms and added terms.)

Search terms which would miss this document record include:

STONE (AU)	Author field preserved intact; need to truncate, as in STONE+(AU).
STONE+	Field not specified, so would default to subject field.
PHIL+(AU)	Author field preserved intact; entry point is at STONE, as in STONE, PHIL.
ALCHEMY (RF)	Reference field preserved intact; need to truncate: ALCHEMY+ (RF).
FRESPANIAN (AT)	Wrong field specified.
FRESPANAN (LA)	Miskeyed.

6.6 PHRASE SEARCHING

In systems which allow the preservation of phrases in the dictionary, search statements or queries containing phrases are quite legitimate. For example,

USER:	LASER FUSION		
SYSTEM:	10	218	LASER FUSION
USER:	GREEK PHILOSOPHY		
SYSTEM:	11	48	GREEK PHILOSOPHY

As with a single-term search, the system allocates a set number and prints the number of items in the database containing the specified phrase.

6.7 COMBINING TERMS AND SEARCH STATEMENTS

Terms and search satements are usually combined in online search systems by using the logical operators AND, OR, NOT; these were formulated by the logician George Boole and are thus known as Boolean operators.

AND is used to link different concepts of a search — for example, FISH and FARMING will retrieve only those records which contain both the term *fish* and the term *farming*.

OR is used to link related concepts of a search — for example, APPLE OR PEAR OR BANANA will retrieve records which include any of the terms *apple, pear, banana*.

NOT is used to exclude concepts from a search — for example, ENERGY NOT SOLAR will retrieve records that contain the term *energy*, but not if they also contain the term *solar*.

Software systems (for example, Dialog, Elhill, Quest, etc.) vary in the way searchers are allowed to combine terms and search statements. Some allow one to enter terms directly — for example,

LION OR TIGER
1   654   LION OR TIGER

Others necessitate the allocation of sets first — for example,

LION
1   289   LION
TIGER
2   482   TIGER
1 OR 2
3   654   1 OR 2

Some allow for a mixture of terms and set numbers — for example,

1 OR TIGER
2   654   1 OR TIGER

Different logical operators may be used in the same statement but the rules determining which operator has precedence varies with different systems. This is usually overcome by the use of brackets:

(TIGER OR LION) AND ZOO
1   34   (TIGER OR LION) AND ZOO

or by splitting the search into smaller steps:

TIGER OR LION
1   654   TIGER OR LION
ZOO AND 1
2   34   ZOO AND 1

NOT logic should always be applied with caution, and certainly not before inspecting results obtained without its use. For example, if for some reason documents on panthers were not required and there were references to papers on several members of the cat family, including both panthers AND lions or tigers, then application of NOT PANTHER* would exclude relevant material. This situation is difficult to overcome (for example, (WELDING AND ALUMINIUM) NOT STEEL), but occasionally the context is clear-cut:

(BLACK AND HOLE*) NOT CALCUTTA

If many sets are to be combined using the same operator, a short-cut may be possible. For example,

1 – 8 /OR   (for 1 OR 2 OR 3 OR 4 OR 5 OR 6 OR 7 OR 8)

Usually there is a choice in the way questions may be assembled, and the searcher is free to use the route with which he/she feels most confident — even if it is a slightly roundabout way. One of the great strengths of online searching is the rapid interaction which is possible between the computer and the searcher — and the continual modification which this allows during interrogation. By and large, it is probably better to assemble the component terms of a question one at a time — ORing related concepts and finally ANDing the different concepts. This step-by-step method of building easily lends itself to diagnostics in the event of unexpected results — and the consequent need for alterations in search strategy (for example, inclusion of additional terms, modification of truncation, correction of erroneous search questions, etc.).

When the online system is required to solve logical operations (AND, OR, NOT) which have been applied to the terms of a query, it uses the accession numbers of document records to arrive at a result. For example, the question TRANSMUT+ AND SPIN would locate the document record described in the previous chapter, but in doing this the system must compare all the accession numbers for *transmut+* and *spin*, and count as successful (hits) only those document records whose numbers are common to both. With OR logic (LION OR TIGER), accession numbers for terms are simply combined, although any occurrences of a number, beyond the first, are ignored. It is an impressive feature of online systems that responses are often so fast, even though a question may involve the comparison of accession numbers for tens — or even hundreds — of thousands of document records.

Users need only concern themselves with the dictionary file and its associated postings or hits, but it is to the inverted file that the system must go to find the accession numbers when logical operations (AND, OR, NOT) are requested. Although accession numbers (sometimes called 'addresses') are of key importance to the internal management of the database operations (searching, logic, printing), users can safely remain oblivious to their actual numerical values.

6 8 PROXIMITY OPERATORS

If a system has been built to include word positions within the document address ('word addressing': Section 5.5), then facilities may also exist for describing word proximities when posing questions. For example, the word sequence *deep spin* may be tracked down first by locating accession numbers which are common to both terms and then by calculating the difference in the word position. Some systems are set to do this automatically on receiving a phrase (for example, *deep spin*); others need to be triggered by a specially formatted question — for example,

DEEP ADJ SPIN   (ADJ = adjacent)
or DEEP (W) SPIN   (where W also means adjacent)

In the record from the previous chapter the accession numbers/word positions for *deep* and *spin* were 1 257 289(008) and 1 257 289(009), respectively, which indicates that the terms are adjacent. Document 1 257 289 could therefore be retrieved by the appropriate search statement. Some systems allow for a 'match' irrespective of the order of terms — that is, a document entitled 'How to spin deep in the heart of Texas' might be retrieved!

It is also possible on some systems to specify the number of words which may intervene between terms — for example,

MANAGEMENT(1W) OBJECTIVES
(to match with 'management by objectives')

Note that for this type of comparison to work properly the software system must count all words in the full text field (that is, including the 'stopped' words), when assigning the word positions. Again, the searcher remains oblivious of the actual word position values, and the software system carries out the necessary checks to locate those records which satisfy the precise proximity requirements.

With some systems it is possible to request that terms be in the same sentence or in the same field. The principle is similar to word addressing, but requires the storage of even more detailed 'address' information at the database building stage. For example,

BEACH(F)POLLUTION
to match with items that contain *beach* and *pollution* anywhere in the same field. In this context word order is usually irrelevant

It should be noted that proximity searching locates phrases purely by arithmetical means. No intellectual effort is expended at the stage of preparing the document for input to the database. Therefore, there is no implication, except by context, that a phrase is necessarily of any special significance.

When applying proximity operators, not all systems allow the use of truncated terms. For example,

BEACH+ ADJ POLLUT+

may hit *beaches polluted, beach pollution,* etc.; and if word order is unimportant, then phrases such as *polluted beaches* and *pollutes beaches* would be equally acceptable. Conversely, a system where truncation was not permitted with proximity operators might simply respond with zero hits — as opposed to an error message.

6.9 STRING SEARCHING

String searching is a technique for locating a string of characters, even if it is completely embedded within a larger term. It is a relatively slow operation, as instead of referring to the inverted file or dictionary the computer has to search the sequential file of bibliographic records. Because of this, string searching cannot be directed at the whole database, but instead is used to search a subset of the database. The subset takes the form of a previously retrieved set of records, as shown in the examples below.

String searching is a very powerful search facility, as it can be used to access embedded characters and other parts of the record which do not have entries in the inverted file or dictionary. It can be used to solve a number of distinct search problems:

(1) Chemical nomenclature
Ordinary search:

USER:	ORGANOMETAL+ AND NICKEL+ AND CARBONYL+		
SYSTEM:	1	58	ORGANOMETAL+ AND NICKEL+ AND

String search:

USER:	ORGANOMETAL+ AND NICKEL+		
SYSTEM:	1	624	ORGANOMETAL+ AND NICKEL+
USER:	FIND :CARBONYL:		
SYSTEM:	2	71	:CARBONYL:

In the second search an extra 13 (that is, 71—58) records have been retrieved (containing words such as *benzenetricarbonyl,* where *carbonyl* is not a dictionary entry point, but is embedded within a larger term).

(2) Vague request. String searching can be useful for 'sharpening up' what may be a vague request. For example, a person might have seen a paper on the transmutation of lead which (s)he now wishes to locate: it is

thought that it appeared in a journal whose title included the words TRANSACTIONS or ACTION. The search could be tackled in this way:

```
TRANSMUT+
              1        586        TRANSMUT+
FIND :ACTION: (JO)
              2        19         :ACTION:
```

(3) Phrase searching. String searching can be used if proximity searching is not available to retrieve specific phrases:

```
WOOD* OR TIMBER*
1             10646            WOOD* OR TIMBER*
SOUTH+ AND AMERICA* AND 1
2             408              SOUTH+ AND AMERICA* AND 1
FIND :OUTH AMER:
3             95               :OUTH AMER:
```

Because string searching is a relatively slow process, it is good technique to reserve it for the last step of a search — and not some intermediate stage where the number of postings may still be relatively high.

6.10 LIMITING SEARCHES

There are usually facilities in a search system to narrow or limit searches. This can be done by using the field search facility for, say, language. For example,

```
SYSTEM:       10         150        CRIM+ AND (8 OR 9)
USER:         10 AND ENGLISH(LA)
SYSTEM:       11         41         10 AND ENGLISH(LA)
```

Other fields which could be used in this way include document type, country in which the work reported was carried out, year of publication, etc.

A field not described so far, but which usually exists in most records, is the 'update' field. This is usually of the form 7903, to indicate, for example, that the record was added to the database during the third merging of input records in 1979. Databases vary in the frequency of being updated — for example, weekly, fortnightly, monthly, quarterly, etc. This field can be very useful when limiting searches.

Sometimes ranging of numeric fields is possible using the operators LESS THAN, FROM — TO, GREATER THAN. This could be useful if a search is required on documents published at a certain time. For example,

JUPITER AND GREATER THAN 1977

Sometimes accession numbers may be used to limit the search. For example,

LIMIT 16/10000 — 20000   (where 16 is a previous result number)

6.11 THE SEARCH SAVE FACILITY

Most systems offer a search save facility. This is a particularly useful device and has two main applications. The first concerns the searching of other databases within a system, once the search strategy has been developed — and saved — in the initial target database. The second application involves the periodic execution of a saved search against the update portions of a database — in effect, providing a current awareness profile and an automatic selective dissemination of information service.

The command for saving a search may be entered at the beginning and/or end of a search session, depending on the system. Some systems offer temporary search saves; these are automatically deleted at the end of the day, but are perfectly adequate for searching several databases during one search session. The more usual procedure is for a saved search to be stored indefinitely, with the user taking positive action to delete it when necessary. Care must be exercised when a saved search is used to examine several different databases, because certain commands are not universally valid. This follows naturally from the description given in the previous chapter of the different treatments afforded to fields in different databases (preservation/non-preservation of phrases; full-text/non-full-text treatment of fields; etc.).

Saved searches are normally exclusive to the individual user, so that other users cannot access them, even if they know the names or labels under which they are stored. This is important from a security viewpoint, where saved searches used for current awareness may be held for many months, or even years, within a system.

Associated with any search save facility are commands for listing, executing and deleting the saved search. There may also be some editing commands, which allow the user to modify the saved search; these are especially useful for the periodic maintenance/updating of long-running SDI profiles.

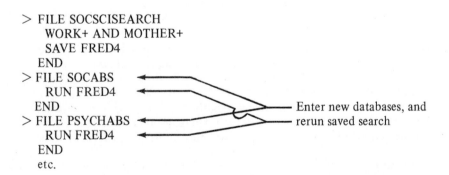

```
> FILE SOCSCISEARCH
    WORK+ AND MOTHER+
    SAVE FRED4
    END
> FILE SOCABS
    RUN FRED4
    END
> FILE PSYCHABS
    RUN FRED4
    END
    etc.
```
Enter new databases, and rerun saved search

In the example the search is saved under a 'label' assigned by the user (FRED4). Some systems automatically assign a label:

User:	SAVE
System:	SSMX8 NOW SAVED

6.12 MULTIFILE SEARCHING

In some systems it is possible to have search terms automatically matched against several databases — using just one command. Depending on the results (postings) for the individual terms, the user can then select the database(s) which look most promising and enter these for the final search. Where logic is involved — for example, the ANDing of terms — postings for the separate terms may be misleading as to the final result, although this is not usually the case. In at least one system it is possible to have search expressions (that is, terms linked by logic) matched in this way. The target databases may either be nominated by the searcher or chosen from a range of database clusters, arranged according to subject coverage.

6.13 SEARCH HISTORY

At any stage of a search most systems can give a concise replay of the search strategy. This is particularly useful during prolonged search sessions, when previous queries and results may be scattered over several feet of printed output. The command (for example, HIST) may invoke a repeat of all previous results or, in some systems, it may be modified to yield only certain sections of the strategy:

HIST 1 — 15   Display first 15 search statements or queries.
HIST 10–25   Display queries 10 — 25 inclusive.
HIST 21 —   Display queries 21 onwards.

Because of the possibility of using any previous result in a later question,

(51 OR DISEAS+) AND 2

this facility is very useful for providing a quick recap (e.g. HIST 1 — 5).

6.14 A COMMON (ALL-PURPOSE) COMMAND LANGUAGE

Watching the development of search languages in the various systems, it is possible to see increasing similarities in the search facilities — and in the commands for activating them. Probably the best example of this is the way in which nearly all major systems now allow the direct combination of terms and/or statement numbers in a single search expression. Another example is the improvement in search save facilities, so that all saved search terms — and not just the final result — are accessible to the searcher. Competitive pressures help to bring about these changes, and users undoubtedly benefit. However, lest the casual observer should think that these changes herald a time, now close at hand, when a common command language will be fully operational, attention should be directed to the complexities of database structure (Chapter 5) and the influence this has on how certain types of questions may be handled or, indeed, whether they may be dealt with at all. While it may be a relatively simple task to develop a limited set of commands for superficially probing a number of different host systems, the task of capturing the diversity – and therefore the power and richness – of the complete range of facilities will be infinitely more difficult. (A description of the 'common command language' for Euronet is given in Appendix 7.)

6.15 CONCLUSION

The search facilities described in this chapter provide tremendously powerful facilities for dissecting a database. In a pictorial analogy, the search process may be seen to cut swathes through the data – from almost any angle (search aspect or concept) – and where these intersect, there is a reasonable chance of finding at least the basic ingredients for relevance:

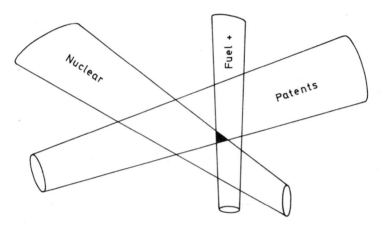

Figure 6.3 Patents on nuclear fuels

Furthermore, because the search is interactive, questions can easily be modified and resubmitted, to cover possibilities (additional vocabulary, etc.) uncovered during the previous step (*Figures 6.4, 6.5*).

The swathes may be massive sections of a database, but such is the computing power available that terms/concepts embracing tens or even hundreds of thousands of documents may be meshed in a single logic expression and the resultant postings (hits) delivered in a matter of seconds. This enormous capacity means that precise definition of terms is often unnecessary, especially when they are to be ANDed with other terms. In a search for joint papers by two authors, for example, it is unlikely that false hits due to the wrong initials would be a serious problem; in any case, they would be easily discernible at the print stage. In a search for joint publications by *TR Brown* and *KL Jenkins*, for example, the search expressions

BROWN+ (AU) AND JENKINS+ (AU)
or possibly
ALL BROWN+ AND ALL JENKINS+

would be perfectly reasonable as a first try, and there is no point in more precise definition of either author, unless the number of hits proves embarrassingly large.

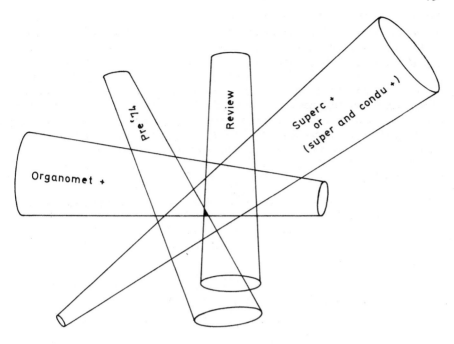

Figure 6.4 Pre-1974 review on organometallic superconductors

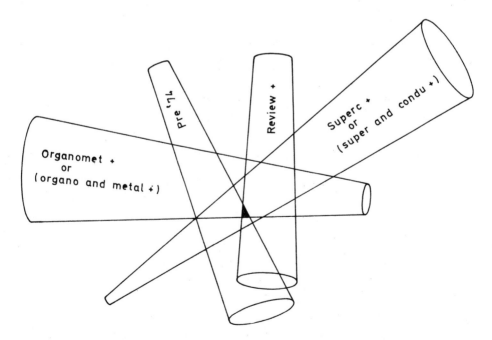

Figure 6.5 Broadening of initial search strategy in Figure 6.4 to allow for occurrences of ... organo metallic ...

Similarly, the *pre-1974* and review criteria (*Figure 6.4*) for organometallic super-conductors could probably be settled by inspection at the print stage, rather than by including them at the search stage.

Figure 6.3–6.5 illustrate searches in which more than two concepts are being linked by AND logic. In practice, these are best dealt with by ANDing one concept at a time, since the final concept(s) may be superfluous if the number of postings is low. Searches can be as simple or complex as the user chooses to make them, but there is no virtue in unnecessary complication. Some of the search facilities described here may be used only rarely, but at least they are there if needed – when trying to crack the particularly difficult nuts.

FURTHER READING

Henry, M. and Young, M. *Prompt Cards for Online Search Languages*, Macmillan, London (1980). ISBN 0-333-29317-7

Chapter 7

Search Preparation and Strategy

7.1 THE TYPICAL ONLINE SEARCH

So far we have considered online searching as an operation which takes place at a computer terminal. This is only part of the picture. Effective searching also requires careful attention to the preparation of the search. And what about the considerable task of following up the results to obtain the source literature? This is rather beyond the scope of this book, but getting the results of the search is not necessarily the end of the operation from the searcher's point of view. The results should be examined to judge whether they are fully satisfactory and to see whether they suggest a further way of developing the search. The overall process of searching, from the receipt of the search request to getting the results, is dealt with in this chapter, with particular attention to search preparation (see *Figures 7.1* and *7.2*). A check list of points is included as Appendix 1, which it will be helpful to refer to from time to time.

Most online searches are carried out by intermediaries (also known as search analysts). The reasons for this are discussed in Chapter 8. This is not only the most typical, but also a most exacting role, since the searcher has the responsibility for the success of searches carried out for other people, colleagues or clients. This chapter is therefore looked at from the standpoint of librarians, information officers or research workers who have, or will have, this specialist intermediary role.

The usual situation is that the enquirer, who may be a student, practitioner, research worker or manager, realises a need for information, and approaches the library or information unit. The enquirer may ask directly for an online search. Or the information staff themselves may decide that this is an appropriate method of dealing with the enquiry. The intermediary's first task is to get full details of the enquiry by discussing it with the enquirer or by getting a written description. He then has to decide what files and systems should be used and draw up a search strategy. This will involve consulting the various search aids — manuals, thesauri, etc. This preparation stage is usually the most time-consuming part of the search and may average about half an hour per search. It will result in a written plan to serve as a guide while the terminal is being used. The next stage is to log on to the system and carry out the search, often with the enquirer also present so that he can assess the progress of the search. The receipt of the results

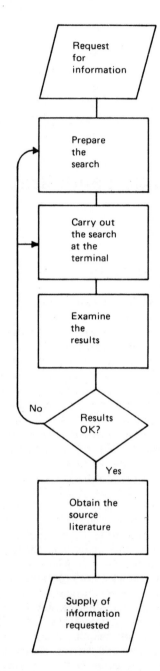

Figure 7.1 The overall searching process

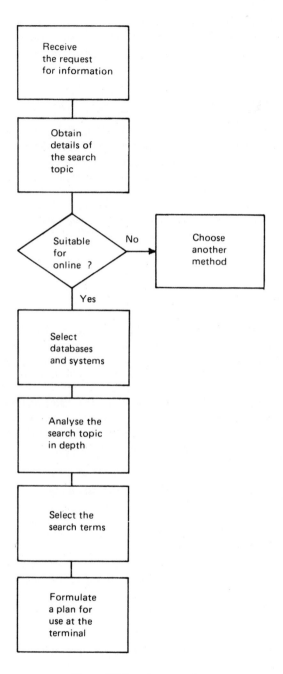

Figure 7.2 Search preparation

is usually the last stage for the searcher but may indicate the need for further searching. The process is not complete for the enquirer, however, until he is able to consult the journal articles, etc., which provide the information he needs.

7.2 BEING PREPARED

Online searching cannot be successful without the use of the relevant manuals, thesauri and other search aids. Getting these and keeping them up to date and in good order is very time-consuming. It is equally necessary to maintain a supply of the system and database newsletters in which changes are announced. To keep up with new techniques of searching and news of new services, journals such as *Online* and *Online Review* are indispensable reading. The exchange of ideas between users, as is facilitated by being a member of a users' group, is also of great value. These activities are an essential part of being prepared for online searching.

7.3 RECEIVING THE SEARCH REQUEST

At the level of the individual search, the initial problem is the communication of the details of the search topic between the enquirer and the intermediary. This is the first part of search preparation.

Getting a clear understanding of the online search topic is a very important aspect, just as it is for a conventional request for information. Where a formal mechanism for making requests is appropriate, the information should be asked for under certain headings (suitable ones are listed in Appendix 1). This is what online search brokers, organisations which carry out searches for payment, would normally do by means of a search request form. More general advice to the intermediary is:

Establish personal contact with the *original* enquirer. Have the enquirer present at the terminal if possible, but at least contact him by telephone.

Make sure you understand the search topic. Get the enquirer to really explain the query and to enlarge on any technicalities. Look up the subject in a reference book if you are not clear about it.

Discuss your search strategy with the enquirer and obtain his help in selecting search terms. He is much more likely to know the terminology of his subject than you are.

Get the enquirer (if present) to comment on the results as they appear on the terminal.

The value of obtaining details of relevant references which are already known to the enquirer is worth emphasising. The titles are a useful source of search terms. They help to indicate what the subject is all about. (The original articles can be consulted if a fuller picture is needed.) It may be possible to use references as search terms in a citation search of one of the files of the Institute of Scientific Information (ISI). They can be examined online to see how they were indexed and so lead to further search terms.

It is important to know how comprehensive a search is required, because this very much affects the search strategy. Getting the enquirer to specify the number of references he wants is a useful way of expressing this. One or two hundred references are usually enough for most enquiries if the subject is well covered in the literature, although if a completely exhaustive search is wanted, thousands of references may be justifiable. Where a subject is sparsely covered, or, for example, the search is required to check out a patent application, it is more difficult to know when to stop searching. This is a needle in a haystack situation. There may be a needle, or more needles, in this or another haystack, but when to stop looking ? The solution is, in consultation with the enquirer, to fix a time or cost limit in advance and try to stick to it. For non-exhaustive searches it is help-ful to know of any categories of references which are particularly desirable or undesirable. Such categories include language, type of literature, date and source journal. There may be limiting devices in the search system which allow these demarcations to be made simply.

How many references the enquirer expects, rather than the number he would like, is another useful piece of information. Assuming that the enquirer is familiar with the literature, this will be a guide as to whether a broad or narrow search strategy is necessary.

Find out also how much information the enquirer has already gathered, so that you know whether you are adding to a mountain or a molehill of existing data.

7.4 DECIDING WHETHER THE ENQUIRY IS SUITABLE FOR ONLINE

An enquiry may not be a suitable candidate for an online search, either because there is no accessible online file which contains the information required or because the information could be obtained more quickly and cheaply from another source. Despite the huge range of files available, they are limited in time-span. Enquiries about topics which are only covered by the older literature will need to be answered by conventional methods of literature searching. Or a different kind of information may be required from that in the file. For example, data are not usually retrievable from a bibliographic file. If the case is marginal and it is decided to go ahead with an online search, it is important to acknow-ledge the limitations of the files; otherwise the results may give a totally mislead-ing impression of comprehensiveness to the enquirer.

Alternatively, the information may be more easily obtained from a library catalogue, textbook or encyclopaedia, by searching an abstract journal or by making a telephone call. It will be some time before an online search is the best way of finding out about everything!

Nevertheless, by providing a thorough coverage of the recent literature an online search is often a useful start to any investigation.

7.5 CHOOSING WHICH FILES TO SEARCH

Which databases to cover and how many depends upon the subject area of the search topic and how comprehensive a search is required. A rule of thumb is to search the biggest and most appropriate databases first. If these do not produce adequate results, the search may be extended. The smaller, more specialised files are generally an advantage when there is a need for a few highly relevant references rather than an exhaustive search. The value of a file depends to a large extent on the source literature it covers. A list of sources is usually available in the corresponding abstract journal. These lists provide a method of comparing files, although the policies for coverage and indexing will also affect what is included and what can be retrieved.

Not having the necessary search aids may affect the decision. For example, it would be difficult to make an effective job of searching Medline or Biosis without the relevant thesauri. This is a good reason to make sure that any aids are obtained which may be needed.

7.6 WHICH SYSTEMS TO USE

Distinguishing between systems on grounds of cost is not as straightforward as it may appear. Cheaper link-up rates may be offset by slower response times or inferior training and support facilities. When considering a particular enquiry, there are certain questions which should be asked about the alternative systems. Do they cover the full range of files you will need to use? Time and money are saved if the whole search can be carried out on one system. Does the system provide an adequate range of search fields for the files you wish to search? Is there a search facility such as string searching or word adjacency searching which would be particularly useful? In practice, users tend to develop a relationship with one or two systems, which they know well and for which they have the relevant search aids, and these are the main factors which narrow down the choice.

7.7 ANALYSING THE SEARCH TOPIC

The search topic is entered at the terminal as a search statement (also known as a search profile), which is a number of search terms linked together by operators. The object of the preparatory stage of the search is to produce a first try at the search statement and to anticipate if possible how this should be varied to meet the responses of the computer. In the formulation of a search statement it is helpful to first of all break the topic into its various concepts.

These concepts are simply pegs on which to hang the search terms. They will usually be found to have an AND relationship, and linking the concepts together gives a rough preliminary search statement in the forms A AND B AND C. . . . For example:

(A. *online*) AND (B. *information retrieval*) AND (C. *computer terminals*)

for the subject of computer terminals for using online information retrieval services (see *Figure 7.3*).

This is a useful approach, because it enables the search statement to be built up systematically and clearly. Note that we are currently regarding these words as concepts rather than search terms. Introducing synonyms, word variants, classification codes, etc., will give a form like:

(A1 OR A2 OR A3. . .) AND (B1 OR B2 OR B3. . .) AND (C1 OR C2 OR C3. . .)

At this point each additional concept narrows the search and omitting concepts broadens the search. If a comprehensive search is required, any concepts which can be justifiably omitted should be. It often seems odd to an enquirer that to leave out what appear to be necessary concepts will make it more likely that no useful references will be missed. He tends to feel that concepts not expressed are not included. But it is obvious from *Figure 7.3* that, for example, excluding concept C does not lead to a diminution of the area of intersection between A and B.

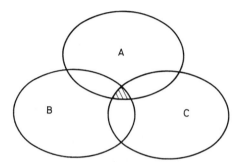

Figure 7.3 The linking of concepts. The shaded area is where the three concepts overlap and have an AND relationship

Some concepts will be found to be implied in the relationship between the others, so that omitting them will improve the output without significantly reducing the proportion of relevant references (that is, the precision). For example:

aphids AND *control* AND *malathion*

(The control of aphids by the insecticide malathion). The majority of references in which the concepts *aphids* and *malathion* co-occur will most likely be about the control of aphids by malathion. The concept of *control*, which is difficult to express, especially in free search terms, may safely be omitted. It could otherwise be expressed as *adverse effects, toxicity*, and so on. In fact there is such a range of possibilities that including the concept could lead to valuable references being missed because it was incompletely expressed.

A concept may, alternatively, be implicit in the nature of the database. With the topic *pollution and arsenic* searched on the Pollution Abstracts database, the concept of *pollution* can be omitted because it can be assumed that most items in the file are on some aspect of pollution anyway. There are other types of bias in databases, such as towards the country of origin of the database, and towards countries of high publication and high research activity, which should be taken into account when constructing the profile (see *Figure 7.4*).

It is important to recognise implicit concepts, because their inclusion will result in a less thorough but more expensive and time-consuming search. The kind of strategy to avoid is one in which a lot of time is spent choosing and entering terms to express a difficult concept which only narrows down the search by about 10 per cent.

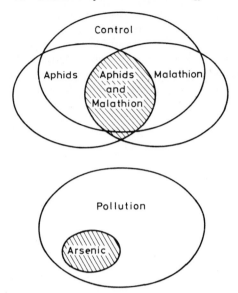

Figure 7.4 Examples of implied concepts: pollution *in the Pollution Abstracts file and* control

One of the advantages of online searching is that concepts and individual terms can be held in reserve and used only when there is a need to regulate the output or precision. Useful elements for narrowing down a search are language (for example, English) or type of literature (for example, review articles).

7.8 THE SELECTION OF SEARCH TERMS

A logical structure for the search statement having been established, the next stage is to find search terms which express the meaning of the various concepts. The variety of possibilities was shown in the previous chapter.

At this stage some of the problems and pitfalls of term selection may be

```
AN - B7 031209; C70016793
TI - CONVERSATIONAL SYSTEMS IN POWER ENGINEERING
AU - GLADYS, H.; CZERNIENKO, A.
SO - ENERGETYKA (POLAND) (EGYAA4), VOL.32, NO.2, PP. 50-2, FEB. 1978, 9 REF.
DT - J (JOURNAL): GR (GENERAL/REVIEW)
LA - POLISH
CC - *3B81108; *3C3340H; 3C74109; 3C7420
IT - POWER SYSTEM COMPUTER CONTROL
ST - POWER ENGINEERING; KONWERS SYSTEM; ON LINE; OFF LINE; COMPUTER DISPLAYS
AB - DISCUSSES ON AND OFF LINE COMPUTER DISPLAYS USED IN POWER ENGINEERING
     DESCRIBES THE 'KONWERS' SYSTEM DEVELOPED IN 1974 FOR THE ODRA 1305
     COMPUTER INCLUDING THE LATEST ADDITIONS. OUTLINES SYSTEM OPERATIONS,
     HIGHLIGHTING ON-LINE COMPUTER CONTROL OF POWER GENERATION AND
     DISTRIBUTION, SYSTEMS USED FOR DIRECT CONTROL OF POWER NETWORKS, AND
     AUTOMATED OPERATION. PROBABLE FUTURE DEVELOPMENTS ARE DISCUSSED.
```

Figure 7.5 The INSPEC record on the SDC system

pointed out. The range of information within a database record which is available for online searching is very wide, and the form of the search terms must match this diversity. Consider the record, in *Figure 7.5*, of the INSPEC file printed out from the SDC system. Of the ten fields shown, all are searchable in part or in whole on SDC. Subject information, with which we are mainly concerned, is contained in five of the fields. The classification codes (CC) and index terms (IT) contain controlled terms which are selected by indexers from controlled lists, the INSPEC classification scheme and thesaurus. The title (TI), supplementary term (ST) and abstract (AB) fields contain uncontrolled subject terms in that they are either natural language or are selected without reference to the thesaurus.

It is common to have these two types of subject information, and they are largely complementary from the searcher's standpoint. Uncontrolled terms allow great flexibility and specificity in profile construction but can lead to ambiguity. They offer little help in searching for broad concepts. The use of the term *pesticides* would not retrieve everything on pesticides, but only those references which referred to pesticides in a general way. Those dealing with particular pesticides, such as malathion, would be missed. Controlled terms, on the other hand, are less flexible because they are limited to a preconceived list of concepts. They may fall behind common use and be unable to express new ideas. They are usually of no use for the selection of names, such as *Lockheed Dialog*, but they make it much easier to select broad concepts. For example, in the INSPEC record in *Figure 7.5* the code C7420 stands for control engineering, and C7410B for power engineering (the 3 at the beginning denotes the edition of the classification scheme). Some systems go a stage further and make it possible to select groups of subject-related terms at one go. This generic capability is the main advantage of the use of controlled terms.

The format in which the information is represented in databases is also an important consideration. Online systems are very fussy about such matters as leading zeros in accession numbers, punctuation in author names and classification codes and how dates are represented.

7.8.1 Searching controlled index terms

Controlled terms include classification codes, such as Dewey, the Biosis Biosystematic Codes or the Predicasts Product Codes, as well as thesaurus terms. Lists of terms or codes are available in book form, so that they can be looked up in advance. It is very important to have on hand the most up to date version of the classification scheme or thesaurus, and in some cases earlier editions are necessary for searching the earlier years of the database. (For example, the INSPEC classification scheme has changed twice in the history of the computerised database.) The main advantage of controlled terms is that they allow the possibility of selecting groups of subject-related terms. This helps to solve the very difficult problem of searching for a broad concept which has many subdivisions and which can be expressed in a wide variety of ways in normal language. It may also provide great economy in the entry of search terms. The Elhill *Explosion* facility is a good example. The MEDLARS thesaurus of Medical Subject Headings is one of the best-known controlled indexing languages. It consists of about 12 000 terms which are divided into 15 subject groups, each group having 7 levels of hierarchy. *Figure 7.6* shows a section of the thesaurus

```
YOHIMBANS                          D3.132.973
  RAUWOLFIA ALKALOIDS              D3.132.973.641
    AJMALINE                       D3.132.973.641.119
    ALSEROXYLON                    D3.132.973.641.223
    RESERPINE                      D3.132.973.641.696
      RESERPINE DERIVATIVES        D3.132.973.641.696.646
        DESERPIDINE                D3.132.973.641.696.646.256
        RESCINNAMINE               D3.132.973.641.696.646.645
        SYROSINGOPINE              D3.132.973.641.696.646.820
    YOHIMBINE                      D3.132.973.641.893
      YOHIMBINE DERIVATIVES        D3.132.973.641.893.743
        CORYNANTHIDINE             D3.132.973.641.893.743.279
        RAUWOLSCINE                D3.132.973.641.893.743.724
```

Figure 7.6 A section of the MEDLARS thesaurus showing a hierarchy

dealing with the *yohimbans* (a group of alkaloids reputed to have aphrodisiac properties). When using Medline, selecting all the *yohimbans* listed here simply requires the entry of EXP YOHIMBANS or EXP D3.132.973.

The *Predicasts* thesaurus which is used to index their files covering economic, product and business information provides similar economy and power of term selection. In the example from their thesaurus in *Figure 7.7* the selection of all the Product Codes (PC) relating to *electronic navigation systems* is achieved by selecting PC = 36624. Groups of terms are selected by using just the stem

```
366 2400   Electronic Navigation Systems
366 2450      Aircraft Navigation Systems
366 2451         Air Navigation Aids
366 2452         Air Traffic Control Equip
366 2453         Aircraft Transponders
366 2454         Instrument Landing Systems
366 2455         Collision Avoidance Systems
366 2457         Turbulence Detectors
366 2460      Marine & Ground Navigation Equip
366 2470      Underwater Navigation Systems
366 2480      Missile & Space Navigation Equip
366 2481         Missile and Space-Borne Nav Equip
366 2483         Missile and Space Ground Nav Equip
366 2484         Missile and Space Nav Support Systems
366 2490      Navigation Support Systems
```

Figure 7.7 A section of the Predicasts thesaurus showing a hierarchy

of the code at the top of the hierarchy. In both of these examples the selection of a group of subject-related terms is carried out in effect by a truncation of the class code.

An alternative arrangement for selecting groups of subject terms is by listing them at the terminal and selecting from the list. The example shown in *Figure 7.8* is from the INSPEC file on the ESA-IRS system. The command EXPAND E6 lists the terms related to the one at E6, NAVIGATION. This is not quite so convenient a method, because it is less easy to plan ahead and requires extra search time for the listing of terms.

Another way in which the use of controlled terms facilitates the selection of broad concepts is by the systematic flagging of certain types of article, such as review, or theoretical study. (This is a feature of the INSPEC file.) The MEDLARS check tags, such as *human* and *animal experiments*, are a similar device. They are applied to large proportions of the database and enable broad distinctions to be made very easily.

Controlled terms help in avoiding ambiguity by the preco-ordination of concepts. In searching for toxic plants, combining the concepts *plants* and

```
                    EXPAND NAVIGATION
            EXPAND NAVIGATION
REF    INDEX-TERM              TYPE  ITEMS  RT
E1     NAVIER-STOKES EQUATIONS-        575   6
E2     NAVIER/STOKES...........          2
E3     NAVIER'S................          2
E4     NAVIGABLE...............          5
E5     NAVIGATING..............          4
E6     NAVIGATION..............       1392  20
E7     NAVIGATION,.............          2
E8     NAVIGATIONAL............        151
E9     NAVIGATOR...............         25
E10    NAVIGATORS..............          7
E11    NAVO3...................         10
E12    NAVSAT..................          3
E13    NAVSTAR.................         14
E14    NAVY....................         97
E15    NAVY'S..................          5
E16    NAV205..................          2
E17    NAX.....................          9
E18    NAXC002.................          2
E19    NAXE....................          2
E20    NAXKI-XNB03.............          2
                                      -MORE-


                    EXPAND E6
            EXPAND NAVIGATION
REF    INDEX-TERM              TYPE  ITEMS  RT
R1     NAVIGATION..............       1392  20
R2     COMPUTERISED NAVIGATION.N        37   3
R3     INERTIAL NAVIGATION.....N       195   2
R4     RADIONAVIGATION.........N       811   6
R5     AIRCRAFT COMMUNICATION..R       235  10
R6     COMPASSES...............R        25   5
R7     DISTANCE MEASUREMENT....R       516   8
R8     DOPPLER EFFECT..........R      1011  13
R9     GROUND SUPPORT EQUIPMENTR        62  10
R10    GROUND SUPPORT SYSTEMS..R       280  13
R11    GYROSCOPES..............R       376   4
R12    LASER BEAM APPLICATIONS.R      2611  24
R13    MARINE SYSTEMS..........R       630   7
R14    RADAR APPLICATIONS......R       770   5
R15    RADIOALTIMETERS.........R        42   5
R16    SHIPS...................R      1069   4
R17    SONAR...................R       653  17
R18    TRACKING................R      1888   6
R19    TRANSPORTATION..........R      2124  21
R20    UNDERWATER SOUND........R       831   9
                                      -MORE-
        1   13409 SELECT R1-R20
        R1: NAVIGATION
```

Figure 7.8 Using the EXPAND command to display and select related terms to NAVIGA-TION on the ESA-IRS system (commands are underlined)

toxicity by AND logic would inevitably lead to the retrieval of many references on toxicity to plants. A controlled term, **TOXIC PLANTS**, avoids this difficulty.

Since controlled terms are applied by indexers after a certain amount of thought, they generally reflect the more important concepts. In some cases this discrimination is enhanced by labelling the terms according to their relevance to the article. In the Energyline file terms are given three levels of weight, and in many other files it is possible to select priority terms usually by prefixing them by an asterisk. These devices make controlled terms particularly useful when the search is for just a few highly relevant references.

However, there are difficulties with controlled terms. The importance of the printed term lists has been mentioned. It is easy to overlook changes made in indexing policy which mean that terms in the current thesaurus do not apply to the full database. Unwittingly the searcher may be confining the search to only a portion of the database.

Other difficulties arise because many thesaurus terms are compound and consist of more than one word. Systems may deal with compound terms in a variety of ways, as was described in the previous chapters. They may be split up into individual words, so that they must be searched by combining the words together; they may be searchable only in a preco-ordinated form; or they may be searchable both as individual words and in compound form. Online services have had changes of policy on this, so that earlier parts of the database required terms to be entered in one form and for the later years in another. The searcher must be aware of these inconsistencies. The most clumsy search strategies are required by the necessity for preco-ordination, particularly when there is no generic searching facility. Some compound terms are extremely long, such as the MEDLARS term PURINE-PYRIMIDINE METABOLISM, INBORN ERRORS, and provide a rather taxing test for the two-finger typist.

Controlled indexing is fine as long as there are terms which represent the search topic. Where they do not, either a broader search may be necessary, using the terms which seem to be closest, or, if it is available, uncontrolled language searching must be used. A useful device in these circumstances is to enter the details of known relevant references at the terminal and see how the indexers dealt with them.

It is common for controlled terms to be put, together with the words from titles, abstracts and uncontrolled index term fields, in a default search field. In this situation they can be searched with the same considerations that apply to searching uncontrolled fields. When necessary, they can be searched separately to provide greater relevance, to help avoid ambiguity, or, where this is available, for their generic searching possibilities.

7.8.2 Searching uncontrolled terms

Uncontrolled terms are intended here to include words from titles, abstracts and uncontrolled index term fields. Words from the corporate source, which contains details of the organisation for which the authors worked, are also in this category. 'Natural language' is a description used in this connection.

Searching uncontrolled terms has some important advantages. Since the words used are those in common use, the search topic can be represented in the profile by the words normally employed to describe it, without the need to translate the subject into codes or the, perhaps slightly out of date or inapt, terminology of a long-established thesaurus. Great flexibility is possible, and names or colloquialisms may be used. When the text of the abstract is searchable, it provides very thorough searching possibilities which may allow references to be retrieved even on quite minor aspects of the article. In searching several databases for the same topic, the profile may need very little modification, and this makes it easier to use the search save procedures. Nor is there the need to be familiar with several different thesauri or classification schemes.

The main disadvantage of uncontrolled terms is that they have no generic capacity. Broad concepts must be represented in the search statement by terms which account for them at a general level and for their subordinate aspects if a comprehensive search is required. In practice, it is often impossible to do this satisfactorily.

Uncontrolled index terms are in fact often governed by some rules. They may be routinely applied to cover certain important elements of the article. For example, in Biosis Previews the names of species mentioned in the text are routinely added as index terms. They may follow certain conventions. In the CA Condensates database it is the policy to add index terms in abbreviated form, so that MOL, CHEM, ANAL and DETN are found as commonly as the full forms of the words. In Biosis Previews many compound words are split up, so that *headache* normally occurs as HEAD ACHE and *prenatal* as PRE NATAL. There are also rules in dealing with punctuation. Hyphens are often omitted, so that ON-LINE becomes ON LINE. When a database is being loaded onto the computer and the inverted files are being built up, the computer system uses a stop list to enable it to discount words, such as prepositions, which have little information value. AND, FOR, FROM, THE, etc., are usually excluded. Where ON occurs on the stop list, the hyphenated form of ON-LINE therefore becomes irretrievable. Coping with this kind of idiosyncratic diversity is one of the most difficult aspects of online searching, especially since the various rules never seem to apply consistently. Just as controlled terms are rather unreliably consistent, uncontrolled terms can be relied upon to be inconsistent. The only safe course in searching them is to allow for any reasonable possibility.

When search terms are being selected, it is obviously important to consider synonyms, narrower terms, variations in spelling and abbreviations. If the search is being carried out by an intermediary, the original enquirer should play an important role, because he is more likely to be familiar with the usual terminology. Variations on the same stem (*retrieval, retrieving*, etc.) are most easily dealt with by means of truncation. The range of possibilities of alphabetically related terms is revealed by displaying terms online by means of commands such as NEIGHBOR, ROOT or EXPAND. Search aids such as the Lockheed *Dialists*, which are equivalent to an EXPAND but available on microfiche, are useful both for the selection of terms and to help judge the point at which a term should be truncated. Because it is important to know the variation in terminology when searching uncontrolled terms, any term list or thesaurus, whether it is related to the database being searched or not, may be of value in finding suitable search terms. The wording of known relevant articles, particularly that in the titles or abstracts, is also an important source which can be used both before the search begins and during the search when relevant items have been retrieved at the terminal.

Online systems generally deal with uncontrolled terms individually, but phrases can be searched for by devices such as the word adjacency facility or string searching. These help to avoid the ambiguity often obtained when using AND logic. For example, *heat pipe* has a very specific meaning with the words together in that order, but many references having nothing to do with heat pipes would contain those two words somewhere in their abstracts. The capability of selecting phrases is an extremely powerful one when the full text of titles and abstracts is available for searching.

7.8.3 Author searching

Author names may appear in a variety of forms. The database producers may have different systems of punctuation and different rules for dealing with such things as prefixes (de, Van, etc.), suffixes (Junior) and double-barrelled names. The authors may vary the number of initials they use. There may be different practices with regard to the inclusion of first names. The safest course, therefore, in searching for authors is to list the online author dictionary.

7.8.4 Selecting highly posted terms

Some terms, such as truncations of common stems such as *effect,* broad classification codes or Explosions, and even individual words such as *properties* in the CA Condensates file, have very large postings in the main files. Selecting and combining these terms requires extra work by the computer which shows itself, particularly at peak times, by slow operation. On grounds of speed and economy, therefore, it is worth bearing in mind certain considerations when dealing with highly posted terms.

First, avoid using them at all if possible. They may come into the category of implicit concepts and turn out not to be necessary. For example, for a search on the toxicity of dieldrin to the stickleback, combining the concepts *stickleback* and *dieldrin* is probably adequate without the addition of the highly posted stem *toxic* and its many alternatives such as *poison, hazard,* etc. Plan to use highly posted terms towards the end of the search, keeping them in reserve until it is clear that they are really needed.

Investigate whether the database or system has special methods for dealing with highly posted terms. Terms may be divided up by year, so that the year becomes a part of the term – for example, HUMAN75, HUMAN76. To select the term ENG (for English language) in Medline, preferred methods are to use NOT FOR (to exclude those in foreign languages), or to carry out a string search for ENG in the language field.

Avoid selecting or combining highly posted terms more than once in a search. This should be possible with careful planning.

The LIMIT command is a common and convenient method for restricting a search by very broad characteristics, such as language, date or type of literature. Date ranging is another device for segmenting the database.

7.8.5 Citation searching

In the ISI databases, Scisearch and Social Scisearch, it is possible to carry out citation searching – that is, using a cited reference as a search term. This method is especially useful for getting started in a field where the terminology is difficult or following up a piece of work for which the only lead is an existing reference. When selecting cited references, it is advisable to inspect and select from the appropriate dictionary at the terminal, because of the difficulty of deciding on the format in which the cited reference will appear.

7.8.6 Selecting search terms – an example

Before selecting search terms, it is necessary to have established the conceptual structure of the search topic and to have decided which system (or systems) and while file (or files) will be searched. The available search fields are a major determinant of the search terms to be used, but the many factors mentioned above and in Appendix 1 need to be taken into account. How comprehensive a search is required will also have a bearing. It may be unnecessary to expend a lot of effort if only a few relevant references on a common topic are required.

For the subject 'online information retrieval', let us assume the need for a comprehensive search of the INSPEC file on the Lockheed system. The subject search fields are controlled and uncontrolled index terms and classification codes. For a search of the index term fields the following terms would be appropriate:

(1) *online:* ONLINE; ON(W)LINE; ON-LINE?; ON LINE?; INTERACTIVE;
     REAL(W)TIME; REALTIME
(2) *information retrieval:* INFORMATION; REFERENCE;
                           BIBLIOGRAPHIC RETRIEV?; SEARCH?
(The ? is a truncation symbol and the W an adjacency operator.)

Note here the use of the adjacency operator to link the words (*real* and *time*, *on* and *line*), which, if they occurred separately, might have a different meaning. Truncation is used where the same stem can, unambiguously, represent the various forms of a word (retrieval, retrieved, retrieving). The second concept, *information retrieval*, would be represented by the logic,

((INFORMATION OR REFERENCE OR BIBLIOGRAPHIC) AND
RETRIEV?) OR SEARCH?

'*Search?*' appears a reasonable alternative to *information retrieval* in this context, since the wording *online searches* or *online searching* might be used.

The problem term is *online*. Strangely enough, all four representations are (at this moment) necessary. *Online* commonly occurs as one or two words. In the earlier years the word ON was a stopword and so cannot be selected by the term ON(W)LINE, but must be selected by ON LINE?, which is a truncation for searching the index term phrases which are a feature of this file. ON LINE? is not, however, sufficient alone, because it does not match with index phrases which contain the term in the middle (*searching on line systems*, etc.). ON(W)LINE is needed for this. Another problem is caused by the hyphen. Hyphens are normally removed, so converting to the two-word form, but some still exist in the file. The truncation is also necessary here. This is a rather extreme case perhaps, but nevertheless a good illustration of the problem of term selection.

The topic could be expressed also by classification codes (C7250 stands for *information storage and retrieval*).

7.9 PREPARING A PLAN

For most searches it is advisable to prepare a written plan to guide you when using the terminal. This will include the search terms to be used and how they are to be combined. It should also anticipate at least two decisions:

(1) What to do if the search turns out to be too broad and produces too many references.
(2) What to do if there are too few references or none.

Ways in which the output may be adjusted are listed in Appendix 1. Broadly speaking, to narrow the search requires the addition of terms by AND logic and the reduction of OR links. Broadening the search involves the opposite. This means in formulating the search plan that some terms among those selected should be earmarked for later inclusion and some for later exclusion, according to how the search develops. The search strategy may also include provision for exploring for further search terms by listing terms online or examining retrieved references. For complicated searches it may be worth producing a script for the search in the following fashion (set numbers are to the left):

```
1–4     ONLINE; ON-LINE?; ON(W)LINE; ON LINE?
5       1–4/OR
6–9     INFORMATION; BIBLIOGRAPH?; LITERATURE; RETRIEV?
10      (6 OR 7 OR 8) AND 9
11      SEARCH?
12      5 AND (10 OR 11)
```

The drawback to this method is that if you make a typing error and create a dud set, the numbering of the subsequent sets is thrown out and this can cause confusion when you are using the terminal.

7.10 AT THE TERMINAL

The procedure when using the terminal conforms more or less to the pattern indicated in *Figure 7.9*. There are three main decision points. The postings for a particular term or combination of terms may show the need to adjust the profile; so may the initial results, the first six or ten references, which can be conveniently displayed at the terminal as titles. When an apparently satisfactory set of references has been formed, they will commonly be printed offline. On the receipt of these results, there may also emerge a need to modify the search.

The search save procedure is an important device for searching several files with the same profile, but differences between files, their subject coverage and terminology will need to be taken into account. This is an especially useful facility when files are segmented by date.

When operating the terminal, the object should be to get on with the search without hesitation, and having a clear plan is an important help in this. It should rarely be necessary to spend time thumbing through thesauri or manuals, or trying to decipher confused notes. There are some further hints which can help save time. Chaining search terms or commands is quicker than entering them separately. Systems generally have much better response times during off-peak use periods. This is particularly noticeable when selecting terms with large postings. If a system is working abnormally slowly, it is better to log off and try another time.

What happens if after all the planning and preparation the search still seems to be getting nowhere? The answer is again to log off and try to sort out the problem offline. Any relevant references should be printed in full first. They may, on further scrutiny, provide a clue as to how to continue.

Consider carrying out the search in stages. This wastes no link-up time when it is possible to temporarily store the profile and can slow down the feverish

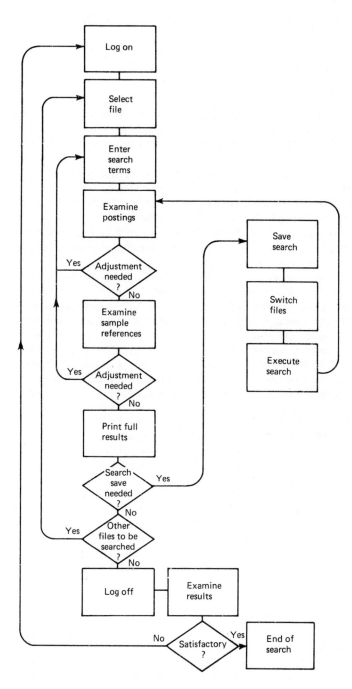

Figure 7.9 The procedure at the terminal

pace of a complicated search to a speed that you can cope with. It also gives an opportunity to consult with the enquirer.

7.11 OBTAINING THE RESULTS

The features of the output which are commonly selectable are its timing, whether to print online or offline; the format, how much of the record you have printed; and the order (the most common arrangement being inverse date order, but it may be possible to sort the output in some other way before it is printed).

Printing offline is generally much less expensive than printing online, and if there is no urgency to get the results, the bulk of the references should be produced offline. However, in the course of the search it will usually be found necessary to print an average of about 15 references to develop the search strategy and to assess the value of the results. The use of a 120 characters per second terminal rather than the more common 30 cps terminal changes this picture somewhat in favour of online printing.

The available formats range from accession numbers only to full citation details and abstract. The more information you get the better, and it is often no more expensive when printing offline to have the full record than to have only part of it. Having abstracts may save a great deal of time that would otherwise be spent looking for unsuitable articles, and in some files the abstracts are so thorough as to make it virtually unnecessary to consult the original. When sampling the results at the terminal the index terms are a great help in developing the search, but for assessing relevance the titles alone are usually sufficient guide. If a large number of references are wanted immediately, it may be possible to print online just the accession numbers of the records which apply to the equivalent abstract journal. The full source details can then be obtained from the abstract journal. However, this is not possible with all databases.

Sorting the output can be very useful. Sorting by journal, for instance, makes it quicker to look up the references in a library catalogue. The range of sort options varies greatly between systems and databases.

Getting the results is not necessarily the final stage of a search. On later examination they may turn out to be less satisfactory than expected and require the search to be done again. Alternatively, they may suggest an interesting new approach, akin to the browsing effect experienced in manual searching. Online searching is essentially an iterative process, and the searcher should at any stage be prepared to continue to refine and improve the search to the extent that seems necessary.

7.12 SEARCHING FOR CHEMICALS

Searching for chemicals warrants separate mention, because in this area the synonym problem and difficulties of ambiguity are exceptionally acute. Many chemicals have a large number of names, particularly when they are marketed as commercial products. This is well illustrated by the record for the insecticide *malathion* from NLM's *Chemline* file (*Figure 7.10*). The entries labelled NI are the preferred *Chemical Abstracts* names for the eighth and ninth collective indexes. Those labelled SY are other synonyms. It is by no means uncommon

```
1
RN - 121-75-5
ON - SEE ALSO: 12737-19-8
ON - SEE ALSO: 12767-62-3
MF - C10-H19-O6-P-S2
N1 - Succinic acid, mercapto-, diethyl ester, S-ester with
     O,O-dimethyl phosphorodithioate (8CI)
N1 - Butanedioic acid, ((dimethoxyphosphinothioyl)thio)-, diethyl
     ester (9CI)
SY - SF 60
SY - 8059HC
SY - ENT 17,034
SY - American Cyanamid 4,049
SY - S-(1,2-Bis(ethoxycarbonyl)etnyl) O,O-dimethyl phosphorodithioate
SY - Carbophos
SY - Compound 4049
SY - Fosfothion
SY - Insecticide no. 4049
SY - Karbofos
SY - Malathion
SY - Malathion LV Concentrate
SY - Mercaptothion
SY - Phosphothion
SY - Ethiolacar
SY - Fosfotion
SY - Malamar 5
SY - Oleophosphothion
SY - Sadophos
SY - Siptox I
SY - Sadofos
SY - Cythion
SY - O,O-Dimethyl S-(1,2-dicarbethoxyethyl) dithiophosphate
SY - Sumitox
SY - Carbetox
SY - Malathion E50
SY - S-(1,2-Bis(carbethoxy)ethyl) O,O-dimethyl dithiophosphate
SY - ((Dimethoxyphosphinothioyl)thio)butanedioic acid diethyl ester
SY - Mercaptosuccinic acid diethyl ester, S-ester with O,O-dimethyl
     phosphorothioate
SY - Carbofos
SY - Malaspray
SY - Prioderm
SY - Zithiol
SY - Ortho Malathion
MH - *MALATHION /(MAJOR 72)
LC - TOXLINE
LO - MEDLARS
```

Figure 7.10 The entry for malathion *from Chemline on Blaise*

for chemicals to have this range of alternative names. The problem of ambiguity arises from the fact that chemical names are, in effect, permutations of the names of sub-structures such as *methyl, amino, alanine* and *ester*. A group of chemical names together in the same abstract or keyword field may provide all sorts of new permutations. Even a name consisting of one term may be highly ambiguous. There is only one substance with the name *aniline*, but there are hundreds of substances which include the word *aniline* as part of their names which would also be retrieved from a free-text file by searching simply for that term. The solution to these problems has been in the development of chemical dictionary files, such as *Chemline* and *Chemname*, which list the alternative names required for free-text searching and in the institution of a unique identifier for each chemical, the CA Registry number. (In the *malathion* record the registry number is labelled RN.) When searching files in which the registry number has been universally applied, specifying chemical names is made very much easier and the question of ambiguity should not arise. (Note that it is usually still worth making sure by including the main distinctive names such as *malathion.*)

Searching for chemicals, then, is usually a two-stage process. There is first of all a search in a dictionary file, using the name you have, the formula or some aspect of the structure, to get the registry numbers and the full range of names of the substance. This information is then used to search the bibliographic database.

FURTHER READING

In this, as in other areas, the magazines *Online* and *Online Review* are indispensable reading. The following items are of particular value.

Obtaining details of the enquiry
Daniels, Linda. 'A matter of form', *Online*, **2**, No. 4, 31–49 (1978) [on request forms]
Somerville, Arleen N. 'The place of the reference interview in computer searching: the academic setting', *Online*, **1**, No. 4, 15–23 (1977)

Concept analysis
'Guide to designing profiles for BIOSIS Previews', In *Biosis Search Guide*, Biosciences Information Service, Philadelphia (1977)
Hall, J.L. *On-line Information Retrieval Sourcebook*, Aslib, London (1977) [see Chapter 3]

Strategy at the terminal
Citroen, Charles L. and Oldroyd, Betty K. 'Study of strategies used in on-line searching', *Online Review*, **1**, No. 4, 295–310 (1977)
Hawkins, Donald T. 'Multiple database searching', *Online*, **2**, No. 2, 9–15 (1978)
Wanger, Judith. 'Multiple database use', *Online*, **1**, No. 4, 35–41 (1977)

Chemical searching
Buntrock, Robert E. 'Chemcorner', *Online* [a regular feature beginning with the July 1978 issue]
Oppenheim, Charles. 'Methods for chemical substance searching online. 1. The basics', *Online Review*, **3**, No. 4, 381–387 (1979)

Of general value
Padin, Mary Ellen. 'Computer ease', *Online* [a regular feature]

Chapter 8

The Role of the Intermediary

8.1 INTRODUCTION

An organisation which decides to use online services such as those described so far in this book must decide who will actually carry out the search at the terminal. There are three main alternatives:

(1) The person with the original need for information (requester).

(2) A librarian or information officer who acts as an intermediary between the requester and the information, but in the absence of the requester.

(3) The intermediary and the requester together.

There has been much discussion as to which is the best solution; in practice, it will vary depending on the circumstances of the organisation, the intermediary and the requester. Anyone who has carried out online searches over a period of time soon becomes aware of the continual developments which can have a crucial effect on both the execution and the outcome of these searches. Likely changes include:

The method of accessing the telecommunications network (for example, different telephone number, identifier, password, etc.).

The search commands available on a system.

The method of charging for a system.

The way a database is loaded on to a system.

The information (structure and content) contained in a record and how it can be searched.

The list of controlled terms or codes used to describe the original document.

The availability of new systems operators that might be of use.

The availability of new databases that might be of use.

In addition to these changes, it is necessary to know what to do when problems arise — for example, engaged telephone lines, a busy network, an inaccessible host computer, 'noise' on the line, a 'dropped' line, a faulty terminal — as well as knowing when are the best times of day for searching specific systems. All this requires a fair amount of reading to keep abreast of developments as well as practice carrying out searches; it has been estimated that two or three searches a week is the minimum necessary to maintain practical fluency. Therefore, it is scarcely a feasible proposition for the average requester to achieve and then maintain the required degree of knowledge and fluency necessary for effective searching. However, there are instances of requesters, perhaps with specialised needs that occur frequently enough, who become good searchers.

In some aspects the discussion as to whether the requester or the intermediary should search for information is common to both online searching and printed index searching. Indeed, some of the changes outlined above will affect the printed index search as well as the online search. However, there is a difference in the cost factor. If a requester carries out a printed index search and takes a long time, there is no direct cost penalty — only a reduction in the work done by this individual. The online search systems operators, such as Blaise, ESA-IRS, Lockheed and SDC, charge for the time spent at the terminal, and this rate is usually several times the combined rate of pay for that period of the requester and the intermediary. Thus, a speedier online search, such as one carried out by an intermediary, will cost less than one carried out by the requester alone.

The majority of people currently involved with online searching believe that an intermediary is necessary, although there are others who argue that requesters should have direct access to information sources. There will be some requesters who are never happy to hand over responsibility for literature searching to a librarian or information officer; such people often feel that no one else is capable of this job and that librarians and information officers are trying to protect their jobs by suggesting that an intermediary is a good idea. However, exploring for references in a new or peripheral area, or assisting in the selection of search terms, the intermediary might be useful in avoiding the narrowness of approach which specialists often develop. On the other hand, there are some requesters who will cheerfully hand over the searching to others and perhaps will not spend enough time thinking about exactly what sort of information is required and will choose not to be present while the search is in progress. Unless the information required is very precise, many subsidiary questions that may arise during the search will remain unanswered, so that much relevant information may not be retrieved. The joint approach, with the intermediary and the requester both present, is probably the best.

In the remainder of this chapter some of the work undertaken to compare the various approaches of who should search will be examined, the functions which may be carried out by an intermediary will be listed and, finally, the characteristics which may be assumed by, and sought for in, a good intermediary will be described.

8.2 COMPARISONS OF SEARCHER ALTERNATIVES

Various studies have been carried out to compare the difference in searching between a requester and an intermediary. A study was carried out by Williams at the University of Manchester Institute of Science and Technology (UMIST) during 1974–75. In a comparison of 38 queries searched by requesters on their own and intermediaries on their own the results can be summarised as follows:

Intermediaries took about 43 per cent of the time taken by requesters to carry out a search.

Intermediaries retrieved about 72 per cent more references than the requesters.

Intermediaries retrieved about 43 per cent more useful references than the requesters.

The precision (that is, number of useful references retrieved/total number of references retrieved) was 59.9 per cent for requesters and 47.5 per cent for intermediaries.

A further set of queries in the study was carried out by requester alone, intermediary alone, and requester and intermediary both present; the results showed that an intermediary took about half the time to carry out a search when the requester was not present, and that a requester searching alone took almost three times longer than the intermediary searching alone. Since charges are still directly related to the time spent online at the terminal, this comparison also relates to the costs for the different modes of operation. Much fuller details of this work are given by Williams and Curtis[1].

The work at UMIST was part of a British Library Research and Development Department project known as the Short Term Experimental Information Network, or STEIN. STEIN ran between 1973 and 1975 and aimed to collect data on the technical, economic and user aspects of the online bibliographic search systems available at the time, so that information workers could assess when, where, how or whether to use such services. In the first volume of the overall report, which deals with the use of non-medical information services, Holmes reports[2] that, of 550 requesters, the preferred modes of search operation were:

Requester to use the terminal unaided, 25 per cent.

Requester to use the terminal with an intermediary present for guidance, 20 per cent.

Intermediary to use the terminal with the requester present for subject guidance, 40 per cent.

Intermediary to use the terminal alone, 15 per cent.

Wanger's survey of 472 organisations in the USA in 1974 found that at 45 per cent of them the requester and the intermediary carried out the search together at the terminal and that at 10 per cent requesters performed searches themselves[3].

Tedd's visits to 12 organisations in Britain and Europe in 1977 showed that all believed that online searching was best carried out by an intermediary[4]. However, opinions differed as to whether or not requesters should be encouraged to be present; some organisations discouraged their presence, because of the increased time (and therefore cost) of searching, even though this might have resulted in 'better' information being retrieved. The average times given by the organisations for carrying out online searches at the terminal ranged from 2–3 minutes to 20 minutes.

8.3 THE FUNCTIONS OF AN INTERMEDIARY

The functions of an intermediary can be divided into the intellectual functions of searching and the management functions of setting up and running the service. Although the former are described in Chapter 7 and in Appendix 1 and the latter in Chapter 9, it is nevertheless worth bringing these functions together in this chapter to indicate some of the work involved.

8.3.1 Intellectual functions

Intellectual functions are:

Obtaining information about the request.
Deciding whether an online search is suitable.
Deciding which databases to search.
Deciding which systems to use.
Analysing the search topic.
Selecting the search terms.
Planning the search.
Carrying out the search and amending the search strategy if necessary.
Receiving the results of the search.
Communicating with the requester.
Recording the details of the search.

8.3.2 Management functions

In many small organisations there will be only one intermediary, and so this person will be responsible for a large number of the functions necessary for carrying out online searches. In organisations with more than one intermediary this work can be shared. The functions might include:

Looking after the literature (manuals, thesauri, newsletters, etc.).
Looking after the equipment (organising maintenance contracts, keeping up supplies of paper, cleaning the equipment, etc.).
Liaising with systems operators and network organisers.
Checking bills for systems, network and telephone use.
Working out charges to be passed on to others and organising this.
Passing on vital information on changes, new features, etc., to others in the organisation.
Keeping up to date (by reading relevant journals and newsletters, by attending relevant conferences and user groups, by trying out new features and potentially useful new databases, etc.).
Publicising the service.
Education.
Training.
Forward planning.

8.4 THE QUALITIES REQUIRED TO BE AN INTERMEDIARY

The key to successful online searching lies in a keen and competent intermediary in the same way as a good reference service in a library depends on a keen and competent reference librarian. In the early days of online searching potential intermediaries tended to select themselves to this job by suggesting that they attend training courses and so on. Now, with the growth of online services in libraries and information units as an extra tool for reference and information work, the task of selecting new or current staff to be trained as intermediaries presents more of a problem.

Wanger[3] reported that many managers chose intermediaries on the basis of library, computer or database familiarity, although some used more subjective characteristics, such as 'the right personality' or a 'logical thorough and analytical mind'. Van Camp[5] expands on some of these personal characteristics, and includes:

Self-confidence.
A logical mind.
Good at communicating with people.
A good salesman.
Knows the subject areas in which most of the searches are undertaken.
Keen enough to supplement formal training with plenty of individual work.
A good memory.
Patience and perseverance.
Efficiency in work habits.
Shares knowledge.

Dolan and Kremin[6] also include self-confidence in their list of requirements, and advise that a potential intermediary should be able to:

Analyse concepts.
Think flexibly.
Think in synonyms.
Anticipate variant word forms and spellings.

This paper also includes a test developed to see whether an individual has the necessary aptitude to become an intermediary.

Another characteristic that is useful in an intermediary is a perceptive, probing and suspicious mind, so that unannounced and strange changes in systems or databases are noticed, all search possibilities are explored and unexpected search results are investigated.

There are some people who, while being very competent librarians or information officers, will never be good intermediaries, because, for reasons which no one as yet clearly understands, they are very frightened and perturbed when using a terminal linked to a computer, This reaction should be recognised by managers, so that such people are not forced into becoming intermediaries.

8.5 CONCLUSIONS

As was stated earlier, there can be no universal decision as to whether it is best for an intermediary to carry out a search with or without the presence of the requester or whether it is best for requesters to carry out searches themselves.

With the access methods, databases and search systems in operation at the present time, it would seem that an intermediary is necessary in most cases, as the total system is not sufficiently oriented towards the requester, and that the presence of the requester while the search is in progress is advantageous.

Williams[7] argues that this situation may change in the future, as several projects are under way to overcome the differences and variations in access methods, databases and search systems. These projects involve developing 'translators' for converting the procedures, conventions and terminology of one system into the equivalent on another system. One example of this work is the common command language to be implemented on host computers on the Euronet network. (More details of this are given in Appendix 7.) Another example of this trend is the work being carried out at the University of Illinois to 'map' databases in a similar subject area so that resources may be shared. For example, a given search might be matched against one database which would provide output – say a Chemical Abstracts Registry Number – which would be automatically matched against another database to provide more output – say a Wiswesser Line Notation – which might be matched with yet another database to provide the required information.

By merging search systems, databases, access methods, and so on, the result may be a drift to the lowest common denominator. However, if it is easy to use and access to the more sophisticated features remains for the experienced searchers, then one might see in the future more requesters doing their own searches and professional intermediaries being used for more special or difficult searches.

REFERENCES

1. Williams, P.W. and Curtis, J.M. 'The use of online information retrieval services', *Program*, **11**, No. 1, 1- 9 (1977)
2. Holmes, P.L. *Online Information Retrieval: An Introduction and Guide to the British Library's Short Term Experimental Information Network Project*. Vol. 1, *Experimental Use of Non-medical Information Services*, British Library, London (1977). ISBN 0-905984-02-1
3. Wanger, J., Cuadra, C.A. and Fishburn, M. *Impact of Online Retrieval Services: A Survey of Users 1974–5*, System Development Corporation, Santa Monica, California (1976). ISBN 0-916368-01-7
4. Tedd. L.A. *Case Studies in Computer-based Bibliographic Information Services*, British Library, London (1979). ISBN 0-905984-30-7
5. Van Camp, A. 'Effective search analysts', *Online*, **3**, No. 2, 18–20 (1979)
6. Dolan, D.R. and Kremin, M.C. 'The quality control of search analysts', *Online*, **3**, No. 2, 8–16 (1979)
7. Williams, M.E. 'Online problems: research today, solutions tomorrow', *Bulletin of the American Society for Information Science*, **3**, No. 4, 14–16 (1977)

Chapter 9

Management Aspects of Online Searching

9.1 THE ROLE OF MANAGEMENT

Assuming that the manager of an information unit has become convinced of the value of online searching, he has a number of hurdles to surmount before a smoothly running online information service can be incorporated into his department. The first step is to persuade higher management to allocate resources for this activity. This must be followed by a persistent educational campaign to make potential requesters of information aware of the facilities on the computerised systems. There are, in fact, two different situations here, depending on whether or not online searching is simply an enhancement of existing information services or an entirely new development. A third problem for the manager is the training of staff to use this new facility. Even keeping up with the huge flow of system documentation is a major burden. Last, once an online information service is established, there are the operational problems of running the service. Some of these problems are discussed by Moureau[1].

9.2 PERSUADING HIGHER MANAGEMENT

In order to persuade others, it is essential that the information manager have a clear view of the advantages of online searching. Perhaps the most significant advantage is the ability to undertake types of search which would not be practicable manually. One example to illustrate this is a search for the use of computers to control lasers in printing, in which the numbers of items for each term are very large. There were some 78 000 items on computing, 22 000 on lasers and 13 000 on printing. The manual task of finding items containing all three terms is clearly impossible. The computer search showed that there were only six references containing all three terms. Also, the computer can undertake relatively complex searches quite easily. For example, there may be four concepts, each containing three to six synonyms, and all four concepts must be present to satisfy the search request.

Another advantage of the online systems is that new types of searching are made available. For example, the ability to truncate a search term — for example, COMPUT: — for terms such as *computing, computer, computation,* etc., or to search for words within a certain proximity of each other, or to look for a string of characters wherever they occur in a piece of text or to search on sections of the record which are not manually indexed. These are the facilities which have been introduced so far, but a computerised search system gives many opportunities for further search methods.

The information manager can also stress the speed and completeness of computer searching. It is very satisfying to obtain the references in answer to a search request within 15 minutes when it could have taken a few hours or even days by manual searching. Furthermore, if manual searching is carried out by the requesters themselves, there is an alarming tendency to be satisfied with a very incomplete scan of the literature. Perhaps online searching can be justified by the costs of failing to find by manual methods information on previous work, which may have already covered the work proposed in a project.

A further point which is worth stressing is the possibility of cross-disciplinary searching. Since files on many subjects are available on the same system, it is possible to transfer a search to a file on a peripheral subject and to uncover references which are outside the requester's normal subject area and are all the more valuable because they would not normally be obtained from the requester's own searches of the literature.

The difficulty in promoting online searching is that the cost is more obvious than with other information services. In contrast, once a book or journal has been purchased, the cost of using it is a hidden cost and the staff costs of gaining access to information are not usually taken into account. On the other hand, there is one feature of many online services which is most attractive. There are usually no joining fees or a small yearly cost, so that nearly all of the cost is incurred as the service is used. Therefore, if there is an abstracting service whose printed cost is high relative to the expected usage, then the occasional access to an online service is a most attractive way of paying for the service.

There is no doubt that the most effective way of interesting people in online searching is to persuade them to try out such a service. The systems operators give demonstrations on request and a carefully planned search for the management on some topic which is highly relevant to them is often very successful. It is usually worth while making a trial run for this type of demonstration, so that a search can be presented which does not have unexpected difficulties. The presence of key management personnel at a demonstration is much more effective than simply presenting the output from a search at a later date. Taking potential large-scale users to exhibitions or demonstrations is another way of generating the pressure that is always necessary to achieve changes in policy.

9.3 PUBLICISING THE SERVICE

If a decision to provide online search facilities is taken, one task of the manager is to tell the customers what is available. Where there has been an information service for some time, this is perhaps a less exacting task, since the queries will come to an information officer who will choose the most appropriate method of answering the query. Even in this situation, however, it is useful to make requesters aware of the particular features of online searching. There may well be searches which are not brought forward, because the requester knows that they would be impracticable as a manual search. When the capabilities of an online search service are made known, this type of query will then be brought to the information service.

It is more difficult to reach a situation where online searching becomes a normal service within an organisation if this is the first occasion on which an information service has been provided. The most effective form of publicity is a satisfied user who enthusiastically shows his search output to his department. However, demonstrations of the systems and explanatory notes are an important part of generating awareness. These are often most effective if they are tailored to a particular audience so that a description of databases which could be useful to an engineer might be circulated on one occasion, and another on the files suitable for a pharmaceutical chemist at another time. Elias[2] and Lipow[3] have discussed the publicity and marketing aspects. Ferguson[4] has written on the difficulties in the university environment.

9.4 TRAINING THE STAFF

Online systems in the UK in 1979 were still relatively expensive, costing around £50 per hour, including communications charges. Therefore, the normal method of access is to use trained intermediaries to carry out searches. They can become familiar with the systems and with the different features of individual databases, so that they are more effective in searching and also more efficient at the terminal, which gives a valuable saving in search costs. At present costs, it is unrealistic to allow the requester to carry out a search himself.

Depending on the size of the organisation, it may be necessary to consider whether a number of information officers or librarians should all be given training so that they can each carry out searches in their own specialist area. The answer depends entirely on the amount of use. It is probably necessary to carry out about a couple of searches a week to maintain familiarity with the systems. If the total amount of searching is around this figure, then only one or possibly two intermediaries should be active. It is, of course, valuable to have a second searcher, so that during holidays and illness there is always someone to carry out searches. This ideal situation is difficult to achieve, because there is career status linked to gaining proficiency in online searching and most staff want to become involved. The need for proficient and cost-effective searching does, however, dictate that the number of searchers should be kept down so that each maintains his expertise by regular searching.

At present the method of training is to attend a course by one of the systems operators who will explain most of the facilities of the system in a one- or two-day course for between $50 and $100. These courses will give a good introduction to one system. It will then be necessary to gain experience by carrying out searches over a period of several hours before real proficiency can be obtained. A company frequently wishes to access several different systems, which may necessitate more than one course. The cost of training staff to a sound level of competence should not be underestimated. There are also training courses for specific databases which will be worth while if there is high use in a particular subject area.

An excellent way of gaining experience is to join one of the many user groups which are now developing. At their meetings there is an opportunity to talk with other users to exchange experience and learn the methods employed by others to use the systems effectively. These meetings also give an opportunity to hear presentations on systems or databases or new developments and often provide an inexpensive way of gaining further knowledge of online systems.

9.5 SETTING UP A SERVICE

Although providing an online search service does not seem a complex operation, there is a surprising amount of administrative detail which must be tackled, particularly if the service is run in a cost-conscious environment — for example, where the costs of the search are chargeable to the user.

The complexity of the administrative work does depend on how the service is operated. If only one system is used and only a few databases are relevant, then overheads can be kept to a low figure, but if complete flexibility is maintained with the opportunity to access any system and database, this is much more expensive.

The first step is to make arrangements with the appropriate telecommunications authorities and the various systems operators to gain access to the database. For some databases it is also necessary to have a special agreement for access which may involve the purchase of the printed version of the information. In addition to the local telecommunications authority, it may also be useful to gain access to the international services such as the International Packet Switched Service of the British Post Office and the Euronet packet switched service inaugurated by the European Commission.

The joining of the services will first generate a collection of contracts, and this paperwork will be followed by much more in the form of operating instructions and manuals for the various services. Some of these manuals must be purchased for $5–$20. There are also guides to the databases, so that it is easy to spend between $50 and $500 to obtain the basic material to start. Then the deluge begins. There are regularly monthly newsletters from each systems operator and occasional information from the database suppliers. As new databases are introduced, there are detailed specifications of search fields and indexing methods sent to the users. The manuals, newsletters, searches, etc., will take a couple of metres or more of shelving to store. This information must all be read and absorbed by the information officer and filed sensibly for future reference.

In the UK the British Library and the Department of Industry have joined together to fund a UK Online Information Centre which is situated at Aslib. This centre provides information and advice to online users in the UK and also acts as the UK Euronet information centre. It has produced a number of pamphlets such as *Going on-line, Terminals suitable for on-line information retrieval, Sources of information on bibliographic databases,* and so on, as well as a monthly newsletter, *On-line Notes.* An information manager in the UK would find the help and advice given by this centre very useful in setting up an online search service. A set of guidelines for the establishment of online services has been produced by Keenan[5].

9.6 RUNNING THE SERVICE

Once the services are in use, there are further clerical procedures to absorb staff time. Each of the systems operators will provide a monthly bill for their services which is often broken down into details of the amount of usage in each file on each occasion of use. There will also be a bill from the telecommunications authority, in addition to which there may be telephone charges to pay. It is prudent to check these charges against internal figures for usage of the services. If there is to be a charge to those asking for the service, it is even more important that there be proper book-keeping methods to keep track of activity. On each occasion of use, the time when the search took place, the duration of the search, the database and system used, the number of prints and the number of packets recorded should be tabulated for later checking. This recording and the checking of the accounts takes a surprising amount of time.

In situations where the cost of a service is charged to the requester, there is further clerical effort to calculate the search cost. This is necessary when the charges are genuine payments by outside bodies, but the clerical overhead of calculating charges should be carefully considered before instituting an internal charging system. The advantage of such a scheme is that usage of the system is more thoughtful when the true costs of searching are made clear to the user. The disadvantage is the expenditure of non-productive effort in book-keeping.

In addition to these clerical overheads, which will absorb about one day per week, there are the activities of the intermediary which are not productive searching but which form a necessary part of the job. The most important of these is the interview between the requester and the intermediary to clarify the purpose of the search and the precise requirements. This is likely to take a minimum of 15 minutes and can easily stretch towards one hour if the requester knows little of online information systems and their particular scope, advantages and characteristics.

There are also the unproductive search sessions caused by system failures or telecommunications difficulties, or even silly mistakes by the terminal operator, which all occur from time to time. When looking at published figures for the cost of searching, these hidden extras need to be considered. It is also necessary on occasions to delete searches which have been stored for future use, and to access the system for news of additions to, and changes in, the available databases.

9.7 RUNNING COSTS

Apart from the cost of staffing the service, there are expenses for subscription charges, equipment, manuals and search aids, and the search charges associated with telephone costs, telecommunications and database charges.

The subscriptions to join the services can be very high for the specialist data-banks in finance and commerce, but for the large bibliographic systems operators the subscription is usually zero or quite small. For example, Lockheed and SDC do not charge for joining the service; Blaise charges £25 per year.

The equipment required is a teletypewriter or visual display unit and a means of communicating with the telephone network, which will be a modem or acoustic coupler. A simple teletypewriter can be purchased for about £800 in the UK and a more sophisticated version with cassette tapes for storing informa-tion, either to send or to receive, will cost a few thousand pounds. The acoustic coupler or modem will cost between £100 and £200 for purchase or yearly hire charge.

The manuals and search aids are not expensive individually, and some of them are provided free by systems operators and database suppliers. However, since there are a large number of databases and a typical price for a manual might be £5, the overall cost can be quite high. These manuals and search aids will, how-ever, amply repay their cost by the more efficient searching which they make possible.

It is important to realise that there are often two parts to the charge for using the telephone lines. There is often a telecommunications network set up specially for data traffic such as Tymnet, Telenet, IPSS (the British Post Office International Packet Switching Service) and Euronet. The costs for using these networks in the UK is coming down from over £20 per hour to a figure over £10, which will reduce to £2–£5 per hour using Euronet. There is also the charge for connection to one of these networks, which is at normal telephone rates. In some countries this means that there is a large disparity between the costs for connection to the network for those close to the node and those at a distance. Also, in several countries there are yearly subscriptions for using these networks.

The remaining charge is for the use of the database, which depends upon which database is used. A charge is levied for the amount of time a database is accessed and also for the number of items printed. This connection charge varies from about £12 to £70 per hour and the print charges are in the region of 4p–25p. In some cases it may be necessary to purchase the printed version to obtain the most favourable rate for access to the files.

9.8 CHARGING FOR THE SERVICE

The question whether there should be a charge for online searches is a complex one which is heavily dependent on the environment in which the searches are carried out as well as the personal opinions of the staff involved. The situations vary from the information brokers, whose livelihood depends upon selling search services, to the public libraries with a strong tradition of free services and the industrial units which already provide information services to their colleagues. Discussion of these problems is provided by Cooper and Dewath[6], Ferguson[7] and Oulton[8].

An organisation which has to recover all searching costs for its users must look at the costs involved very carefully. Many of the published figures do not realistically express the costs involved. It is necessary to take account of clerical time for receiving newsletters and maintaining knowledge of the systems, which will take about one day per week. Due allowance must also be made for attempts to use the system which are thwarted either by failures in the system or by equipment malfunction or just operator error. These factors are in addition to the expected overheads of discussions with requesters of searches and the clerical operations of logging usage and calculating the charges for each session. A true costing will also take into account rental or depreciation charges on equipment and may have to make provision for general overheads of running a business, such as accommodation, postage, telephones, etc.

Given a situation where charges must be recovered, there is the question of whether a uniform averaged charge should be made for a search regardless of the actual cost. This has the advantage that firm figures can be given before the search is undertaken, but does not allow the more reasonable situation of payment in proportion to the actual expenses incurred. With payments per file varying from $25 per hour to $150 per hour and output varying from one or two references to several hundred, it is fairer to make the actual charge bear a closer relationship to the resources used.

The situation in an industrial environment can be quite different. If the effort of creating and running an internal charging system is a substantial exercise, it may seem unreasonable to spend resources on such an activity. However, there are arguments suggesting that some form of notional costing of resources is useful. First, it is necessary to appreciate the high cost of the resource involved. A team of information officers can spend many times more than their salaries by using the online services. Second, it may be necessary to avoid showing the information unit as a section absorbing large sums for no tangible return. Notional transfers of resources to the information unit will provide a measure of the value placed on the service by its users.

In public libraries there are other factors to be considered. There is a long-standing tradition of free provision of services, and if charging is proposed for online services, then a case must be made for a new departure in charging practices. The arguments to support charging lie in the high value of each search and the difficulty of attaching a value to its purpose. Whereas a book costing £10–£20 may be borrowed 10–20 times, giving a low cost per occasion of use, the cost of each online search will typically be many times larger than book costs per loan. In an industrial or university setting a search will normally have a serious intent related to research or production. Searches in a public library will be more varied in nature, and some of them will be for social or recreational purposes. Should this type of search have equal priority with the more technical need in research and industry?

The decision on charging will be very dependent on individual circumstances, so no firm recommendations can be made. However, in taking the decision two factors should be fully considered: the cost of the clerical and accounting machinery for charging; and the effects of a charging policy on the objectives of the service.

9.9 THE IMPACT ON STAFF

In general, the development of online searching within an information unit is favourably received. Staff are keen to learn how to use the systems and seem to feel their professional status is enhanced if they acquire this skill. Indeed, this can create difficulties if some members of staff are involved in online searching and others are not. If the volume of searching is small, it may be sensible to limit the searching to one or two members of staff, so that the searchers become efficient and cost-effective, but the management problems of having some staff in a favoured position must be faced.

The main difficulty caused by the introduction of online searching is an increase in the number of inter-library loans. This has both a staffing and an economic implication. If the library and information units are separate, there may be resentment that one section are being given more attractive employment which is creating more work for those without the new job enhancement. The effect of introducing online services is considered by Atherton[9] and Dougherty[10].

9.10 THE DEVELOPMENT FUNCTION

Once an information unit has passed through the initial phases of introducing online searching – the persuading, training, publicity and administration – there is the task of maintaining momentum and gaining the best advantage from available facilities. It must be accepted that the learning stage will be here for some time to come. The problem of training staff will be a continuous one. There are an increasing number of job opportunities for online searchers, so the mobility of staff is high and training of new staff may well be a regular occurrence. There is also the need to train existing staff in new databases and new systems. The need to explain the particular characteristics of online searching to those requesting searches will also be a constant requirement for some time to come.

It will also be useful if someone within an information unit pays particular attention to the developing technology for information access. For example, there will almost certainly be terminals emerging at a modest price with exactly the kind of intelligence to make online searching more economic and effective. It may be that a higher level of computer knowledge would be useful to take advantage of some of these developments. New networks based on satellite communications will be appearing. Small computers with programs to establish a search description by a dialogue with the user may be produced, so that the requester himself can more easily carry out a search. The rate of change and the diversity of information access which is likely to emerge in the future means that to make the best use of information systems the manager must develop the ability to assess the technological possibilities which are becoming available.

REFERENCES

1. Moureau, M.L. 'Problems and pitfalls in setting up and operating an online information service', *Online Review*, 2, No. 3, 237–244 (1978)
2. Elias, A. 'Marketing for online bibliographic services', *Online Review*, 3, No. 1, 107–117 (1979)
3. Lipow, A.G. 'User education and publicity for online services', in Watson, P.G. (Ed.), *Online Bibliographic Services – Where We Are, Where We're Going*, pp. 67–77, American Library Association, Chicago (1977)
4. Ferguson, D.G. 'Marketing online services in the University', *Online*, July (1977)
5. Keenan, S.K. *How to Go Online – Guidelines for the Establishment of Online Services in Public Libraries*, British Library Research and Development Department Report No. 5533, London (1980)
6. Cooper, M.D. and Dewath, N.A. 'Effect of user fees on the cost of online searching in libraries', *Journal of Library Automation*, 10, No. 4, 304–319 (1977)
7. Ferguson, D.G. 'The costs of charging for information service', in Watson, P.G. (Ed.), op. cit., pp. 60–66, American Library Association, Chicago (1977)
8. Oulton, A.J. 'Factors affecting end-user charges for online bibliographic information retrieval services in public libraries', in *Third International Online Information Meeting, London 4–6th December 1979*, pp. 35–44, Learned Information, Oxford (1979). ISBN 0-904933-21-0
9. Atherton, P. 'Online bibliographic services in academic libraries; some observations', in Watson, P.G. (Ed.), op. cit., pp. 24–30.
10. Dougherty, R.M. 'Management implications of introducing innovative reference services', in Watson, P.G. (Ed.), op. cit., pp. 85–91.

Chapter 10

Education and Training

10.1 INTRODUCTION

When the problems of education and training for online bibliographic searching are considered, it is necessary to be aware of the different functions of the two. Williams[1] sees education for online use of databases as being concerned with the fundamental principles and basic knowledge of information science and how they relate to search strategy formulation, bibliographic database structures, users' needs, and so on, whereas training is concerned with details of specific databases and search systems, their interaction and ways of optimising their use.

As the number of available databases, systems operators and command languages increases, so too do the problems of training. A chapter on the education and training aspects of online searching appears for the first time in the 14th issue of the *Annual Review of Information Science and Technology.*

Those to be educated and trained about online searching include not only potential intermediaries, but also potential requesters or users. In this chapter the term 'searcher' will be used to cover both types of person, although it must be remembered that the content of an education or training programme may well be different for both types of person.

The importance of the training process should not be underestimated by the searcher or by the organisation to which (s)he belongs. Adequate time and money should be allocated for initial training, practice sessions, attendance at relevant courses and keeping up with developments. Attendance at a refresher course is advisable if for some reason a searcher has not carried out any online searches for a substantial period, as databases might change structure and systems operators might change the command language and the way in which a database is searched on their system.

Papers by Caruso, Stanley, Wanger and Martin on training and retraining are included in reference 2; also, there are many useful papers on user education and training in reference 3 and some in reference 4.

10.2 WHO IS INVOLVED IN EDUCATION AND TRAINING?

10.2.1 Academic institutions

First, several academic institutions aim to make future searchers aware of on-line bibliographic searching by including the topic in the education of under-graduates. The University of California at San Diego has experimented with offering undergraduates free use of online search services for 7 months and has shown that many undergraduates have sophisticated information needs[5]. In Sweden the Royal Institute of Technology has developed a course on library use and information retrieval which is an integral part of studies in the school of mechanical engineering. This is described by Sabsay in reference 3.

Second, library schools are increasingly including online searching in their curricula, although the time allocated to the topic will vary from course to course. Harter[6] reports on a survey of instruction in online searching in American library schools in 1977. In the UK the British Library Research and Development Department has encouraged the teaching of online searching to library school students and since 1975 has funded many projects on the teaching of this subject. Tedd has produced an overview of this teaching in 1979[7]. As well as educating future librarians and information officers, library school teachers are also involved in the education and training of others in online searching; for example, by giving courses to students of other disciplines within the institution, holding workshops for local librarians and professional association branches and running special training courses for specific organisations.

10.2.2 Database producers

Most people agree that training in the use of a particular database is best given by the database producer, although for databases with a relatively simple struc-ture or content such special training is scarcely necessary. Thus, when a new database becomes available online, it is usual to have appropriate training sessions. British database producers such as the Commonwealth Agricultural Bureaux and the Institution of Electrical Engineers have run training sessions in North America, for example. Sometimes special posts of 'education specialist' are created; Engineering Index Inc., for instance, has such a post. The training techniques developed by ISI and Biosis over the years are described by Collier and Elias, respectively, in reference 3. However, as more databases and more services become available, especially via Euronet, it will be difficult for the database producers (especially the smaller ones) to train searchers in the use of their database on a particular system.

10.2.3 Individual organisations

When one or more people have been trained and have become experienced in online bibliographic searching, they are frequently given the task of training others within the organisation. In the UK this has happened at, for example, the Ministry of Agriculture, Fisheries and Food, ICI and the Unilever Research Port Sunlight Laboratory and is described by Tedd[8], while the techniques used within the Philips Research Laboratories in Holland are described by Schulkes in reference 3.

10.2.4 International organisations

One of the aims of UNISIST is to train and educate information specialists and users; online bibliographic searching is included and UNISIST's activities in this area are described by Tocatlian in reference 3.

It was the 1976 annual conference of EUSIDIC – European Association of Scientific Information Dissemination Centres – which generated so many of the papers which have been cited so far in this chapter. Both they, and their American counterpart, ASIDIC, are involved in the education of online bibliographic searching.

The Euronet launch team, while not undertaking specific training themselves, will be promoting Euronet and co-ordinating various training activities.

10.2.5 National organisations

In many countries national organisations involved in information work have also become involved in education and training for online searching. In the UK an online information centre which is funded by the British Library and the Department of Industry was established at Aslib in 1979. Among the aims of this centre is the promotion and monitoring of the education and training facilities for online searching in the country. In France the work of the Bureau National de l'Information Scientifique et Technique (BNIST) in this area is described by Rozenstroch in reference 3, and in Norway the work of the Norwegian Centre for Informatics is described by Tedd[8]. In Belgium the national body for Scientific policy (SPPS) has funded work at the National Centre for Scientific and Technical Documentation in order to make the scientific community aware of online searching in preparation for Euronet. This involved: seminars and demonstrations on sites for potential users; preparation of leaflets and booklets in Dutch and French to supplement prime sources of information; and specific training at various levels.

10.2.6 Professional Societies

In the UK organisations such as the Library Association run short courses on online bibliographic searching, whereas the British Computer Society and the Institute of Information Scientists have set up special interest groups for online information retrieval. The United Kingdom Chemical Information Service (UKCIS), which is part of The Chemical Society, organises linked courses run by the database producers and the systems operators. This is a useful way to learn about searching a particular database on a particular system. In France the Association Française de Documentation Automatique en Chemie (AFDAC) offers basic and advanced training courses on a regular basis. In North America the American Library Association, the American Society for Information Science and the Canadian Association for Information Science are also involved in this area.

10.2.7 Systems operators

For education and training in a particular command language the systems operators usually provide good courses. However, the systems operators cannot be expected to give full details on how to search efficiently all databases accessible via the system. Training courses are frequently of two types — one for new users and another for advanced users. Both types of course are held at regular intervals in many parts of Europe and North America.

10.2.8 User groups

As more people become involved in online searching, the growth of user groups is evident. In the UK there are several groups in different parts of the country. These groups run courses themselves and also organise conferences or seminars on training so that their members become aware of the problems and possibilities. In the Netherlands the online user group has established an official training centre which is rented out to those wishing to hold training sessions. The centre does not have any permanent staff; it has about five terminals and video facilities to enable 25–30 attenders of a course to watch demonstration searches.

10.3 ASPECTS IN THE DESIGN OF COURSES

Obviously, the aim of teaching about online bibliographic searching will vary, as will the level of teaching. The time available for the course will also vary and will influence the design of the course. Training courses such as the new user training course run by SDC may last for two full days, whereas the time available for this topic in an academic course might vary from 1 or 2 hours to 60 hours. Also, the amount of money available for running the course will vary. Many of the organisers of courses on online bibliographic searching charge a fee which is higher than the normal fee for courses in order to cover the cost of giving participants 'live' experience of searching. This extra charge cannot usually be made on an academic course, and if money is not available, other methods, such as recording searches, may be used. This, in turn, influences the design of the course.

In general terms, there are five main components of a course on online bibliographic searching: general introduction, specific introduction, demonstration search, live search and assessment of search results. The choice of components to be included in a particular course will depend on the type of course: a training course would probably include little general introduction but would include the remaining components, whereas a library school course might include some general introduction and a demonstration, or some specific introduction and a live search with assessment might be added if time and money permitted. The course organiser should monitor participant reaction to the course and be ready to restructure and revise the content of the course as appropriate.

10.3.1 General introduction

Before course participants carry out a live search themselves, a certain amount of general introduction to online searching is necessary. This can be covered in lecture or seminar sessions, although films might be used or participants given background reading material.

Topics covered in the general introduction might include:

The objectives of bibliographic searching.

A comparison with manual methods.

The historical background to online searching.

An overview of existing online search systems.

An overview of the existing databases available for online searching.

A description of the types of commands necessary for online searching, including Boolean logic.

A description of the equipment (terminal, modem, etc.) required.

An explanation of the use of telecommunications networks.

An explanation of how inverted files are formed and used.

10.3.2 Specific introduction

The course organiser must know which system(s) and database(s) the participants will want to use, since in the main only information relating to those systems and databases will be appropriate. Printed material produced by the systems operator or the database producer can be used if it is at the right level, in the right language, etc.; otherwise special handouts may need to be prepared. Workbooks such as those by Bourne[9], Stockey and Basens[10] and Markey and Atherton[11] might also be used if appropriate.

Decisions need to be made and information given in the following three areas:

(1) Terminal keyboard. It cannot be assumed, especially in the UK, that course participants will be familiar with a typewriter keyboard. Therefore, an introduction to the keyboard and, if possible, to online interaction with a computer should be available. Alternatively, some time spent on an ordinary typewriter might be useful for participants.

(2) Command language. It is necessary to decide how many of the more sophisticated commands and techniques are to be taught – for example, string searching (on ORBIT or Elhill), word proximity searching (on Dialog or Quest), term truncation, etc. If these are not covered, then the full potential of online search systems may not be appreciated; on the other hand, too much detail at an early stage may confuse. The phased approach adopted by some systems operators of having 'new user' and 'advanced user' courses is perhaps best, if time permits. A leaflet summarising the commands, the logging on and off procedures and special characters is useful to have at the terminal.

(3) Database(s). In most cases the database or databases to be used in training will be obvious because of the background of the course participants. If this is not so, a database should be picked which is economical and can exemplify various features, such as controlled versus uncontrolled search terms, searching parallel printed indexes, searching by a variety of fields, and so on.

It is also necessary to consider in how much detail to describe the coverage of the database, the content of the bibliographic record and the indexing policy of the database producer. In addition, the ways of searching the database on the system must also be covered – for example, searchable and printable fields, file size, the frequency with which the database is updated, methods of dealing with authors, abbreviations, special photo typesetting characters, etc.

10.3.3 Demonstration search(es)

Before carrying out a live search themselves, the course participants will probably see or take part in a demonstration search or searches. The topic of the search is important and should be chosen to appeal to course participants, perhaps by including a search for a 'local' author or work published from a 'local' institution.

Various methods of demonstrating searches, both recorded and live, are described by Tedd and Keen[12]. These include the use of videotape, digital cassettes, audio cassettes, etc., which will be described in some more depth in the next section. A table showing the relative costs, in terms of system cost and course organisers, for varying sizes of group is also given in reference 12.

When organising group demonstrations, it is necessary to ensure that there are ample TV monitors so that participants can clearly see what is happening; also, if possible, participants should be given an annotated hand-out of the demonstration search.

10.3.4 Live search

Most courses involve the participants doing a live search, and so a decision needs to be made on the subject of these searches. A variety of approaches may be used:

Participants choose their own topic.
Participants choose from a list, perhaps graded by the course organiser.
Participants all do the same search, chosen by the course organiser, on different databases.
Participants carry out a search for a 'real' enquirer.

Another factor in organising the 'live search' part of the course is to decide how much time each person is allowed to have online and, if there is a limited supply of terminals, what the remainder of the participants should be doing. One approach might be to split the participants into groups of, say, four, so that they can search co-operatively.

10.3.5 Assessment of search results

This part of the course might involve the course participants in assessing the relevance of retrieved references and discussing ways in which the search strategies might have been improved. If the group size is small, say less than 15, this might be organised in a seminar session; otherwise the organiser should select particular searches and discuss them in a more formal manner.

Another analytical approach involves the course organiser's measuring the use and misuse of each command in each search. In this way information can be gained as to which commands were misunderstood, underused, etc., so that the teaching of those commands can be improved.

In academic courses a widely used method of formally evaluating how much a student has understood about online searching is by a question in an examination paper. Other methods of evaluation might include the comparison of an online search with a printed index search of the same query, or the comparison of the use of a particular database on, say, three systems operators.

10.4 AIDS IN TEACHING

Various aids can be used in the teaching of online bibliographic searching. Although live 'hands-on' experience of searching, with expert guidance available if required, is perhaps the ideal way to learn, this may not be an economical (in time and money) solution. Thus, many course organisers make use of some form of recorded search — perhaps on slide, overhead transparency, digital cassette, videotape or paper.

There are several advantages to using recorded searches for demonstration purposes, the main one being that the course organiser is freed of the difficulty of getting into and using the system and so can concentrate on the teaching function. Other advantages include: no problem of computer inaccessibility; no telecommunications network problems; no computer system failures; no telephone line failures; and cheaper. It can, however, take some appreciable amount of the course organiser's time to prepare a sample search. A suitable topic and the level of commands to be included having been chosen, some time must be spent online developing a series of commands which will exemplify all the points the course organiser wishes to make.

The course organiser who makes use of such aids should ensure that participants do not think that they are being taught totally by machine, and ample time for answering questions and amplifying points made should be given.

When choosing teaching aids, various technical aspects should be considered:

Suitability of the medium to the subject.
Cost (in time and money) of acquiring or making the aid.
Equipment required to use the aid.
Technical staff required to run the equipment.
Whether or not the aid has been produced in a standardised format which can be used on the available equipment.
Possibility of reproducing the aid, if it has been prepared 'in house'.

Before the more technical teaching aids which can be used are described, it is perhaps worth mentioning a teaching technique that has been used at the University of London and elsewhere. The medium required consists of a piece of paper and a pencil. The trainee writes a command that might be given to the search system and the trainer writes the system response. In this way the trainer can adjust the search so that the trainee has to work out what to do if there are too many or too few references, etc.

10.4.1 Audio and digital recording

A special training device, known as Mediatron, has been developed by Mellordata in conjunction with the University of London[13,14]. This device enables the recording of audio and digital signals on to a single cassette and also allows for a link with a slide projector to give a full multimedia aid. Recorded searches can be played back via a visual display unit and a TV monitor for large groups or just via a VDU for individual demonstrations. The device costs about £500 and prepared cassettes are available from Alina Vickery at the University of London. The Mediatron can also be used to guide a trainee through a prepared recorded search and thus give some hands-on experience. Mediatrons are now used in several educational establishments.

Alternatively, searches can be recorded using a digital cassette or paper tape attached to the terminal. In this case a commentary might be given live by the

```
                        This is a recorded demonstration of on-line
                        searching of a database.Our search topic is
                        'bilingual education in Wales'.We shall use the
                        ERIC database on the Lockheed Dialog system.
                         Every now and then you will be asked to type a
                        specific command. When you have done this please
                        press the orange return button on the keyboard
                        and then the cont start button on the panel.
                         Do not worry if you cannot type too well-there is
                        no hurry. Good luck!
                        We shall start by choosing the ERIC database
                              Please type BEGIN 1



?    BEGIN 1

           30nov78 1:45:15 user 7244
Filel*:ERIC 66-78/007
           Set Items Description (+=OR;*=AND;-=NOT)
           --- ----- -------- ---- ----------------

                        We know that the late Jac L. Williams was
                        interested in bilingual education in Wales and so
                        our first approach is to retrieve items written
                        by him.  Because these may be referred to in
                        different ways we shall use the EXPAND(shortened
                        form E)command.  Please type E AU=WILLIAMS, JAC
                        note in ERIC there is always a,and a space
                        between surname and forename or initial.



?    E AU=WILLIAMS, JAC
R F  I dex-term            Type Items RT
E1    AU=WILLIAMS, J. R.------      2
E2    AU=WILLIAMS, J. R. PARRY      4
E3    AU=WILLIAMS, J. SHERWOOD      5
E4    AU=WILLIAMS, J.D.-------      2
E5    AU=WILLIAMS, J.H., JR.--      1
E6    AU=WILLIAMS, JAC--------
E7    AU=WILLIAMS, JAC L.-----      2
E8    AU=WILLIAMS, JAC. L.----      1
E9    AU=WILLIAMS, JACK D.----      1
E10   AU=WILLIAMS, JACK F.----      2
E11   AU=WILLIAMS, JACK K.----      2
E12   AU=WILLIAMS, JAMES------      1
E13   AU=WILLIAMS, JAMES 9.---      2
                        We see that there is nothing by Williams, Jac
                        but there are 2 items by Williams, Jac L. (E7) and
                        1 item by Williams, Jac. L. (E8). The break key
                        on the keyboard was used to interrupt the listing
                        of further irrelevant authors.
                         To pick up E7 and E8 we use the SELECT (shortened
                        form S) command.  Please type SE7-E8
```

Figure 10.1 Example of a HOARS demonstration

trainer or recorded on a separate audio cassette. The use of the two separate cassettes is described by Tedd and Keen[12], while part of an annotated search developed by Tedd is shown in *Figure 10.1*. This last technique is known as HOARS (hands on annotated recorded search). The recorded search is edited to include a description of the search process and, if necessary, stop codes after each system prompt, so that when it is being played back the trainee can type in the appropriate command.

A drawback to all these hands-on recorded methods of demonstration is that, irrespective of what command the trainee types, the system will respond as though it had been correct.

10.4.2 Computer-assisted instruction

To date, little work has been carried out in this area, although Moghdam[15] concludes that 'an online tutorial program, built as an integral part of the information retrieval system, is seen as the ideal alternative to back-up to live help'. The nearest example to this at present is perhaps Medlearn. Medlearn, available via the US National Library of Medicine in Washington, provides online training for Medline and is described by Eisenberg *et al.*[16].

The Trainer online training package developed by Caruso at the University of Pittsburgh[17, 18] provides programmed instruction and practice for potential users of Lockheed and SDC. The specially prepared computer programs (in Fortran) emulate the Dialog and ORBIT software and use a sub-set of various databases accessible on Lockheed and SDC.

Various smaller computer-assisted instruction packages exist. A student at Sheffield University has developed a program in BASIC, known as FOSSILS, which aims to give an idea of how online searching works by guiding students through two prepared searches on Lockheed using the ERIC and SSCI databases. FOSSILS is now used successfully by several library schools in the British Isles. The program is similar to one developed at Trent Polytechnic Library, which guides one through a search on the NTIS database on ESA-IRS.

At Leeds Polytechnic a number of self-instructional packages have been prepared using a Hewlett Packard HP2645A 'intelligent' terminal. By using programmable keys the student can interact with the terminal and be led to different pieces of text recorded on to the terminal's cassettes, depending on the answer given to a question. Packages have been developed giving tutorials on Blaise and Medline, and a series of questions based on the use of Medline on Blaise.

Another example of a computer-assisted system for education and training is Lockheed's Ontap (Online Training and Practice) facility. Trainees can search a prescribed topic on the 1975 sub-set of the ERIC database and can compare retrieved references with those located by an 'expert' searcher.

It is likely that with microcomputer systems, such as the PET, APPLE, RML 380 Z and the Tandy TRS 80, being used as 'super' terminals their processing capability will be used for education and training purposes as well as for enhancing the whole search process. Several education and training organisations in the UK are now using microcomputer systems for this purpose.

10.4.3 Printed material

Printed material is a very important teaching aid for online searching. Some course organisers may find the printed material produced by others such as systems operators or database producers suits their needs; others may wish to produce their own. In general, the information given in a printed form will fall into several categories:

(1) Information about the system. This may include a general description of the system and how particular databases may be searched on the system. Systems-operator-produced material such as newsletters, pocket-sized reference cards or the large manual giving full details of the system might be made available for course participants.

(2) Information about the database. Each systems operator produces some documentation about the use of each database on their system. Also, many database producers are now preparing guides on the use of their database on the different services. In addition, the newsletters, lists of subject headings and thesauri published by the database producers might be made available for course participants.

(3) General information about search techniques. Course organisers may ask participants to read appropriate textbooks or journal articles to assist in this area. Also, annotated sample searches and copies of recorded searches might be used.

Workbooks such as references 9—11 also fall under the category of printed material and can be useful teaching aids.

10.4.4 Other aids

There are a number of other audio and visual aids that can be of use in education and training for online searching.

Transparencies used with an overhead projector may be produced by the course organiser or may be produced more professionally, to the course organiser's specification, or may be bought from outside. A search could be prepared on a set of these overhead transparencies (blown up from the original output to ensure legibility) and could be used to describe the steps in searching and the use of various commands. Transparencies of sample records from different databases are also useful to show the difference in structure and also the differences in output formats of the systems operators. Attachments, such as those for producing 'animation' or for showing 'books' of overhead transparencies, can be acquired for the projector.

Films, which are usually produced by external organisations, can be useful. These are usually more general in nature and so are best used in the introduction part of a course. *Access*[19], made in 1975 at Stanford University, deals with the use of online systems for information retrieval in general (for example, camp sites, best restaurant in town, guitar players) and also includes a Lockheed search.

Videotape can be used to record the progress of an online search. A video camera might be placed behind the searcher to record all that happens on the terminal (a VDU terminal is best for this purpose), and a voice commentary might be simultaneously recorded to guide future viewers through the search. Alternatively, a 'silent' videotape could be made with a commentary being added live by the course organiser when the videotape is played back to students or trainees. A more sophisticated videotape could also be made which includes shots of the searcher, the thesauri used, the telephone and modem, the full text of a relevant retrieved document and blow-ups of important parts of the search. This type of videotape can take some time to produce. Yet another use of videotape might be to record some of the stages of a 'real' search and use the dialogue and non-verbal communication techniques to help in teaching about the reference interview. Although videotape is a useful teaching aid, for both large groups and individuals there are serious standardisation problems which might affect the use of externally produced videotapes on 'local' equipment.

Thirty-five mm slides used on their own or with an audio tape (a tape–slide presentation) can be made in-house to the course organiser's specification, or be bought from elsewhere. The audio and visual aspects of a tape–slide presentation are usually automatically synchronised by a pulsing mechanism on the audio tape. There can be standardisation problems with this, but they are fairly easily overcome. Slides or tape–slide presentations can be used to record a search, to demonstrate logging on and off details or to describe a particular database or system, and so on. A tape–slide which describes the stages of an online search from when a requester first realises a need for information to its acquisition has been made by Tedd[20].

Some experimental work on the use of viewdata for learning about online searching is being undertaken in the UK.

10.5 CONCLUSIONS

This chapter has described some of the organisations involved in education and training for online searching and given some practical details for anyone involved in designing or running such courses.

The ways in which searchers are educated and trained varies. In organisations where members of staff have several years of experience of online searching these people often train new searchers in that organisation, and this means that the training can be linked to the particular systems and databases used by that organisation. On the other hand, if an organisation is using online search services for the first time, the new searcher may attend suitable courses offered by the organisations described in this chapter; but if no suitable course were available, then the new searcher might learn by practising at the terminal. Self-instruction was the common way of learning about online searching in the early days – that is, the early 1970s. In the future it is hoped that there will be a variety of formal training courses available for new searchers, which will take into account the background of the searcher and the likely use to be made by the searcher (that is, requester versus intermediary). Apart from the current set of courses that are available, more general ones on search strategy formulation, the reference interview, a general introduction to the terminology and technology of online searching and an overview of search features on different systems might be useful for the new searcher.

REFERENCES

1. Williams, M.E. 'Education and training for online use of databases', *Journal of Library Automation,* 10, No. 4, 320–334 (1977)
2. Kent, A. and Galvin, T.J. (Eds). *The Online Revolution in Libraries.* Marcel Dekker, New York (1978). ISBN 0 8247 6754 3
3. MacCafferty, M. (Ed.) *User Education – Towards a Better Use of Information Resources; Proceedings of the EUSIDIC Conference, Graz 1–3 December, 1976,* EUSIDIC and Aslib, London (1977) (European User Series No. 4). ISBN 0 85142 096 6

4. Watson, P.G. (Ed.) *Online Bibliographic Services — Where We are, Where We are Going,* American Library Association, Chicago (1977)

5. Maina, W.E. 'Undergraduate use of online bibliographic retrieval services: experience at the University of California, San Diego', *Online,* 1, No. 2, 45–59 (1977)

6. Harter, S.P. 'An assessment of instruction provided by library schools in online searching', *Information Processing and Management,* 15, No. 2, 71–75 (1979)

7. Tedd, L.A. 'The teaching of online searching in UK schools of librarianship and information science — some facts and figures', *Third International Online Information Meeting, London 4–6th December 1979,* Learned Information Oxford (1979). ISBN 0-904933-21-0

8. Tedd, L.A. *Case Studies in Computer-based Bibliographic Information Services* (British Library Research and Development Department Report No. 5463), British Library Research and Development Department, London (1979). ISBN 0 905984 30 7

9. Bourne, C.P. *DIALOG® Lab Workbook,* Institute of Library Research, University of California, Berkeley (October 1976)

10. Stockey, E. and Basens, S.J. *An Introduction to Database Searching: A Self-instructional Manual,* Graduate School of Library Science, Drexel University, Philadelphia (1977)

11. Markey, K. and Atherton, P. *Online Training and Practice Manual for ERIC Database Searchers,* ERIC Clearinghouse on University Resources, Syracuse University (June 1978)

12. Tedd, L.A. and Keen, E.M. 'Methods of teaching online bibliographic searching: experience at the College of Librarianship, Wales', *Information Processing and Management,* 14, No. 6, 453–463 (1978)

13. Vickery, A. and Batten, A.M. 'Development of multimedia teaching packages for user education in online retrieval systems', *Online Review,* 2, No. 4, 367–374 (1978)

14. Pratt, G. and Vickery, A. 'The development of multimedia teaching aids for users of computer-based information retrieval systems', *Program,* 11, No. 1, 10–15 (1977)

15. Moghdam, D. 'User training for online information retrieval systems', *Journal of the American Society for Information Science,* 26, No. 3, 184–188 (1975)

16. Eisenberg, L.J. *et al.* '*MEDLEARN* — a computer assisted instruction (CAI) program for MEDLARS', *Bulletin of the Medical Library Association,* 66, No. 1, 6–13 (1978)

17. Caruso, E. 'Hands on online: bringing it home', *Online Review,* 2, No. 3, 251–268 (1978)

18. Caruso, E. 'A TRAINER for online systems', *Online,* 1, No. 4, 28–34 (1977)

19. *Access,* a film by John Nutt, Department of Communication, Stanford University, California (1975). 16 mm, 20 min

20. *Online searching,* a tape slide program by Lucy Tedd, Media Services Unit, College of Librarianship, Wales (1979). 80 slides, 1 tape cassette, 14 min

Note to the Appendices

The only way to appreciate the variety of online information systems, their scope and the different methods of treatment is to study the available systems and see demonstrations of them. The problem of familiarisation, however, is made difficult by the rapid rate of change in the systems and the databases they provide. The authors were placed in the dilemma of either giving no information on individual systems to guide potential users or giving details of the systems that would inevitably become progressively outdated by the passage of time.

It was decided to give the details that were current in early 1979 to give readers a survey of the online information area. However, it must be strongly emphasised that some of these details will already be dated by the time this book is published. For precise information users must consult a current system manual which is being regularly updated. However, there are some details which are more stable than others. The list of databases will probably be fairly accurate but incomplete; there are new databases regularly on the systems. The system commands also tend to be stable, with the addition of new facilities from time to time. The numbers and names of databases do change – in particular, when a large and growing file is split into two separate files. The data on the size of files and the size of the updates is the most variable item, particularly for some databases which are still developing their coverage. Changes that have taken place since the original setting of these appendices have been incorporated, where possible, at the proof-reading stage, in early 1980. Thus, details of new databases provided by each system operator have been added at the end of the relevant appendix.

If these appendices are to be used for reference purposes, they should be carefully updated whenever changes take place. Some space has been allowed for this purpose.

Appendix 1

A Check List for Search Preparation and Search Strategy

This check list is aimed primarily towards the intermediary who has a responsibility to the enquirer to maintain a high standard of searching but it also indicates the many considerations there are for effective searching of online databases.

A1.1 HAVE THE NECESSARY SEARCH AIDS

Which include:

System manuals and updates.
Database producers' manuals and updates.
System newsletters.
Database newsletters.
Term frequency lists.
Thesauri and classification schemes (up to date).
Independently produced searching guides.
Appropriate dictionaries, glossaries and other reference works.

A1.2 OBTAIN INFORMATION ABOUT THE ENQUIRY

Make sure that you understand the enquiry and appreciate what the enquirer wants by:

Questioning the enquirer as thoroughly as necessary.
Consulting encyclopaedias, other reference works and known relevant references.

The following headings are useful for the collection of information from the enquirer:

A brief summary of the search topic.
A list of the words or phrases normally used to describe the search topic.
Details of several recent relevant references.
How comprehensive a search is required.
How many references the enquirer expects there to be.
Any limitations by date, language, etc.
The urgency of the search.
Whether the search is confidential.

A1.3 DECIDE WHETHER ONLINE SEARCHING IS A SUITABLE METHOD OF DEALING WITH THE ENQUIRY

Are there databases which cover the subject?
Do they provide the kind of information required?
Do they go far back enough?
Would another source (textbook, abstract journal, encyclopaedia, library catalogue, telephone call) be better or cheaper?
Would an online search be a worthwhile preliminary step even though it could not provide the full answer?

A1.4 DECIDE WHICH DATABASES TO SEARCH

According to:

Subject coverage.
Journal coverage.
Record content.
Indexing attributes.
How comprehensive a search is required.
Cost.
Accessibility.

A1.5 DECIDE WHICH SYSTEMS TO USE

According to:

Database coverage. (Does one system cover all those you intend to search?)
How the relevant databases are dealt with (as regards record content, segmentation, etc.).
Search fields. (Does the search have a particular requirement?)
Search devices and other similar features. (Does the search have a particular requirement?)
Performance (for example, response rate is affected by local time; urgent searches require speedy offline print distribution).
Print formats.

Cost.
Accessibility.

A1.6 ANALYSE THE SEARCH TOPIC

Break the enquiry into its logical components.
Exclude unnecessary concepts.
Check your analysis with the enquirer if possible.

A1.7 SELECT THE SEARCH TERMS

According to:

The search topic.
How comprehensive a search is required.

Using:

Information supplied by the enquirer.
Thesauri and classification schemes.
Term frequency lists.
Known relevant references (online or offline).
Reference works.
The printed form of the database.
Chemical dictionary files.
Online term displays where advisable.

With a knowledge of the systems and files to be searched including:

Search devices.
Indexing policies.
Search fields available.
Default field options.
Field labels.
Whether controlled terms should be entered in pre- or post-co-ordinated form.
How hyphens and other punctuation marks are dealt with.
Word segmentation policy.
Stop words.
Term formats (author names, journal names, etc.).
Limiting to priority terms.
Limiting by date, language, file segments, etc.
Generic term selection devices.
Potentially highly posted terms.
Potential ambiguity.
How long controlled terms have been valid.
The consistency with which rules for dealing with words or punctuation signs, etc., are applied.

Checking that:

All necessary forms and spellings of a word are used.

All necessary synonyms, broader terms, narrower terms and abbreviations are included.

Optional rules for dealing with terms are allowed for (for example, hyphens or not, segmentation or not).

Truncation is at the most suitable point.

A1.8 PLAN THE SEARCH

Check that you know the system commands, search devices, correction routines, etc.

Prepare the initial profile.

Avoid unnecessary use or combination of highly posted terms.

Avoid ambiguity.

Decide what to do if the search is too broad or too narrow.

Anticipate other decision points.

Aim to avoid online information gathering or exploring for search terms when this can be carried out more cheaply beforehand.

Consider carrying out a search in stages.

Prepare a clear plan.

If using a search save procedure, check for:

Compatibility of search terms.
Compatibility of search fields.
Varying ambiguity problems.
Varying implicit concepts.

Enter the search in the cheapest file.

A1.9 CARRY OUT THE SEARCH

Be expeditious.
Be flexible.
Use off-peak times if possible.
Chain commands.
Use the fastest available speed.
Be prepared to log off when an impasse is reached or the system is performing badly.

A1.10 TO NARROW THE SEARCH IF NECESSARY

Reduce the number of ORed terms.
Include additional ANDed terms or new concepts.
Check for ambiguous terms or truncations.
Restrict the use of broad classification codes.
Use specific controlled terms.
Use specific natural-language phrases.
Use priority labelled terms.

Restrict the search to titles or controlled index fields.

Limit by date or language.

Limit by type of literature (books, reviews, etc.).

Restrict the search to the most appropriate file or file division.

A1.11 TO BROADEN THE SEARCH IF NECESSARY

Reduce the number of AND links and concepts.

Increase the number of ORed terms (word variants, synonyms, broader and narrower terms).

Use more truncations and explosions if appropriate.

Search the full record, including abstracts if possible.

Search the full range of appropriate files.

Check for the erroneous use of NOT logic.

Check that the terms used allow for the peculiarities of the files and systems (see Section A1.7, above).

A1.12 OBTAIN THE RESULTS

Use the most suitable print formats (for example, accession numbers for speed online, titles for sampling online, abstracts for information offline).

Consider sorting possibilities.

Check that the results are decipherable by the enquirer and that he can interpret abbreviations of journal names.

Make sure the enquirer knows what search terms were used and what databases covered in case he needs to follow up the search elsewhere.

Get the results to the enquirer without delay.

Be prepared to repeat the search if the results are unsatisfactory or suggest a new approach.

A1.13 COMMUNICATING WITH THE ENQUIRER

It is usually advantageous for the enquirer to be present at the terminal, first to discuss the search and then to assess the (preliminary) results.

Explain the searching process to the enquirer. It will help him to appreciate how best to submit future enquiries.

Maintain good 'customer' relations.

Do not allow the procedure of the search to be determined by an inexperienced enquirer. Assume a strong role.

Inform the enquirer if you know of any other useful sources of information on his search topic.

A1.14 RECORDING THE DETAILS OF SEARCHES

Consider recording the details of all searches and keeping duplicate print-outs of terminal interactions.

Maintain confidentiality.

Appendix 2

Blaise

A2.1 SOFTWARE SYSTEM

Elhill III C, United States National Library of Medicine, plus Blaise programs, including Editor

A2.2 ADDRESS

Blaise Marketing,
7 Rathbone St,
London W1P 2AL

Tel: 01-636 1544

A2.3a ABBREVIATIONS FOR SEARCHABLE FIELDS FOR MEDICAL DATABASES

AU	Author
BX	Vocabulary backward cross-reference
CN	Citation number
DC	Descriptor code
DE	Descriptor entry version
DT	Data tags
ED	Entry date
IS	ISSN
IT	Index terms
JC	Journal title code
LA	Language
LI	Special list indicator
MC	MeSH class number
MH	MeSH heading, descriptor print version
PD	Publication date
PL	Place of publication
PN	Place of publication class number
QA	Topical qualifier abbreviation
QE	Qualifier entry version
QT	Qualifier type
RN	CAS registry number
SB	Journal sub-set
SH	Mesh sub-heading, qualifier print version
SI	Secondary source ID
ST	Source and time frame
SU	Name as subject
TA	Journal title abbreviation
TW	Text words from title or abstract field
YP	Year of publication

A2.4a AVAILABLE MEDICAL DATABASES

Database name	Brief details	Approximate cost (£) Per hour	Per offline print
CHEMLINE	A database of synonyms and CAS registry numbers for chemical names	50	0.15 per page
MEDLINE National Library of Medicine	The US Bureau of Medicine biomedical database, including *Index Medicus*	30	0.10 per page
SDILINE	Current month's MEDLINE records	30	
BACK 75	As for MEDLINE, but with off-line printing and searching		
BACK 72	As for MEDLINE, but with off-line searching and printing	£2 per search profile	0.10 per page
BACK 69	As for MEDLINE, but with off-line searching and printing		
BACK 66	As for MEDLINE, but with off-line searching and printing		
TOXLINE	The US National Bureau of Medicine database on toxicology and allied subjects	50	0.15 per page
TOXBACK	As for TOXLINE, but with off-line searching and printing	£2 per search profile	0.15 per page
CANCERLIT National Cancer Institute	Cancer literature	30	0.10 per page
CANCERPROJ	Current cancer research projects	30	0.10 per page
CLINPROT	Clinical investigations of new anti-cancer agents and treatment	30	0.10 per page
MESH Vocabulary	Information on all medical subject headings and qualifiers	30	0.10 per page
RTECS National Institute for Occupational Safety and Health	Toxicity data	30	0.10 per page

Date	Approximate size	Update	Searchable fields
Current	243 000	Quarterly	19 fields
1976–	632 000	Monthly 23 000	(AU), (CN), (ED), (IS), (JC), (LA), (LI), (MC), (MH), (PD), (PL), (PN), (SB), (SH), (SU), (TA), (TW), (YP)
Current month	23 000	Monthly 23 000	As above
1975	385 000	None	As above
1972–1974	671 000	None	As above
1969–1971	649 000	None	As above
1966–1968	545 000	None	As above
1974–	458 000	Monthly 8000	(AU), (DT), (IS), (IT), (JC), (KW), (LA), (YP), (RN), (SI), (ST), (TW)
1940–1973	379 000	None	As above
1976–	160 000	Monthly 4000	(AU), (ED), (IS), (JC), (JT), (LA), (PT), (SI), (TW), (YP)
Last two years	20 000	Quarterly 2000	(ED), (TW) + 16 others indicating research workers, sponsors, etc.
Current	1 168	4-monthly	(ED), (TW) + 20 others indicating research workers, sponsors, etc.
Current	14 000	Annually	(BX), (DC), (DE), (MC), (MH), (QA), (QE), (QT)
Current	36 000	Quarterly	(RN), (TW) + 17 others indicating chemical and toxic information, etc.

A2.3b ABBREVIATIONS FOR SEARCHABLE FIELDS FOR NON-MEDICAL DATABASES

BL	Blaise number
CN	Corporate author
CT	Control tag
CW	Corporate word
DC	Dewey Decimal Classification
DP	Date of publication
ED	Entry date
HC	Corporate name added entry
HM	Meetings name added entry
HP	Personal name added entry
HW	Personal name added entry
IC	Information codes
LC	Library of Congress Classification
MN	Meetings name
MW	Meetings word
PD	Précis term
PN	Personal name
PS	Subject index number
PU	Publisher
PW	Précis word
SH	Subject heading
SW	Subject word
TW	Text word
WH	Corporate author word
WM	Meetings name word

A2.4b AVAILABLE NON-MEDICAL DATABASES

Database name	Brief details	Approximate cost (£)	
		Per hour	Per offline print
LCCMARC	Information on books and serials catalogued by the US Library of Congress for the current period	30	0.10 per page
LCRMARC	As above, for earlier data	30	0.10 per page
UKC	Information on books and serials catalogued by the British Library for the current period	30	0.10 per page
UKRMARC	As above, for earlier data	30	0.10 per page

Date	Size	Update	Searchable fields
1974–	660 000	Monthly 10 000	(BL), (CN), (CT), (CW), (DC), (DP), (ED), (HC), (HM), (HP), (HW), (IC), (LC), (MN), (MW), (PD), (PN), (PS), (PU), (PW), (SH), (SW), (TW), (WH), (WM)
1968–1973	267 000	None	As above
1974–	190 000	Monthly 3000	As above
1950–1973	457 000	None	As above

A2.5 SUMMARY OF BLAISE COMMANDS
(Alternatives are shown in parentheses)

Command	Function	Example
"COMMENT	Message to operator	
"DIAGRAM ("DIAG)	Displays search structure	
"EDIT	Transfers to Editor sub-system	
"ELEMENTS APPLY ("ELEMENTS INCLUDE)	Selects elements for searching	"ELEMENTS APPLY AU
"ELEMENTS CANCEL	All elements are searched	
"ELEMENTS DEFAULT	Only default elements are searched	
"ELEMENTS EXCLUDE	Excludes some elements from search	"ELEMENTS EXCLUDE TW
"ERASEALL ("ERSLL)	Erases all search statements	
"ERASEBACK ("ERSBK)	Erases last search	
"ERASEBACK number	Erases back to specified statement	"ERSBK 5
"EXPLAIN ("EX)	Explains last message	
"EXPLAIN item	Explains command or message	"EXPLAIN FIND
"FILE name	Selects named database	"FILE MEDLINE
"FILES?	Lists available databases	
"FIND terms ("FD)	Enters search statement	"FIND NORTH SEA
"FINISHED	Defines end of search formulation	
"HELP	Calls for assistance	
"MESHNO item ("MNO)	Displays the MeSH classification number	"MESHNO KIDNEY
"MESHTERM number	Displays MeSH term for a given number	"MESHTERM C6.689.202
"NEIGHBOR term ("NBR)	Displays adjacent terms in the index	"NBR OIL
"NEIGHBORDET term ("NBRDET)	As above but includes all forms of search terms	"NBRDET OIL
"NEWS	Displays the news	
"OFFSEARCH	Changes to offsearch usage	
"OFFSEARCH CANCEL	Returns to on-line usage	
"PRINT ("PRT)	Gives output from the search	"PRT TI, AU, 4
"PURGESEARCH name	Deletes a stored search	"PURGESEARCH FARQ
"RENAME item } "TO item ("RNM) }	Changes name of commands, etc.	"RNM FILE TO BASE
"RESTACK ("RSTK)	Deletes all except last search	
"RESTACK number ("RSTK)	Deletes all except named statement	"RSTK 13
"RESTART ("RST)	Erases search and restarts	
"STOP	End of searching	
"STORESEARCH	Changes to storesearch usage	
"STORESEARCH CANCEL	Cancels the search being stored	
"SUBHEADINGS APPLY ("SUBS APPLY)	Creates sub-heading for all main headings	
"SUBHEADINGS CANCEL ("SUBS CANCEL)	Cancels any sub-headings	

"SUBHEADINGS DISPLAY ("SUBS DISPLAY)	Display current sub-headings	
"TREE item	Gives MeSH number and the position in the tree	"TREE KIDNEY
"USERS	Gives number of active users	
"VERSION item ("VERS)	Changes length of specified message	"VERS SHORT
"VERSION item ALL	Changes length of all messages	"VERS SHORT ALL

Note: Search statements can be entered directly — i.e. without being preceded by a command. For example, COMPUTER AND LIBRARY

Appendix 3

ESA-IRS

A3.1 SOFTWARE SYSTEM
    QUEST
A3.2 ADDRESSES

European Space Agency,
ESRIN/IRS,
Via Galileo Galilei,
00044 Frascati,
ITALY

Tel: 06/942 2401

United Kingdom:

B.A. Kingsmill,
Dialtech Service,
Technology Reports Centre,
Orpington,
Kent, BR5 3RF

Tel: 0689 32111 Ext. 255 TWX 896866

Belgium:

Mr E. Lapeysen, CNDST,
4 Bd de L'Empereur, 1000,
Bruxelles

Tel: (02) 513 6180 TWX 21157

Denmark:

Mr D. Nag,
DTB Library,
Anker Engelunds Vej 1, 2800 Lyngby

Tel: (02) 883 088 TWX 37148

France:

Miss C. Gruson, ANRT,
101 Avenue R. Poincaré, 75116,
Paris

Tel: (01) 533 4036

Ireland:

Miss E. Butterley, IIRS,
Ballymun Rd,
Dublin 9

Tel: (01) 370101 TWX 5449

Spain:

Mr R. Baiget, INTA RED/INCA,
Serrano 187,
Madrid 2

Tel: (01) 450 5800 TWX 42608

Sweden:

Mr A. Nord,
KTH Library,
Valhallavagen 81,
10044 Stockholm

Tel: (08) 787 8970 TWX 10389

A3.3 ABBREVIATIONS FOR SEARCHABLE FIELDS

AB	Abstract
AF	Affiliation of first author
AU	Author
BC	Biosystematic code
BN	Biosystematic code Name
CA	Card alert, cited authors
CC	Classification code, corporate source code, orientation code, category, section cross-reference, section/sub-section
CF	Cosati code
CN	Cross code name
CO	Coden, country
CR	Cited references
CS	Corporate source, corporate authors
CT	Controlled terms, keywords, subject headings
CT*	Major keywords
CY	Country
DE	Descriptor
DT	Document type
ET	English title
FT	French title
GT	German title, geographic location
ID	Identifiers
JA	Journal issue
JN	Source journal
LA	Language
NF	Non-fragments
NP	Non-patents
PA	Patents
PB	Publisher
PC	Patent classification
PT	Patentee
PY	Publication year
RN	Report number
S	Section numbers
SC	Corporate source code
SN	ISSN
TC	Treatment codes
TI	Title
UP	Update code
UT	Uncontrolled terms, keywords, free terms
YR	Date

Notes: (1) Individual words (apart from stop words) have been entered in the on-line dictionary for fields prefixed by /.
      (2) For fields suffixed by = , the entry in the online dictionary is the complete field.

A3.4 AVAILABLE DATABASES

Database name	Brief details	Approximate cost (AU)[a]	
		Per hour	Per offline print
ALUMINUM (9) American Society for Metals	All aspects of aluminium (excluding mining), including production, casting, fabrication, properties and uses	37	.11
BIOSIS (7) Biosciences Information Service	Biological abstracts and the Bioresearch index on the life sciences	39	.11
CHEMICAL ABSTRACTS CONDENSATES (2)	Chemical abstracts covering chemistry, chemical engineering and the life sciences	36	.15
COMPENDEX (4) Engineering Index Inc.	Most branches of engineering, including some management, mathematics, physics and instruments	50	.13
ENVIROLINE (11) Environment Information Centre	All aspects of the environment: management, law, economics, biology, chemistry, etc.	68	.19
INSPEC (8) Institution of Electrical Engineers	Information on physics, electrotechnology, computers and control	44	.11
ISMEC (10) Data Courier Inc.	Mechanical engineering, including energy and power, transport and handling	60	.15
METADEX (3) American Society for Metals	Comprehensive data on materials, processes, properties, products, forms and influencing factors for metals	60	.15
NASA (1)	Scientific and Technical Aerospace reports from NASA and International Aerospace Abstracts	30	.11
OCEANIC (15) Data Courier Inc.	Biology, fisheries, geology, oceanography, engineering, diving, government and legal aspects	60	.15
PASCAL (14) CNRS	Covers wide area of science, including physics, chemistry, earth sciences and metals	40	.13
USGRA (6) National Technical Information Service	US Government-sponsored research in aeronautics, agriculture, astronomy, social sciences, chemistry, electronics and many other disciplines	36	.11

Date	Approximate size	Update	Searchable fields
1968–	61 000	Monthly 600	/AB, AU=, CC=, CS=, /CS, CT, /TI
1972–	1 360 000	Monthly 20 000	AU=, BC=, BN=, CC=, CN=, CO=, JN=, /TI, /UT
1969–	3 312 000	Monthly 34 000	AU=, CC=, CO=, /CS, LA=, /NF, /NP, /PA, PC=, SN=, /TI, /UT
1969–	740 000	Monthly 10 000	AU=, CA=, CO=, /CS, /DE, /DE*, /ID, ID*, JA=, /TI
1975–	75 000	Monthly 1500	/AB, AU=, CC=, CS=, /CS, /CT, DT=, /TI, UP=
1971–	1 024 000	Monthly 10 000	AU=, CC=, CO=, /CS, /CT, LA=, PB=, /TI, /UT
1973–	76 000	Monthly 1000	AU=, CC=, CO=, CS=, /CS, /CT, DT=, JN=, LA=, /TI, /UT
1969–	272 000	Monthly 2500	AU=, CC=, /CT, /TI
1962–	945 000	Monthly 5000	AU=, CC=, /CS, /CT, /CT*, RN=, SC=, /TI
1964–	102 000	Bimonthly 1200	/AB, AU=, CS=, /CS, /CT, LA=, PY=, /TI, UP=, /UT, YR=
1973–	1 424 000	Monthly 40 000	AU=, CC=, /CS, /CT, /DE, /ET, /FT, /GT, LA=, /OT, /TI
1970–	453 000	Monthly 5000	CC=, CF=, /CS, /DE, /DE*, /ID, /ID*, /TI

Database name	Brief details	Approximate cost (AU)[a]	
		Per hour	Per offline print
AQUALINE (25) UK Water Research Centre	Water, waste water and aquatic environment	43	.18
CAB (16) Commonwealth Agricultural Bureaux	Agricultural sciences	54	.11
ENERGYLINE (19) Environment Information Center Inc.	Energy, linked to printed *Energy Information Abstracts*	68	.19
FRANCE-ACTUALITÉ Microfor Inc.	Articles published in the French press	45	.11
FSTA * International Food Information Service	Food science and technology		
PNI	Pharmaceutical, cosmetic and medical industry	67	.18
POLLUTION (18) Data Courier Inc.	Pollution and the environment, linked to *Pollution Abstracts*	60	.15
RAPRA * Rubber and Plastics Research Association	Commercial, engineering and research aspects of rubber and plastics		
WTI * World Transindex	Translation announcements by International Translation Centre, CEC, and CNRS		

[a]AU: International Accounting Units are used for billing purposes by IRS. In 1980 1 AU = £0.63356 *or* $1.4.

Date	Approximate size	Update	Searchable fields
1974–			/AB, AU=, CC=, CN=, /CS, /CT, LA=, PY=, /TI + some others
1972–	900 000	Monthly	/AB, AU=, CC=, CS=, /CT, LA=, PB=, PY=, /TI, UP= + some others
1971–	41 400	Monthly	/AB, AU=, CC=, CS=, /CS, /CT, /CT*, DT=, /TI
1978–		Monthly (2100)	/AB, AU=, CC=, JN=, /TI, /UT + some others
1969–	160 500	Monthly	
1974–	30 000	Monthly	
1970–	67 500	Monthly (500)	/AB, AU=, CC=, CO=, /CS, /CT, LA=, PY=, /TJ, /UT + some others
1974–	60 000	Monthly	
1978–			

Notes: (1) Databases marked * are planned.
      (2) ESA-IRS also has several databanks – e.g.
               ELECOMPS   – details of electronic components
               ELSPECS   – electronic specifications
               LEDA   – information obtained from satellites
               SPACECOMPS – inforn ation on components for spacecraft use

A3.5 SUMMARY OF QUEST COMMANDS
(Alternatives are shown in parentheses)

Command	Function	Example
BEGIN	Gives heading for start of search	BEGIN
BEGINn	Select or change files	BEGIN8
COMBINE (C)	Combine terms to form new set	C 1 OR 2
DISPLAY SETS (DS)	Prints summary of search	DS, DS5
EXPAND (E)	Displays adjacent terms in the index	EXPAND STEEL
END	Summarises the usage	END
END/SAVE	Saves the search strategy	END/SAVE
.EXECUTE	Executes a saved search	.EXECUTE
.FILEn	Selects file and keeps previous search history	.FILE3
.INTERSECT	Gives matrix display showing hits retrieved	.INTERSECT (2, 4, 5)*(6, 8)
KEEP (K)	Saves items in special set	K 2/1−12
LIMIT (L)	Restricts set in various ways	L 3/75−77
LOGOFF	Ends search and disconnects	LOGOFF
PAGE (P)	Continue index display	P
PRINT (P)	Print offline	P
.RECALL	Displays saved search	.RECALL A2
.RELEASE	Deletes saved search	.RELEASE
SELECT (S)	Selects terms to create sets	S ZEBRA
..SET SESAME ON (..SET EUROLANGUAGE ON)	Enter commands on the Euronet common command language	
..SET SESAME OFF (..SET EUROLANGUAGE OFF)	Revert to Quest command language	
TYPE (T)	Print items at the terminal	T 2/1/4−20
M101	Sends message to computer	M101/WHEN WILL FSTA BE AVAILABLE
? CHARGES	Database fees	
? command	Details of a particular command	? SELECT
? COVERAGE	Database subject coverage	
? FIELDS	Searchable fields	
? FILES	Available files	
? FILE number	Details of a particular file	? FILE 18
? FORMAT	Type and print formats available	
? NEWS	Latest news	
? QUEST	Description of Quest commands	
? SESAME	Description of common command language	
? UPDATES	News of updates	

Appendix 4

Infoline

A4.1 SOFTWARE SYSTEM
    BASIS — Modified

A4.2 ADDRESS

Infoline Limited,
Brettenham House,
Lancaster Place,
London WC2E 7EN

Tel: 01-836 1876   Telex: 261176

A4.3 ABBREVIATIONS FOR SEARCHABLE FIELDS

AC Accessions number
AY Accession number year
CL Derwent classification
IC IPC
IN Inventors
KS Plasdoc key serial numbers
KT Plasdoc key terms
MC Manual codes
PA Patent country
PC Patentee code
PN Patent number
PR Priority country
PY Priorities
RR Ring index numbers
TT Title terms, additional search words
UP Update code

A4.4 AVAILABLE DATABASES

Database name	Brief details	Approximate cost (£)	
		Per hour	*Per offline print*
BIOSIS Biosciences Infor- mation Service	Biological abstracts and Bioresearch index on the life sciences		
CASEARCH Chemical Abstracts Service	Chemical abstracts covering chemistry, chemical engineering and the life sciences	32	0.065
CAREGISTRY Chemical Abstracts Service	Chemical compounds	32	
COMPENDEX Engineering Index Inc.	Most branches of engineering, including some management, mathematics, physics and instruments		
INSPEC Institution of Electrical Engineers	References on physics, electrotechnology, computers and control		
RINGDOC Derwent Publications	References to pharmaceutical literature		
WPI Derwent Publications	The World Patents Index of patents from all major industrial countries		

The particulars of these files were not fully available at the time of writing.
Further details can be obtained from Infoline.

Date	Approximate size	Update	Searchable fields
1972-	2 600 000	Fortnightly 35 000	
1963–	1 550 000	Monthly 38 000	AC=, AY=, CL=, IC=, IN=, KS=, KT=, MC=, PA=, PC=, PN=, PR=, PY=, RR=, TT=, UP=,

A4.5 SUMMARY OF INFOLINE COMMANDS
(Alternatives are shown in parentheses)

Command	Function	Example
CANCEL PRINTS	To delete offline prints requested but not yet MAILED	
DISPLAY (TYPE, DI, D, TY, T)	To display, or print online, retrieved records	DISPLAY F1/1–10
EXPAND (NEIGHBOR, EX, E, NBR)	Displays adjacent terms in the index	EXPAND AIRCRAFT
FILE (FI, F)	To select a file	FILE WPI
LIST (LS)	To display all, or some, sets created since the last FILE	LIST 7–10
LOGOUT (LOGOFF, END, STOP)	To end the session	
MAIL (MA)	To despatch offline prints requested from PRINT	
PRINT (PR)	To request offline prints of all, or selected parts of, retrieved records	PRINT 1 AT, TT/1–10
SELECT (COMBINE, FIND, SE, S, CO, C)	To select, or combine, terms	S COMPUTER AND LIBRARY
SORT	To sort records from a retrieved set into a specific order	SORT SET = 4 AU
TITLE (TL)	To assign a title to office prints	TITLE AIR POLLUTION
PROFILE START (P START)	To denote the start of a search strategy to be saved	
PROFILE NEW (P NEW)	As above, but set numbering restarts at 1	
PROFILE SAVE name (P SAVE)	To give a name to a saved search	P SAVE FRED1
PROFILE RUN name (P RUN)	To recall and execute a saved search	P RUN FRED1
PROFILE SUSPEND name (P SUSPEND)	To suspend a search session you want to interrupt and resume later	P SUSPEND FREDA
PROFILE RESUME name (P RESUME)	To resume a suspended profile	P RESUME FREDA
PROFILE DELETE name (P DELETE)	To delete a profile which has been SAVED	P DELETE FRED1
PROFILE RENAME name AS name (P RENAME)	To rename a stored profile	P RENAME FREDA AS FRED
PROFILE COPY name AS name (P COPY)	As above, but original profile remains	P COPY FREDA2 AS FREDA3
PROFILE LIST (P LIST)	To list all profiles for the user's ID	
PROFILE LIST name (P LIST)	To list contents of a particular profile	P LIST FREDA3
PROFILE LIST SUSPEND name (P LIST SUSPEND)	To obtain a listing of the complete contents of a suspended session	P LIST SUSPEND FRED2
PROFILE EDIT (P EDIT)	To edit saved profiles	
EXIT	To terminate P EDIT, retaining modifications	
KILL	To terminate P EDIT, discarding modifications	

Appendix 5

Lockheed

A5.1 SOFTWARE SYSTEM
Dialog

A5.2 ADDRESSES

Lockheed Information Systems,
3460 Hillview Avenue,
Palo Alto, CA 94304
USA

Tel: 800/227 1960

Lockheed Information Systems,
Suite 201, Crawford Savings Building,
1400 Summit Avenue,
Oak Brook Terrace,
IL 60181, USA

Tel: 312/629-7416

Lockheed Information Systems,
200 Park Avenue, Suite 303 East,
New York, NY 10017,
USA

Tel: 212/682-4630

Lockheed,
900 17th Street N.W.,
Washington DC 20006,
USA

Tel: 202/872-5971

Ms C. Pagis,
Lockheed Information Systems,
5th Floor,
37–39 Oxford Street,
London W1R 2LL

Tel: 01-439 1680

A5.3 ABBREVIATIONS FOR SEARCHABLE FIELDS

AA   Asset amount, author affiliation
AB   Abstract, note
AC   Legislative authority code, country of patent application, area code, activity code, assignee code
AG   Asset greater than, grant greater than
AI   Alloys index
AL   Asset less than, grant less than
AM   Grant amount, contract amount
AN   Assignee name, acession number, agency name, abstract number
AP   Approach
AR   Authority record
AS   Agency state, agency state code, agency/service abbreviation
AT   Asset type, article type
AU   Personal author, inventor
AV   Availability on microfiche, availability
BC   Biosystematic code, branch city
BN   Biosystematic name, branch name, bureau number, book number, ISBN
BS   Branch state
BZ   Branch zip code
CA   Card alert, cited author, call number
CC   Concept code, corporate source, category code, country code, contractor company code, class code, geographic code
CF   Cosati field
CG   Contributions greater than, corporate source location
CH   Clearinghouse code
CL   Patent classification number, classification code, contributions less than, classification group, conference location
CM   Community code
CN   Contract/grant number, concept name, country name, geographic name, name match, class name, corporate source name, company number
CO   Coden, company, corporate source, contractor company name
CP   Contract number prefix, country of publication
CR   Cited reference, *CA* reference, contributions received, cited author
CS   Corporate source, contractor state, contractor state code
CT   Conference title
CY   Conference year
DC   Descriptor code, UDC number
DD   Dewey Decimal number
DE   Descriptor
DF   Single-word descriptor, domestic or foreign recipient
DG   Degree year
DN   Document number
DO   Donor
DS   Division/station code
DT   Document type, date, date of contract, publication date
EC   Event code, element count
ED   Edition, errata data
EG   Expenditure greater than

EI	Internal revenue service number
EL	Expenditure less than
EN	Event name
ES	Establishment data, element symbol
EV	Errata volume
EX	Employee size, expenditure, exchange
FC	Foundation city
FG	Funding greater than
FL	Funding less than
FC	Foreign patent number, foundation name
FR	Federal region
FS	Foundation state, field of science
FT	Foundation type
FU	Actual funding
FY	Fiscal year
GA	Grant amount
GC	Group code, auxiliary descriptor code
GE	Geographic descriptor
GG	Grant greater than
GI	Gallery index
GL	Grant less than, geographic location
GN	Grant number, number of grants, group number
GP	GPO number
GR	Growth rate, grade
GS	Tag, auxiliary descriptor, geographic descriptor
HC	Headquarters city, hardware capability code
HE	Historical period ending date
HI	Highest grant
HN	Headquarters name, hardware capability name, section heading
HP	*CA* parent index name, historical period
HS	Headquarters state, historical period starting date
HX	Headquarters code
HZ	Headquarters zip code
ID	Identifier
IN	Investigator name
IS	Issue number, journal announcement
IV	Investigator
JA	Journal announcement
JC	Journal coverage, journal code
JN	Title of publication, journal name, country of granted patent
JO	Journal name, journal announcement, journal citation, journal
LA	Language, loan amount
LC	Licensing country, Library of Congress card number
LM	Limitation
LN	Number of loans
LO	Location, lowest grant, location code
MA	Matching gifts, microfilm address
MC	Measure code
MF	Molecular formula
MN	Number of matching gifts, measurement name, manufacturer's name, meeting number

NA	Name of program, named person
NM	*CA* index name modification
NN	NICSEM accession number
NO	NAL call number
NP	Publisher
NT	Descriptive note, note
NU	Number of program
OB	Objectives
OC	Old category code, OCLC number
ON	Officer's name
PA	Patent assignee, purpose and activities, program amount
PB	Publisher, publications
PC	Product code, phase code
PD	Publication date, process date
PG	Performing organisation place
PI	Country of patent, periodic index term
PN	Bureau/project number, patent number, phase name, product name, number of programs
PO	Country of original patent, performing organisation, performing organisation code
PP	Place of publisher, progress period
PR	Progress report
PS	Program sponsor, institution
PT	Phase type
PU	Publisher
PX	PACS code
PY	Publication year
PZ	Performing organisation zip code
QC	Quick code
RC	Recipient city, review classification
RI	Title
RN	Report number, ID number, abstract number, recipient name, record number, CAS registry number
RP	Research problem area code
RS	Recipient state
RT	Recipient type, registration type
SA	Sponsoring agency, scholarship amount
SB	*CA* substituent index name, source publication
SC	Corporate source code, section code, subject category, system category code, *CA* section, sponsor code, source code, subject code, section heading code, SIC code
SD	Search date, sales in million $, start date
SE	Series note, series, series statement
SF	Special features, sub-file
SG	Sponsoring organisation place
SH	Section heading
SL	Summary language
SM	Search month, share of market, sub-commodity code
SN	Number of scholarships, subject name, ISSN, SSIE number
SO	Source

SP	Sponsoring program, sponsor
ST	Stereochemical descriptor, system category name, state/country abbreviation, section heading
SY	Synonyms, search year
SZ	Sponsoring organisation zip code
TC	Tag code
TD	Termination date
TI	Title
TN	Trade name
TX	Taxonomic descriptor
UC	Universal decimal code
UD	Update
VL	EC volume number
WT	Work type
YA	Year authorised
YR	Year, year of publication, degree year, journal year
ZP	Foundation zip code

Notes: (1) Individual words (apart from stop words) have been entered in the online dictionary for fields prefixed by /.

(2) For fields suffixed by =, the entry in the online dictionary is the complete field.

(3) For databases that have different rates for subscribers and non-subscribers of the linked printed publication the two rates have been shown with the non-subscriber rate in parentheses.

A5.4 AVAILABLE DATABASES

Database name	Brief details	Approximate cost ($)	
		Per hour	Per offline print
ABI/INFORM (15) Data Courier Inc.	Management and administration	75	0.20
AGRICOLA (10) National Agricultural Library	Journal and monographic literature on agriculture	25	0.05
AIM/ARM (9) Ohio State University	Index to vocational and technical education, employment, job training and manpower economics	25	0.10
AMERICA (38) ABC-Clio Inc.	US and Canadian history, area studies and current affairs	65	0.15
APTIC (45) US Environmental Protection Agency	Air pollution, its effects, prevention and control, including social, political, legal and administration aspects	35	0.10
ART MODERN (56) ABC-Clio Inc.	Art history, biographies of artists, artistic media	60	0.10
ASFA (44) FAO, Rome	Aquatic sciences and fisheries	35	0.15
ASI (102) Congressional Information Service	American Statistics Index of US Government statistical publications	90	0.15
BHRA FLUID-ENGINEERING (96) British Hydromechanics Research Association	Fluid engineering, including statics and dynamics, and laminar and turbulent flow	65	0.15
BIOSIS PREVIEWS (5) (55) Biosciences Information Service	Biological abstracts and Bioresearch index on the life sciences	45	0.10
CA SEARCH (2) (3) (4) *Chemical Abstracts* Service	Chemical abstracts and the general subject headings and the *CA* Registry Numbers	70	0.20
CA PATENTS (43) *Chemical Abstracts* Service + Lockheed	Correlates patents from different countries for the same invention. Chemical and chemical engineering patents	45	0.12
CAB ABSTRACTS (50) Commonwealth Agricultural Bureaux	Agriculture and biology, including dairy science, forestry, plant breeding, mycology, fertilisers, rural sociology, etc.	35	0.25
CIN (19) American Chemical Society	Chemical industry notes from Predicasts. Business information on the chemical industry	60	0.20

Date	Approximate size	Update	Searchable fields
August 1971–	80 400	Monthly 1200	/AB, AU=, CO=, /TI, UD=
1970–	1 134 000	Monthly 12 000	/AB, AU=, CC=, /CS, /DE, DT=, JA=, JN=, LA=, LO=, NO=, OC=, RN=, SC=, SM=, SY=, /TI, UD=
1967–1976	17 500	None	AC=, AU=, BN=, CN=, /DE, DN=, GC=, GN, /ID, IS=, JO=, PS=, RN=, SC=, SP=, /TI, UD=
1964–	51 000	Quarterly 3000	/AB, AU=, JO=, RN=, /TI, UD=, YR=
1966–1978	89 000	None	/AB, AU=, CN=, /CS, /DE, DT=, /ID, JO=, LA=, MS=, PD=, RN=, /TI, UD=
1974–	31 000	Semiannually 3500	/AB, AU=, /DE, DT=, GI=, JO=, /TI, UD=
1975–	6 800	Monthly	AU=, CC=, CS=, /DE, DT=, /GE, LA=, PD=, /TI, /TX, UD=
1973–	55 000	Monthly	
1974–	33 000	Quarterly	
1969–	2 765 000	Monthly 20 000	AU=, BC=, BN=, CC=, CN=, CO=, /DE, JN=, /TI, UD=
1967–	4 000 000	Biweekly 12 000	AC=, AU=, CL=, CO=, /CS, /DE, JN=, LA=, NP=, PA=, PN=, SC=, /TI, UD=
1972–	134 802	Semiannually 20 000	PN=, UD=
1973–	825 000	Monthly 10 000	/AB, AU=, /CS, /DE, DT=, /ID, JO=, LA=, PB=, PD=, RN=, SC=, SF=, SL=, SN=, /TI, UC=, UD=
1974–	230 000	Weekly 1000	/AB, CC=, CN=, CO=, /DE, DT=, EC=, EN=, JO=, UD=

Database name	Brief details	Approximate cost ($)	
		Per hour	*Per offline print*
CHEMNAME (31) *Chemical Abstracts* Service + Lockheed	Thesaurus for chemicals giving registry numbers, molecular formula, synonyms and substance index name	70	0.20
CHILD ABUSE AND NEGLECT (64)	US Department of Health, Education and Welfare. Research projects and service programs	35	0.10
CIS/INDEX (101) Congressional Information Service	Working papers, hearings, reports, etc., of Congress	90	0.15
CLAIMS/CHEM (23) IFI/Plenum Data Corporation	US chemical patents and some from Belgium, France, UK, West Germany and the Netherlands	95	0.15
CLAIMS/CLASS (124) IFI/Plenum Data Corporation	Classification codes and titles for US Patent Classification System	90	0.10
CLAIMS/US PATENTS (24) IFI/Plenum Data Corporation	US patents and some from Belgium, France, UK, West Germany and the Netherlands	95	0.15
CONFERENCE PAPERS INDEX (77) Data Courier Inc.	Details of conference papers, proceedings and publications	75	15
COMPENDEX (8) Engineering Index Inc.	Engineering and technological literature	65	0.10
COMPREHENSIVE DISSERTATION ABSTRACTS (35)	University Microfilms international subject, title and author guide to most US dissertations	55	0.12
CRIS (60) USDA Cooperative State Research Service	Current Research Information System on agricultural projects now current	40	0.10
DISCLOSURE (100) Disclosure Inc.	Public company reports filed with the SEC	90	3.00
ECONOMIC ABSTRACTS INTERNATIONAL (90)	Information on markets, industries and economic data. Marketing data for specific industries	65	0.20
EIS INDUSTRIAL PLANTS (22) Economic Information Systems	Information on 90% of US industrial activity	90	0.50
EIS NONMANUFAC- TURING ESTABLISH- MENTS (92) Economic Information Systems	Information on 85% of US establish- ments in non-manufacturing sectors	90	0.50

Date	*Approximate size*	*Update*	*Searchable fields*
–	434 000	–	CN=, /DE, /EC, GN=, HP=, /ID, MF=, NM=, PI=, RN=, SB=, ST=, SY=, UD=
1965–	7 000	Annually	/AB, AU=, CS=, /DE, FR=, JA=, RN=, SF=, ST=, /TI, UD=
1970	110 000	Monthly	
1950–1970	250 000	None	AC=, AN=, CL=, CR=, FN=, PN=, /TI, UD=
–	15 000	–	
1971–1977	485 000	None	/AB, AC=, AN=, AU=, CL=, CR=, FN=, PD=, PN=, PY=, /TI, UD=
1973–	500 000	Monthly	AU=, CL=, CS=, CT=, CY=, /DE, JA=, MN=, SC=, SP=, /ST, /TI, UD=
1970–	642 000	Monthly 6000	/AB, AU=, CA=, CO=, /CS, /DE, /ID, JA=, /TI, UD=
1861–	608 000	Monthly 3300	AU=, /CS, /DE, DG=, /TI, UD=, YR=
1974–	26 000	Monthly 2000	AC=, /AP, AS=, CM=, /DE, DS=, FS=, IV=, LO=, /OB, /PB, PD=, PN=, PO=, PP=, /PR, /RI, RP=, SD=, SM=, ST=, TD=
1977–	11 000	Weekly	CN=, CO=, DT=, EX=, RT=, SC=, UD=
1974–	65 000	Monthly	/AB, AU=, BN=, CS=, DC=, /DE, DT=, GC=, GL=, JN=, LA=, PU=, PY=, SE=, /TI, UD=
Current	130 000	Quarterly	BC=, BN=, BS=, BZ=, CC=, CN=, /DE, EX=, HC=, HN=, HS=, HX=, HZ=, PC=, PN=, SD=, SF=, SM=
Current	200 000	Quarterly	As above

Database name	Brief details	Approximate cost ($) Per hour	Per offline print
ENERGYLINE (69) Environment Information Centre Inc.	*Energy Information Abstracts* and *Energy Index* material on scientific and policy aspects, etc., of energy	90	0.20
ENVIROLINE (40) Environment Information Centre Inc.	All aspects of the environment: management, law, economics, biology, chemistry, etc.	90	0.20
EPB (68) Environmental Studies Institute	The *Environmental Periodicals Bibliography* on human ecology, land resources, health, etc.	60	0.15
ERIC (1) National Institute of Education	Educational Resources Information Centre. Research and literature on education	25	0.10
EXCEPTIONAL CHILD EDUCATION ABSTRACTS (54)	Literature on the education of handicapped and gifted children	25	0.10
EXCERPTA MEDICA (72) (73) Excerpta Medica	Abstracts and citations in medicine and related disciplines	55	0.15
FOODS ADLIBRA (79) K and M Publications	Food technology and packaging, including research, patents and government regulations	55	0.10
FOUNDATION DIRECTORY (26) Foundation Center	Foundations with assets of 1 million $ or more, or make grants of $100 000 or more annually	60	0.30
FOUNDATION GRANTS INDEX (27) Foundation Center	Information on grants of more than 400 major foundations	60	0.30
FROST AND SULLIVAN (50) Frost and Sullivan	Information on US Department of Defense contracts	90	0.25
FSTA (51) International Food Information Service	Food science and technology abstracts. Also includes agriculture, chemistry, physics, etc.	65	0.15
GEOARCHIVE (58) Geosystems	Geoscience material, including journals, books, conferences, geological maps, new minerals and names	70	0.20
GPO MONTHLY CATALOG (66) US Government Printing Office	Catalogue of US Government publications. Reports, proceedings, hearings of all US Government agencies	35	0.10

Date	Approximate size	Update	Searchable fields
1971–	41 400	Bimonthly 800	/AB, AU=, AV=, /CS, /DE, DT=, RC=, RN=, /SB, /TI, UD=
1971–	84 000	Monthly 800	/AB, AU=, AV=, /CS, /DE, DT=, RC=, /SB, /TI
1973–	80 000	Bimonthly 4000	AU=, CS=, /DE, JN=, PY=, /TI, UD=
1966–	319 500	Monthly 2500	/AB, AC=, AU=, CH=, CN=, /CS, /DE, DT=, GC=, /ID, IS=, JO=, /NT, PN=, RN=, /SA, SC=, /TI, UD=, YR=
1966–	275 000	Quarterly 750	/AB, AU=, AV=, BN=, CC=, CH=, CN=, /DE, /DF, GC=, /ID, JO=, /NT, PD=, PS=, RN=, SP=, /TI, UD=, VL=
1974–	1 002 000	Monthly	/AB, AU=, CO=, CP=, CS=, DC=, /DE, /GS, /ID, JN=, LA=, MN=, PY=, SC=, SE=, SF=, /ST, TC=, /TI, /TN, UD=
1974–	30 000	Monthly 2000	/AB, CO=, /DE, DT=, JN=, PA=, PN=, PY=, /TI, UD=
Current year	3 200	Semiannual revision	AA=, AG=, AL=, AT=, CR=, CG=, CL=, /DE, /DO, EG=, EI=, EL=, /ES, EX=, FC=, /FN, FS=, FT=, GA=, GG=, GL=, GN=, HI=, LA=, LM=, LN=, LO=, MA=, MN=, /ON, /PA, PA=, PN=, SA=, SN=, ZP=
1973–	47 000	Bimonthly 200	/AB, AG=, AL=, AM=, CC=, /DE, DF=, /FN, FS=, /LM, LO=, RC=, /RN, RS=, /RT, US=, YA=
1975–	190 000	Quarterly 15 000	/AB, AC=, AM=, /AN, AN=, AS=, CC=, CN=, CO=, CS=, DT=, HC=, /HN, HN=, NA=, NU=, PC=, /PN, PN=, PT=, SC=, /ST, UD=
1969–	160 500	Monthly 1500	/AB, AU=, CS=, /DE, DT=, JO=, LA=, PD=, RN=, SL=, /TI, UD=
1969–	250 000	Monthly 5000	AN=, AU=, BN=, DC=, /DE, DT=, GC=, /GS, JA=, JC=, JN=, LA=; PU=, PY=, /TI, UD=
1976–	35 000	Monthly 1700	/AB, AU=, BN=, CA=, CL=, CO=, CS=, CT=, CY=, DC=, DD=, /DE, ED=, GL, GP=, JN=, LA=, LC=, NA=, /NT, PU=, SE=, SN=, /TI, UD=

Database name	Brief details	Approximate cost ($)	
		Per hour	*Per offline print*
HISTORICAL ABSTRACTS (39) ABC-Clio Inc.	Covers the history of the world from 1450 to present, excluding US and Canada	65	0.15
INSPEC (12) (13) Institution of Electrical Engineers	Covers physics, electrotechnology, computers and control	55	0.15
IPA (74) American Society of Hospital Pharmacists	Development and use of drugs and professional pharmaceutical practice	50	0.15
ISMEC (14) Data Courier Inc.	Mechanical engineering, including energy and power, transport and handling	75	0.15
LISA (61) Learned Information	Library and information science	50	0.10
LLBA (36) Sociological Abstracts Inc.	Language and language behaviour abstracts	55	0.15
MAGAZINE INDEX (47) Information Access Corporation	Items from 370 magazines on a wide range of topics	45	0.10
MANAGEMENT CONTENTS (75)	Accounting, finance, industrial relations, marketing, operations research and public administration	70	0.15
METADEX (32) American Society for Metals	Comprehensive data on materials, processes, properties, products, forms and influencing factors for metals	80	0.12
MGA (29) American Meteorological Society	Meteorological and geoastrophysical abstracts of foreign and US literature	50	0.10
MLA BIBLIOGRAPHY (71) Modern Language Association	References on modern language, literature and linguistics	55	0.15
MRIS Abstracts (63) Maritime Research Information Service	Arctic operation, cargo handling, ships, navigation, ports, propulsion, trade, etc.	45	0.10
NATIONAL FOUNDA-TIONS (78) The Foundation Centre	Contains details of all US foundations, including small and local agencies	60	0.30
NICEM (46)	National Information Centre for Educational Media database on non-print material	70	0.20

Date	Approximate size	Update	Searchable fields
1973–	54 000	Quarterly 1900	/AB, AU=, JO=, RN=, /TI, UD=, YR=
1969–	1 045 000	Monthly 12 500	AU=, CN=, CO=, /CS, /DE, /ID, JN=, LA=, PA=, PI=, PN=, PO=, RN=, SC=, UD=
1970–	49 500	Bimonthly	/AB, AU=, CS=, /DE, /HN, JN=, LA=, PY=, SL=, /TI, UD=
1973–	79 500	Monthly 1000	AU=, CO=, /CS, /DE, /ID, JN=, LA=, RN=, SC=, UD=
1969–	30 000	Bimonthly	/AB, AN=, AU=, /DE, JN=, LA=, /NT, PY=, /SH, /TI, UD=
1973–	25 000	Quarterly 1200	/AB, AU=, CA=, CO=, /CS, /DE, DT=, /ID, JO=, PD=, SC=, /TI, UD=
1977–	98 000	Monthly 5000	AT=, AU=, CO=, /DE, GR=, /ID, JN=, /NA, /NT, PD=, PN=, PY=, SH=, SY=, /TI, UD=
1974–	40 000	Monthly 1500	/AB, AU=, DC=, /DE, DT=, JC, JN=, /TI, PY=, UD=
1966–	318 000	Monthly 2500	AI=, AU=, CC=, CN=, /DE, DT=, ES=, GN=, /ID, JA=, JO=, LA=, PD=, PI=, RN=, SC=, /TI, UD=
1970–	30 000	Irregular	/AB, AU=, CP=, /CS, /DE, DT=, JA=, LA=, /TI, UD=
1976–	70 000	Annually	AU=, DC=, /DE, DT=, HE=, HP=, HS=, JN=, /NT, PU=, PY=, SE=, SF=, SN=, /TI, UD=
1970–	16 750	Monthly 250	/AB, AU=, CG=, CN=, CS=, /DE, JN=, PY=, RN=, SC=, /TI, UD=
Current	20 000	Annually	AB=, AC=, AG=, AL=, AM=, CM=, /CO, CP=, CR=, EG=, EI=, EL=, EX=, FC=, /FN, FS=, FT=, GA=, GG=, GI=, GL=, LI=, /ON, OT=, QD=, UI=, ZP=
1964–	250 000	Biennially	/AB, AN=, AU=, CN=, /CS, /DE, DT=, /ID, JO=, LA=, MS=, PD=, PN=, RN=, /TI

Database name	Brief details	Approximate cost ($)	
		Per hour	Per offline print
NICSEM/NICIS (70)	Descriptions of equipment for use with handicapped children	35	0.10
NTIS (6) National Technical Information Service	US Government-sponsored research in aeronautics, agriculture, astronomy, social sciences, chemistry, electronics and many other disciplines	35	0.10
OCEANIC ABSTRACTS (28) Data Courier Inc.	Biology, fisheries, geology, oceanography, engineering, diving, government and legal aspects	75	0.15
ONTAP ERIC (201)	Training file using 1975 ERIC database with evaluation facility	15	Not available
ONTAP CA SEARCH (204) Chemical Abstracts Service	A training file for new users of CA SEARCH	15	Not available
PAIS INTER-NATIONAL (49) Pais Inc.	Public Affairs Information Service on political science, international relations, economics, law, sociology, etc.	60	0.15
PIRA (48) Paper Industry Research Association	Information on paper and packaging, including management	55	0.15
PNI (42) Pharmaceutical News Index Data Courier Inc.	Items from weekly pharmaceutical newsletters. Legislation, company news, etc.	90	0.20
POLLUTION ABSTRACTS (41) Data Courier Inc.	Air pollution, water pollution, solid wastes, noise, pesticides, radiation, etc.	75	0.15
POPULATION BIBLIOGRAPHY (104) Carolina Population Centre	Covers literature on family planning, demography, population policy, law and research	55	0.10
PSYCHOLOGICAL ABSTRACTS (11) Am. Psych. Assoc.	Coverage of psychology and other behavioural sciences over a wide range of subject areas	65	0.10
PTS F and S INDEXES (18) (98) Predicasts Inc.	Information on companies, products and industries internationally, sales and profit forecasts and events	90	0.20
PTS FEDERAL INDEX (20)	Federal activity, including regulations, bills, speeches, reports, decisions, orders, contracts, etc.	90	0.20
PTS FEDERAL INDEX WEEKLY (21)	Current information for one month of above file	90	0.20

Date	Approximate size	Update	Searchable fields
1974–1977	35 000	None	/AB, AU=, BN=, CS=, /DE, ED=, LA=, LC=, NN=, /NT, OC=, PU=, PY=, SE=, /TI, UD=
1964	676 000	Biweekly 2500	AU=, CC=, CF=, CN=, CP=, /CS, /DE, /ID, JA=, RN=, RP=, TI=, UD=
1964–	180 000	Bimonthly 1000	/AB, AU=, /DE, /DF, JA=, LA=, /TI, UD=, YR=
1975	32 000	None	/AB, AC=, AU=, CH=, CN=, /CS, /DE, DT=, GC=, /ID, IS=, JO=, /NT, PN=, RN=, /SA, SC=, /TI, UD=, YR=
Selection only	15 000	None	AC=, AU=, CL=, CO=, /CS, /DE, DT=, /ID, JA=, JN=, LA=, NP=, PA=, PN=, PY=, RN=, SC=, /TI
1976–	67 000	Quarterly 1500	/AB, AN=, AR=, AU=, BN=, CS=, /DE, DT=, JN=, LA=, PP=, PU=, SE=, SF=, /TI, UD=, YR=
1975–	35 000	Monthly	/AB, AN=, AU=, /DE, DT=, DU=, JA=, JN=, LA=, PY=, SF=, SO=, /TI, UD=
1975–	27 000	Monthly	CO=, /DE, JO=, /TI, UD=, YR=
1970–	67 500	Bimonthly 1000	/AB, AU=, CL=, CO=, CS=, CT=, /DE, DT=, /ID, JN=, LA=, PU=, PY=, /TI, UD=
1966–	41 000	Bimonthly 1000	AN=, AU=, BN=, CA=, /DE, DT=, ED=, GL=, /ID, JN=, LA=, LC=, /NT, PU=, PY=, SE=, SL=, SN=, /TI, UD=
1967–	270 000	Monthly 2000	/AB, AU=, CL=, CO=, /CS, /DE, /ID, JA=, JN=, LA=, SC=, /TI, UD=, YR=
1972–	1 055 500	Monthly 12 500	/AB, CC=, CN=, CO=, /DE, DT=, EC=, EN=, JO=, LC=, PC=, PN=, SF=, UD
1976–	65 000	Monthly 12 000	/AB, AU=, CC=, CN=, /CS, CT=, DT=, EC=, EN=, JO=, PC=, PN=, UD=
Current month		Weekly	

Database name	Brief details	Approximate cost ($)	
		Per hour	*Per offline print*
PTS INTERNATIONAL ANNUAL TIME SERIES (87)	50 key series for 50 non-US countries. Historical and forecast data in population, GNP, employment, products, etc.	90	0.20
PTS INTERNATIONAL STATISTICAL ABSTRACTS (86)	Forecasts for all countries of the world on general economics, industry, products, etc.	90	0.20
PTS PROMT (16)	Market information from news-papers, magazines, journals; reports, etc., on trade, products, legislation, etc.	90	0.20
PTS US ANNUAL TIME SERIES (82)	Historical and forecast data for population, GNP, employment, products, etc.	90	0.20
PTS US REGIONAL TIME SERIES (83)	Regional series on the lines of the international ones	90	0.20
PTS US STATISTICAL ABSTRACTS (81)	Published forecasts for the US, including historical base, short-term forecast and long-term forecast	90	0.20
PTS WEEKLY (17)	These are the current files which go to F and S and PROMT files	90	0.20
RAPRA ABSTRACTS (95) Rubber and Plastics Research Association	Commercial, technical and research aspects of the rubber and plastics industry	65	0.15
RILM (97) City University, New York	Abstracts of literature on music, both specialist and interdisciplinary	65	0.15
SCISEARCH (34) (94)	Institute for Scientific Information files on science and technology. Searching by citation is possible	30 (120)	0.10 (0.20)
SOCIAL SCISEARCH (7)	Institute for Scientific Information files on social sciences, behavioural science. Searching by citation is possible	30 (120)	0.10 (0.20)
SOCIOLOGICAL ABSTRACTS (37) Soc. Abs. Inc.	Sociology and related disciplines in the social and behavioural sciences	55	0.15
SPIN (62) American Institute of Physics	Physics, mathematical and statistical physics, astronomy, astrophysics and geophysics	35	0.10

Date	Approximate size	Update	Searchable fields
1972–	130 000	Quarterly	
Current	244 000	Monthly 2000	AU=, CC=, CN=, /CS, CS=, /DE, DT=, EC=, EN=, GR=, JO=, MC=, MN=, PC=, PN=, QC=, SF=, YR=
1972–	280 000	Monthly 3000	/AB, CC=, CN=, CO=, /DE, /DF, /DF*, DT=, EC=, EN=, JO=, PC=, PN=, SF=, TN=, UD=
1971–	30 900	Monthly	
1971–	42 000	Irregular	
1971–	150 000	Quarterly	AU=, CC=, CN=, /CS, CS=, /DE, DT=, EC=, EN=, GR=, JO=, MC=, MN=, PC=, PN=, QC=, SF=, YR
Current month	15 000	Weekly	/AB, /DE, DT=, JO=, SF=, UD=
1972–	85 000	Monthly	/AB, AN=, AU=, CS=, CY=, /DE, DT=, GL=, /ID, JA=, JN=, LA=, PA=, PN=, PY=, SC=, /TI, /TN, UD=
1967–	50 000	Irregular	/AB, AN=, AU=, CS=, /DE, DT=, JA=, JN=, LA=, PU=, PY=, SF=, /SH, SH=, /TI, UD=
1974–1977(34) 1978– (94)	2 184 000	Monthly 42 000	AU=, CR=, /CS, DT=, JO=, LA=, /TI, UD=
1972–	70 000	Monthly 7500	AU=, CR=, /CS, DT=, JO=, LA=, /TI, UD=
1963–	99 000	Quarterly 2000	/AB, AC=, AU=, CN=, CO=, /CS, /DE, /ID, JC=, JO=, LA=, PD=, SC=, /TI, UD=
1975	70 000	Monthly 2000	AA=, /AB, AU=, CO=, DT=, ED=, EV=, /ID, JA=, JN=, MA=, PX=, PY=, /TI, UD=, WT=

Database name	Brief details	Approximate cost ($)	
		Per hour	*Per offline print*
SSIE (65) Smithsonian Science Information Exchange	Government and privately funded research projects started in the last 2 years	90	0.20
TSCA INITIAL INVENTORY (52) EPA	List of chemical substances relevant to the 1977 Toxic Substances Control Act	45	0.15
USPSD (93) University of Pittsburgh	United States Political Science Documents. Political, social and policy sciences	65	0.15
WELDASEARCH (99) The Welding Institute, Cambridge	Covers joining of metals and plastics and metal spraying and cutting	65	0.15
WORLD ALUMINUM ABSTRACTS (33)	All aspects of aluminium (excluding mining), including production, casting, fabrication, properties and uses	50	0.10
WORLD TEXTILES (67) Shirley Institute	Literature on textile technology, production, management, etc.	55	0.10
AQUACULTURE (112)	The growing of marine, brackish and fresh-water organisms	35	0.15
CHEMSEARCH (30) Chemical Abstracts Service	Dictionary listing of the most recently cited chemical substances in CASEARCH (4). Companion to CHEMNAME (31)	55	0.16
CLAIMS/US PATENTS ABSTRACTS WEEKLY (125) IFI Plenum Data Co.	Current month's input for file 25	95	0.50
CLAIMS UNITERM (223, 224, 225) IFI Plenum Data Co.	US chemical and chemically related patents	300	0.15
CONFERENCE PAPERS INDEX (77) Data Courier Inc.	Scientific and technical papers presented at major US conferences	75	0.15
ENCYCLOPEDIA OF ASSOCIATIONS (114) Gale Research Co.	Non-profit US membership associations of national scope	55	0.15

Date	Approximate size	Update	Searchable fields
Current 2 years	205 000	Monthly 9000	/AB, CN=, /DE, FG=, FL=, FU=, FY=, IN=, PG=, PO=, /PR, PZ=, SD=, SG=, SN=, SZ=, TD=, /TI, UD=
Current	43 000	Irregular	CN=, /DE, /EC, EC=, GN=, /ID, MF=, PI=, RN=, SY=
1975–	10 800	Quarterly 900	/AB, AU=, /DE, /GS, /ID, JN=, NA=, /NT, PY=, /TI, UD=
1967–	45 000	Monthly 400	/AB, AU=, /DE, JN=, LA=, /NT, PY=, /TI, UD=
1968–	64 000	Monthly 550	/AB, AU=, CO=, /CS, DC=, /DE, DT=, JA=, JO=, LA=, PD=, RN=, SC=, /TI, UD=
1970–	76 000	Monthly 700	AN=, AU=, CS=, /DE, DT=, JA=, JN=, LA=, PN=, PY=, SF=, SO=, /TI, UD=
1970–	4300	Irregular	/AB, AU=, /DE, /GS, JN=, PY=, SO=, /TI, UD=
Latest 6 weeks	45 000	Biweekly	CN=, /DE, /EC, EC=, GN=, HP=, MF=, NM=, PI=, RN=, SB=, ST=, UD=
Current month	6000	Weekly	/AB, AC=, AN=, AU=, CL=, CR=, FN=, PD=, PN=, PY=, /TI, UD=
(223) 1950–70 (224) 1971–77 (225) 1978–	265 000 148 515 39 000	None None Quarterly	/AB, AC=, AN=, AU=, CL=, CR=, FN=, PD=, PN=, PY=, /TI, UD=, UN=, UT=
1973–	670 000	Monthly	AU=, CL=, CS=, CT=, CY=, /DE, /ID, JA=, MN=, SC=, SP=, /ST, /TI, UD=
Current	15 000	Annually	/AB, FY=, GL=, OF=, /ON, ON=, SF=, /SH, SH=, UD=, ZP=

Database name	Brief details	Approximate cost ($)	
		Per hour	Per offline print
FOREIGN TRADERS INDEX (105) U.S. Dept. of Commerce	Directory of manufacturers, retailers, wholesalers, etc., in 130 countries outside US	45	0.25
NATIONAL NEWS-PAPER INDEX (111) Information Access Corp.	Front-to-back-page indexing of 3 major US newspapers	75	0.10
NEWSEARCH (911) Information Access Corp.	Current month's input for National Newspaper Index (111) and Magazine Index (47)	95	0.10
ONTAP CHEMNAME (231) Chemical Abstracts Service	Training file containing corresponding chemical substance information for records in ONTAP CASEARCH	15	Not available
PHILOSOPHER'S INDEX (57) Philosophy Documentation Centre	Philosophy	55	0.15
SURFACE COATINGS ABSTRACTS (115) Paint Research Association	Paints and surface coatings	65	0.15
U.S. PUBLIC SCHOOL DIRECTORY (120) National Center for Education Statistics	Details such as district, type, no. of teachers, no. of students, etc., for US schools		

Date	*Approximate* size	Update	*Searchable fields*
Not known at time of going to press			
1979–	150 000	Monthly 1500	AT=, AU=, CI=, CO=, /DE, ED=, GR=, /ID, JN=, /NA, /NT, PD=, PN=, PY=, SF=, SL=, /TI, UD=
Current month	Varies	Daily 1200	AT=, AU=, CI=, CO=, /DE, ED=, GR=, /ID, JN=, /NA, /NT, PD=, PN=, PY=, SF=, SL=, /TI, UD=
–	?	–	CN=, /DE, /EC, GN=, HP=, ID, MF=, NM=, PI=, RN=, SB=, ST=, SY=, UD=
1940–	56 000	Quarterly 1500	/AB, AU=, /DE, DT=, JA=, JN=, LA=, NA=, PU=, PY=, /TI, UD=
1976–	25 000	Monthly 700	/AB, AU=, DT=, JA=, JN=, PA=, PN=, PY=, /SH, SH=, /TI, UD=
Current	80 000	Annually	

A5.5 SUMMARY OF DIALOG COMMANDS
(Alternatives are shown in parentheses)

Command	Function	Example
BEGIN	Gives heading for start of search	BEGIN
BEGINn	Select or change files	BEGIN7
COMBINE (C)	Combine terms to form new set	C 3 AND 7
DISPLAY (D)	Print on VDU screen	D 3/2/1—23
DISPLAY SETS (DS)	Prints summary of search	DS, DS8
END	Summarises the usage	END
END/SAVE	Saves the search strategy	END/SAVE
END/SAVETEMP	Saves the search strategy temporarily	END/SAVETEMP
END/SDI	Saves a strategy for regular use on updates for files	END/SDI
EXPAND(E)	Displays adjacent terms in the index	E COMPUTER
EXPLAIN	Explains commands and gives information	? FILE 62, ? COMMANDS, ? NEWS, ? EXPLAIN
.EXECUTE nnnn	Executes entire search strategy for saved search number nnnn	.EXECUTE BAP5
.EXECUTE STEPS nnnn	Executes each line for saved search number nnnn	.EXECUTE STEPS EF51
.EXECUTE STEPS nnnn/n	As above, but up to statement number n	.EXECUTE STEPS 25A9/12
.FILEn	Selects file and keeps previous search history	.FILE8
KEEP(K)	Saves items in special set	K 3/4—10
LIMIT(L)	Restricts set in various ways	LIMIT 6/ENG
LIMITALL (LALL)	Limits all sets in various ways	LALL/FOR
LOGOFF	Ends search and disconnects	LOGOFF
PAGE (P)	Continue index display	PAGE
PRINT (PR)	Print off line	PR 6/6/4—78
PRINT−(PR−)	Cancel previous PRINT before end	PR−
.RECALL nnnn	Displays saved search number nnnn	.RECALL EA48
.RELEASE nnnn	Deletes saved search number nnnn	.RELEASE M8A3
SELECT(S)	Selects terms to create sets	S INFORMATION, S TOY AND CAR
.SORT	Sorts output according to specified parameters	.SORT
TYPE (T)	Prints a set at the terminal	T 3/2/1—12
.COST	Gives elapsed time and cost since last BEGIN	

Appendix 6
SDC

A6.1 SOFTWARE SYSTEM
  ORBIT

A6.2 ADDRESSES

SDC Search Service,
System Development Corporation,
2500 Colorado Avenue,
Santa Monica, CA 90406
USA

Tel: 213/829-7511

401 Hackensack Avenue,
Hackensack, NJ 07601,
USA

Tel: 201/487-0571

900 Commerce Drive,
Oakbrook, IL 60521,
USA

Tel: 312/325-6363

Ms E. Crockett,
SDC Search Service Inc.,
28 Boulevard de Grenelle,
Suite 301 bis,
Paris 75015,
France

Tel: 33 (1) 575 57 75

7929 Westpark Drive,
McLean, VA 22101,
USA

Tel: 703/799-9850

Information Services,
International-Dentsu Ltd,
7–13 1 Chome, Tsukiji,
Chuo-Ku, Tokyo,
104 Japan

Infomart,
Suite 1506,
One Younge St,
Toronto,
Canada

Tel: 416/366-3904

A6.3 ABBREVIATIONS FOR SEARCHABLE FIELDS

AAB	Analytical abstract
AB	Abstract
AC	Accession number
AN	Accession number
AOS	Author organisational source
AU	Author
AV	Availability
AW	Awardee
AY	Accession number year
BI	Basic index
BN	International Standard Book Number
CA	Cited author
CALL	Library of Congress call number
CC	Category code name
CEN	Century
CG	Contract/grant numbers
CHAN	Clearing house accession number
CI	City
CJ	Cited journal
CL	Derwent classes
CN	NAL call number
CNO	Congressional Record number
COCO	Committee code
CORD	Co-ordinates
CP	Cited page
CS	Congress and session number
CV	Cited volume
CY	Cited year
DD	Deadline data, Dewey Decimal number
DEG	Degree
DT	Document type
EC	Event code
EY	Entry year
FR	Foreign
FS	File segment
FUND	Funding
HE	Heading note
IC	International patent classification
ICC	Issue category code
IN	Principal/associate investigators
IS	Issue
IT	Index terms
IW	Index words
JC	Journal citation, journal coden
LA	Language
LC	Library of Congress card number
LO	Location, location (country)
ME	Main entry (author)

NO	Notes
NU	Document/report/bill numbers
ON	Order number
OS	Organisational source
OSCO	Organisational source code
PA	Patent countries, patent assignee
PC	Patent classification, patentee/company code
PCC	Primary category code
PD	Publication date
PL	Patent location
PN	Patent number, project number
PR	Priority country
PY	Publication year, priority number
RN	Report number
RNO	Number of rings
RPR	Rings present
RSD	Ring system description
SCC	Secondary category code
SE	State
SF	Substituent fragment
SI	Superintendent of document/item number
SN	Source name
SO	Source
SOCO	Source code
SPO	Sponsoring organisation
ST	Supplementary terms
STAT	Citations to statutes at large
STF	Stereochemistry fragment
TA	Title annotation
TC	Taxonomic codes
TI	Title words
TN	Task number
TT	Title terms
UP	Update code
VOL	Volume
WT	Witness terms
XR	Cross-reference index terms

Notes: (1) For fields prefixed by / the entry in the online dictionary is the complete field.

(2) The fields which have been used to create entries in the Basic Index (BI) – i.e. individual words (apart from stop words) from these fields have been entered into the online dictionary– are indicated in parentheses.

(3) For databases that have different rates for subscribers and non-subscribers of the linked printed publication the two rates have been shown with the non-subscriber rates in parentheses.

A6.4 AVAILABLE DATABASES

Database name	Brief details	Approximate cost ($)	
		Per hour	Per offline print
ACCOUNTANTS American Institute of Certified Public Accountants	Accounting, auditing, taxation, data processing, finance, investment, management	65	0.10
AGRICOLA US National Agricultural Library	Agriculture, rural sociology, human nutrition, animal science, forestry, natural resources, entomology	35	0.06
APILIT American Petroleum Institute	Petroleum refining, petrochemicals, air and water conservation, trans- portation and storage, petroleum substitutes	65 (85)	0.11 (0.20)
APIPAT American Petroleum Institute	Refining patents from USA, Belgium, Canada, France, Germany, UK, Netherlands, Italy, Japan, South Africa	65 (85)	0.11 (0.20)
ASI Congressional Informa- ation Service Inc.	Statistical publications of the US Government. Social, economic and demographic data	90	0.25
BIOCODES Biosciences Informa- tion Service	Contains Biosis Previews codes, names and cross-references	35	0.10
BIOSIS, BIO6973 Biosciences Information Service	Research review and documenta- tion and retrieval of biological and biomedical information	65	0.10
CAS7276, CAS77 Chemical Abstracts Service	Comprehensive coverage of chemistry, including chemical engineering	60	0.12
CBPI Information Access	Canadian industry, including technical, political and financial information	55 (75)	0.10 (0.10)
CDI University Microfilms International	Doctoral dissertations from US and elsewhere. Multidisciplinary coverage	55	0.12
CHEM7071 Chemical Abstracts Service	Some coverage as CAS77 and CAS7276 but without merger of CASIA	60	0.12
CHEMDEX Chemical Abstracts Service	Details of chemical compound names and registry numbers	60	0.12
CIN Chemical Abstracts Service	Business literature in chemical industry; production, pricing, sales, products, government and commercial activity	70	0.10

Date	Approximate size	Update	Searchable fields
1974–	60 000	Quarterly 3000	/AN, /AU, /DT, /JC, /IT, /IW, /TI, /OS, /UP (NO in BI)
1970–	1 296 000	Monthly 12 000	/AN, /AU, /CN, /DT, /FR, /FS, /LA, /OS, /PCC, /PD, /SCC, /SN, /UP (AB, IT, TI in BI)
1964–	270 000	Monthly 1500	/AN, /AU, /CC, /IT, /OS, /UP
1964–	126 000	Monthly 700	/AN, /AU, /CC, /IT, /PN, /UP
1973–	57 600	Monthly 1000	/AN, /CC, /DT, /IS, /IT, /OSCO, /SI (AAB, AB, ANO, HE, TI in BI)
Current	1 200	None	
1974– 1969–1973	1 200 000 1 000 000	Monthly None	/AN, /AU, /CC, /FS, /JC, /TC, /UP (IT, TI in BI)
1972–1976 1977–	2 500 000 1 200 000	None Biweekly 12 000	/AN, /AU, /CC, /CI, /DT, /FS, /ISSN, /IT, /IW, /JC, /LA, /LO, /OS, /PC, /PCL, /PN, /PR, /RN, /TI, /UP
1975–	265 000	Monthly 4400	/AN, /AU, /CC, /IT, /IW, /JC, /TI, /UP
1861–	536 000	Monthly 3000	/AN, /AU, /CC, /CEN, /DEG, /FS, /ICC, /LO, /OS, /UP (TI in BI)
1970–1971	600 000	None	/AN, /AU, /CC, /DT, /JC, /LA, /LO, /OS, /PC, /PL, /PN, /UP (IT, TI in BI)
1972–	400 000	Monthly 30 000	/IT, /MF, /MFF, /NF, /NM, /NMF, /P, /PF, /RN, /RNO, /RPR, /RSD, /S, /SF, /STF
1975–	258 000	Weekly 1000	/AN, /CC, /EY, /JC, /PD, /UP (AB, TI in BI)

| Database name | Brief details | Approximate cost ($) | |
		Per hour	Per offline print
CIS INDEX Congressional Information	US Congress and Senate publica- tions, public laws, added annually. Multidisciplinary and topical	90	0.25
CNI Information Access	Index to items of news from Canadian newspapers	55 (75)	0.10 (0.10)
CONF Data Courier Inc.	Scientific and technical papers at various meetings	75	0.15
COMPENDEX Engineering Index Inc.	Most branches of engineering, including some management, math- ematics, physics and instruments	65	0.10
CRECORD Capitol Services Inc.	Current coverage of Congressional Record, Bills, Reports, legislation, speeches, committees, etc.	80	0.15
ENERGYLINE Environment Information Centre	Energy economics, fuel, power, transport, US policy, environment, resources	90	0.20
ENVIROLINE Environment Information Centre	Environmental studies, including pollution, energy, population, etc.	90	0.20
ERIC US National Institute of Education	Education, counselling, career education, educational management, exceptional children, language, reading, tests, teacher education	35	0.08
FEDREG Capital Services Inc.	Contains citations from *Federal Register Abstracts*	80	0.25
FSTA International Food Information Service	Food science, microbiology, toxicology, economics, packaging, laws and standards	65	0.12
GEOREF American Geological Institute	Geosciences, including economics, engineering, chemistry, chronology, morphology and physics aspects	75	0.20
GRANTS Oryx Press	Details of grant programmes by federal, state, local, commercial and private foundations in over 88 disciplines	60	0.35
INFORM ABI of Data Courier Inc.	Business management, including accounting, administration, econ- omics, international trade, business law, taxes, training and other fields	65	0.10
INSPEC, INSP6976 Institution of Electrical Engineers	Material from physics abstracts, electrical and electronics abstracts, and computer and control abstracts	45	0.10

Date	Approximate size	Update	Searchable fields
1970–	104 300	Monthly 1000	/AN, /COCO, /CS, /DT, /IS, /IT, /SI, /SOCO, /STAT, /WT (AAB, AB, TI in BI)
1977–	244 000	Monthly 6000	/AN, /AU, /DT, /IT, /IW, /JC, /PD, /PY, /TI, /UP
1973–	515 000	Monthly 9000	/AN, /AU, /CC, /DT, /IT, /IW, /JC, /NA, /OS, /PD, /PY, /TI (AB in BI)
1970–	656 000	Monthly 6000	/AN, /AU, /CC, /JC, /OS, /UP (IT, ST, TI, XR in BI)
1976–	160 000	Weekly 1750	/AN, /CC, /CNO, /CS, /PD, /PY, /SO, /UP (TI in BI)
1971–	41 400	Bimonthly 800	/AN, /AU, /CC, /DT, /OS, /UP (AB, IT, TI in BI)
1971–	84 000	Monthly 800	/AN, /AU, /AV, /CC, /DT, /IT, /IW, /JC, /OS, /TI, /UP (AB in BI)
1966–	280 000	Monthly 2500	/AN, /AU, /CC, /CHAN, /DT, /FS, /IS, /IT, /IW, /JC, /LA, /LO, /NU, /OS, /SPO, /TI (ST in IT) (AB in BI)
1977–	56 000	Weekly 1500	/AN, /CC, /IS, /PD, /PG, /PY, /TI, /UP, /VOL
1969–	170 000	Monthly 1500	/AN, /AU, /CC, /IT, /IW, /JC, /LA, /OS, /PN, /TI, /UP (AB in BI)
1967–	427 000	Monthly 4000	/AN, /AU, /CC, /CEN, /DT, /EY, /IS, /IT, /IW, /JC, /LA, /NU, /OS, /TI (CORD, NO in BI)
Current	1 500	Monthly replacement	/AN, /CI, /DD, /DT, /LO, /OS, /SE, /UP (AB, IT, TI in BI)
1971–	99 000	Monthly 1200	/AN, /AU, /DT, /ISSN, /IT, /IW, /JC, /LA, /TI (AB in BI)
1969–	1 500 000	Monthly 13 000	/AN, /AU, /CC, /DT, /FS, /IT, /IW, /JC, /LA, /LO, /NU, /OS, /PC, /TI, /UP (AB in BI)

Database name	Brief details	Approximate cost ($)	
		Per hour	Per offline print
ISMEC Data Courier Inc.	Mechanical engineering, including energy, power, transport and handling	65	0.12
LABORDOC International Labour Organisation	Various areas in finance, management, labour and industry	75	0.15
LIBCON/E 3—M	English-language material from monographs and audiovisual material, including Marc records from Library of Congress	120	0.25
LIBCON/F 3—M	As for LIBCON/E, but foreign material	120	0.25
LISA Library Association, England	Library and information science, promotion, organisation, publishing, bookselling, reading and reprography	50	0.10
MANAGEMENT Management Information Services	Accounting, banking, economics, finance, regulations, industrial relations, marketing, production, government, etc.	65	0.10
NTIS National Technical Information Services	US Government-sponsored research in aeronautics, agriculture, astronomy, social sciences, chemistry, electronics and many other disciplines	45	0.08
OCEANIC Data Courier Inc.	Oceans	55	0.10
PAPERCHEM Institute of Paper Chemistry	Literature on pulp, paper and board manufacturing and utilising industry	80 (110)	0.15 (0.15)
P/E NEWS American Petroleum Institute	Covers major publications in the petroleum and energy fields	95	0.11
POLLUTION Data Courier Inc.	Air pollution, water pollution, solid wastes, noise, pesticides, radiation, etc.	65	0.15
PSYCHABS American Psychological Association	Coverage of psychology and other behavioural sciences over a wide range of subject areas	60	0.10
QUEBEC Microfor Inc.	Extracts from three major French-language newspapers on many topics	75 (85)	0.10 (0.10)
RINGDOC Derwent Publications	Extensive coverage of the pharmaceutical literature	Available from Derwent	

Date	Approximate size	Update	Searchable fields
1973–	90 000	Monthly 1200	/AN, /AU, /CC, /DT, /IT, /IW, /JC, /LA, /LO, /NU, /OS, /PC, /TI, /UP
1965–	98 000	Monthly 600	/AN, /AU, /CC, /CO, /DT, /IT, /IW, /LA, /NU, /OS, /ST, /TI
1968–	1 055 000	Weekly 3800	/BN, /CALL, /CEN, /DD, /LC, /ME, /UP,
1965–	1 071 000	Weekly 7000	As for LIBCON/E
1969–	40 000	Bimonthly 700	/AN, /AU, /CC, /IT, /IW, /JC, /LA, /NO, /TI, /UP (AB in BI)
September 1974–	70 000	Monthly 1000	/AN, /AU, /JC, /UP (AB, IT, TI in BI)
1970–	540 000	Biweekly 2300	/AN, /AU, /CC, /IS, /NU, /OS, /SPO, /UP, (IT, ST, TI in BI)
1964–	180 000	Bimonthly 1000	/AN, /AU, /IT, /IW, /JC, /LA, /OS, /TI, /UP (AB in BI)
1968–	134 000	Monthly 1000	/AN, /AU, /AV, /DT, /OS, /PC, /PN, /UP (AB, IT, TI in BI)
1975–	104 000	Weekly 500	/AN, /IT, /JC, /UP
1970–	67 500	Bimonthly 1000	/AN, /AU, /OS, /UP (IT, ST, TI in BI)
1967–	270 000	Monthly 2000	/AN, /AU, /CC, /DT, /IT, /IW, /JC, /LA, /OS, /TI, /UP (AB, ST in BI)
1973–	180 000	Monthly 2000	/AN, /AU, /CC, /IT, /IW, /NU, /OS, /TI (ST in IT)
July 1964–	700 000	Monthly 4000	

Database name	Brief details	Approximate cost ($)	
		Per hour	Per offline print
SAE ABSTRACTS Society of Automotive Engineers	Self-propelled vehicles, including fuels, manufacturing, safety, noise, management, testing, etc.	80	0.15
SSIE Smithsonian Science Information Exchange	Covers ongoing and recently completed research in a wide range of science, engineering and technology	110	0.25
TITUS Institut Textile de France	Information on the textile industry for managers, engineers and technicians, patents, standards, data and regulations, etc.	75	0.15
TULSA University of Tulsa	Literature and patents on oil and natural gas; exploration, development and production	75	0.15
WPI World Patent Index	Covers patentee codes, title terms, Derwent classes and code patent numbers, etc.	Available from Derwent	
BUSINESS Infomart	Business and government related information published in major Canadian newspapers	65 (85)	0.20 (0.20)
COLD Cold Regions Research and Engineering Lab.	All disciplines dealing with Antarctica, Antarctic Ocean and sub-Antarctic islands		
CRDS Derwent Publications	Synthetic organic chemistry	Available from Derwent	
ELCOM Cambridge Scientific Abstracts Inc.	Electronics and communications		
FOREST Forest Products Research Society	Wood products	80	0.15
NEWSPAPER INDEX Bell and Howell	General news from major US newspapers	80	0.15
PESTDOC Derwent Publications	Agricultural chemicals	Available from Derwent	
PROMT Predicasts Inc.	Market information from newspapers, etc., on trade, products, legislation	90	0.50
SAFETY SCIENCE ABSTRACTS Cambridge Scientific Abstracts Inc.	Science of safety	75	0.15

Date	Approximate size	Update	Searchable fields
1965–	12 000	Quarterly 200	/AN, /AU, /CC, /IT, /IW, /JC, /OS, /TI, /UP, (AB in BI)
1974–	540 000	Monthly 9000	/AN, /CI, /IN, /IT, /OS, /ST, /UP
1970–	162 000	Monthly 1500	/AN, /AU, /DT, /IT, /IW, /JC, /LA, /OS, /PC, /PN, /UP (AB in BI)
1965-	270 000	Monthly 1500	/AN, /AU, /IT, /TI, /UP
1963–	1 500 000	Monthly 22 000	/AC, /AY, /CL, /IC, /MC, /MP, /PC, /PN, /PR, /PY, /RR, /TT
1979–	3 600	Monthly	/AN, /AU, /CC, /DT, /IT, /IW, /JC, /NA, /TI
1962–	60 000	Quarterly	/AN, /AU, /CC, /CO, /DT, /FS, /IT, /IW, /LA, /OS, /TI, /UP
1944–	100 000	Quarterly	
1977–	60 000	Monthly	/AN, /AU, /LA, /OS, /TI, /UP
1947–	12 000	Twice yearly	/AN, /AU, /CC, /FS, /IT, /IW, /LA, /OS, /TI, /UP
1976–	800 000	Monthly	/AN, /CC, /IT, /IW, /JC, /TI, /UP
1968–	100 000	Quarterly	
1972–	400 000	Weekly	/AN, /CC, /CO, /DT, /EC, /FS, /IT, /IW, /JC, /LA, /PC, /TN
1975–	90 000	Bimonthly	/AN, /AU, /LA, /OS, /TI, /UP

Database name	Brief details	Approximate cost ($)	
		Per hour	Per offline print
SOCIAL SCIENCE CITATION INDEX ISI	Journal literature and cited references in the social sciences	65	0.10
SPORT Sport Information Resource Centre	Sport	70	0.15
USCA Washington Representative Services	US Government contract awards	85	0.15
USPSD University of Pittsburgh	American political science journals	65	0.15

Date	Approximate size	Update	Searchable fields
1977–	375 000	Monthly 10 000	/AA, /CA, /CC, /CJ, /CP, /CV, /CY, /DT, /JC, /LA, /ON, /OS, /TI
1975–	45 000	Quarterly 2500	/AN, /AU, /AV, /DT, /IT, /IW, /JC, /LA, /NU, /OS, /TI
1978–	8 000	Monthly	/AN, /AW, /CC, /CI, /CN, /FS, /FUND, /SE, /SPO, /RN, /TI
1975–	15 000	Quarterly 750	/AN, /AU, /CA, /IT, /IW, /JC, /TI, /UP

A6.5 SUMMARY OF ORBIT COMMANDS
(Alternatives are shown in parentheses)

Command	Function	Example
BACKUP (ERSK, ERASEBACK, ERASE BACK)	Erase last statement	
BACKUP TO n (as above)	Erase statements to and including the given number	BACKUP TO 10
COMMENT	Message to SDC	
DELETE name (PURGE name)	Delete stated SAVEd or STOREd search	DELETE FREDA
ERASEALL (ERSLL, ERASE ALL)	To erase all searches	
EXPLAINitem (EXP, ?)	Describes databases, messages, commands, procedures, etc.	EXPLAIN ERIC ? COMMENT
FILE name	Connects to named database	FILE NTIS
FILES ?	Lists available databases	
FIND term (FD)	Enter search statement	FD OIL AND ENERGY
FINISHED	To indicate end of STORE or SAVE search statements	
HELP	To obtain assistance	
HISTORY (HIST, HIS, DIAGRAM, DIAG)	Displays previous searches	HISTORY 6–10
KEEP (RESTACK, RSTK)	Save one or more searches temporarily	KEEP 5, 10, 21
NEIGHBOR term (NBR)	Displays adjacent terms in the index	NBR WHITE NBR WHITE (AU)
NEWS	Prints latest news	
ORDER document service name	Enter order for full text copies	ORDER ERIC
PRINT instructions (PRT)	Prints result of the search as indicated	PRT 4 TI, AU
RECALL name	Ask for given SAVEd or STOREd search to be run	RECALL FREDA
RENAME name TO name (RNM)	Change the name of a command, operator, etc.	RENAME FILE TO BASE
RESTART (RST)	Erases searches and restarts	
SAVE name	Saves previous search statements until the end of the day	SAVE FREDA
SAVE OLD name	As SAVE, but only for statements for which postings have been received	SAVE FREDA1
SDISEARCH	Enter a STOREd search profile for SDI on specified databases	
SENSEARCH (SENS)	To search specified fields of a retrieved set for a specific string occurring within a sentence	SENS/TI:COW:MOON:
SHOWSDI	List all SDI profiles	
SHOWSEARCH	List all SAVEd and STOREd searches	
STOP	End session	
STORE name	As SAVE, but stored until DELETEd	STORE FREDA
STOREOLD name	As SAVEOLD, but stored until DELETEd	STOREOLD FREDA1
STRINGSEARCH (STRS)	To search for a specific string in a retrieved set	
SUBHEADINGS (SUBS)	Enter one or more sub-headings	SUBS AU
SYNONYM (SYN)	To create a second name or abbreviation for system keywords	SYN BASE FOR FILE

TERMINAL (TERM)	To store information for USERID to be applied at login	TERM STORAD
TIME (TIME INTERVAL, TIME I, TIME RESET, TIME R)	To obtain various timing information	

Note: Search statements can be entered directly — i.e. without being preceded by a command. For example, COMPUTER AND LIBRARY

Appendix 7

Euronet

The information in this appendix has been reproduced by the kind permission of the Euronet Launch Team of the Commission of the European Communities.

Euronet-DIANE: the new on-line service
> A new European service is now starting operations to offer a wide variety of computerised information files on-line to researchers, engineers, scientists and managers. This service brings together new and existing information services as partners on the same network:

1. The partners

— *some 23 hosts in the European Community offering on-line socio-economic, Scientific and Technical Information (STI) interactive retrieval services. Together they form DIANE, Direct Information Access Network for Europe;*
— *the Community's telecommunications authorities (PTTs), operating the Euronet international data transmission network, which links all the Nine countries together;*
— *the Commission of the European Communities, sponsoring the project and common services for the on-line user.*

2. Which hosts?

The up-to-date list of the hosts which are or will be service suppliers on DIANE, and of the data-bases they will offer, is available on a separate fact sheet. Most of these hosts are already operating on-line services through existing telecommunications facilities. A growing number are now linking to Euronet or preparing a connection.

3. The network

The Euronet network has entry points in all the Community countries. Using the latest packet-switching technologies, it offers fast, reliable and low-cost data transmission. Tariffs for the network are based only on volume and time, and do not depend on distance; they are appreciably lower than existing international tariffs in Europe.

4. The users

On-line STI users will benefit from the modern telecommunication facility and its tariffs, which ensure low-cost and equal access to any DIANE host from anywhere in the Community.

They will also benefit from the common services developed under sponsorship by the Commission:
— *Common Command Language on DIRS 3 (DIMDI, ECHO, FIZ-TECHNIK, INKA) and on IRS software. It is under implementation on MISTRAL, STAIRS, UNIVAC, and is planned for GOLEM software;*
— *toll-free automated enquiry service available on-line via Euronet (Network Adress 0234307813);*
— *multi-lingual aids;*
— *central user forum;*
— *multi-lingual Euronet DIANE Launch team for user assistance.*

Finally, users will benefit from the impetus given — already being implemented — to the development and improvement of on-line STI services in Europe, for the European user.

Information reproduced in these fact sheets is as announced by the host services, who are responsible for the operation of their services. The CEC disclaimes liability for any mistakes or omissions.

Hosts

All the hosts named below will offer their services as part of the DIANE facility. Hosts which are already operational can of course be accessed now, through existing facilities (indicated by "now" in the column headed Availability). Please check with them the date of their Euronet connection. The list of data bases shows as "operational" those which can be accessed on line now, and as "planned" those which will be mounted by the host in due course.

Hosts	Availability	Data bases to be offered on line
ARDIC-CIDA, Paris	Now	**Operational:** Pluridata
BLAISE, London	Now	**Operational:** CANCERLINE (CANCERLIT, CANCERPROJ, CLINPROT); CHEMLINE; LC MARC (Current / Retrospective); UK MARC (Current / Retrospective); MEDLINE (and BACKFILES); MeSH; RTECS; SDILINE; TOXLINE & TOXBACK
		Planned: BEI; CONFERENCE PROCEEDINGS INDEX; ISDS; RBUPC
CATED, Paris	Now	**Operational:** ARIANE
CED, Rome	To be announced	**Operational (in house):** Legal data bases. ALBO; BID; CEE; CIVILE; CONSTA; CORTEC; COSTIT; DOTTR; LEXR; LEXS; MERITO; PENALE; REBI; REBIS; RIV; TITLEX; TIT 1; TIT 2; TRIBUT
CERVED, Padua	Now	**Operational:** IBIS; ITIS; SANI; SANP; SAOE; SDOI; SIBB; SIBV
		Planned: SDON
CILEA, Milan	To be announced	**Planned:** ALICE; GEODIM
CISI, Paris	Now	**Operational:** CISI-BIR; CISI-BRUIT; CISI-ELECNUC; CISI-MEDIAM; CISI-MEDIAP; CISI-PI; CISI-TRANSINOVE
		Planned: CISI-AFO; CISI-OFCE; CISI-SCE
CTI, Brussels	Now	**Operational:** EPIC, INIS
Datacentralen, Copenhagen	To be announced	**Planned:** AGREP; CAS NAMES; CASEARCH; COMPENDEX; ENDOC; ENEX; ENREP; ENVIROLINE; POLLUTION
DIMDI, Cologne	Now	**Operational:** BIOSIS PREVIEWS; CANCERLIT; CANCERPROJ; EMBASE/EXCERPTA MEDICA; FSTA; MEDLARS (incl. MEDLINE, SDILINE, BACKFILES, FILE 64/65); MeSH (incl. German translation); PA; SCI SEARCH; SOCIAL SCISEARCH
		Planned: ARZ-DB; CAB ABSTRACTS/ANIMALS; CHEMLINE; CLINPROT; HEALTH; IDIS FILES/SOCIAL MEDICINE; IPA; LIT-KRAN; NAR; SUSIS; TOXLINE & TOXBACK

EurOnet
DIANE

ECHO Service, Luxembourg	To be announced	**Planned:** AGREP; EABS; ENDOC; ENREP; EURODICAUTOM; EUROFILE; Referral and Enquiry Services
ERGODATA, Paris	To be announced	**Planned:** ERGODATA
European Patents office, The Hague	To be announced	**Operational (in house):** PATENT REGISTER
FIZ-Technik, Frankfurt	Now	**Operational:** DKI; DOMA; DRE; DZF; ZDE **Planned:** DKF
GID, Frankfurt	Now	**Operational:** BIBLIO-DATA; BUL-L; DKI; FSTA; PSYCHOLOGICAL ABSTRACTS; SDIM **Planned:** NAR
INFOLINE, London	Now	**Operational:** WPI **Planned:** BIOSIS; CA REGISTRY NAME FILE; CASEARCH; COMPENDEX; INSPEC; NPL-SGTE; RINGDOC; WORLD PATENTS LATEST (WPI)
INKA, Karlsruhe	Now	**Operational:** BAUFO; COMPENDEX; EDB; INKA-CONF; INKA-DATACOMP; INKA-NUCLEAR; INPADOC-IFS & IPG; INSPEC; NTIS; ORLIS; RSWB; SDIMi
		Planned: ENSDF; INKA-ASTRO; INKA-CORP; INKA-HEP; INKA-MATH; INKA-MATHDI; INKA—PHYS; INKA—PLASMA; INKA—SPACE; INKA—SURVAC; SDIMii
Institut Textile de France, Paris	Now	**Operational:** TITUS
IRS, Frascati	Now	**Operational:** ALUMINUM; BIOSIS; CAB; CHEMABS (CASEARCH); COMPENDEX; ELECOMPS; ELSPECS; ENERGYLINE; ENVIROLINE; EUROFILE (EUSIDIC); FRANCE ACTUALITE; INSPEC; INSPEC INFORMATION; ISMEC; LEDA; METADEX; NASA; NTIS; OCEANIC; PASCAL; POLLUTION; SPACECOMPS
		Planned: AB/INFORM; AQUALINE; CONFERENCE PAPERS INDEX; FSTA; PHARMACEUTICAL NEWS INDEX; RAPRA; SATELDATA
JRC, Ispra	Planned	**Planned:** ECDIN; EUROCOPI
SPIDEL, Paris	Now	**Operational:** AFEE; BIIPAM; CETIM; CIS-BIT; DAFSA; EDF-DOC; KOMPASS; MERLIN-GERIN I (Economy); MERLIN GERIN II (Electricity); PASCAL (Metallurgy, Mechanical Engineering); SGB **Planned:** AGREP; AGRIS; ENDOC; ENREP

EurOnet DIANE

Télésystèmes-Questel, Paris	Now	**Operational:** BIPA; CANCERNET; CBAC; EDF
		Planned: CASEARCH; FRANCIS; GEODE; IALINE; INPI-Brevets; NORIANE; PASCAL; RESEDA; TELEDOC; TITUS; URBAMET
Thermodata, Grenoble	Now	**Operational:** THERMODATA

Detailed information on present access facilities, or planned availability through Euronet DIANE, and on the data bases offered, should be obtained directly from the host organisations. For general information about the project, write to: Euronet DIANE Information, Commission of the European Communities, Directorate General 13, Luxembourg BP 1907.

DATA BASES

The list below gives a brief description of the data bases available now, or in the future, from DIANE HOSTS; more detailed information should be obtained from the hosts themselves (separate fact sheets list the hosts with their data bases, and their addresses).

AB/INFORM	Business management and administration
AFEE	Water pollution and related subjects
AGREP	Permanent Inventory of Agricultural Research Projects in the Community
AGRIS	Agricultural science and technology
ALBO	Register of Italian barristers and solicitors
ALICE	Catalogue of books in the Italian language — all subjects
ALUMINUM	World Aluminium Abstracts
AQUALINE	All aspects of water research and engineering
ARIANE	Building and construction engineering data bank
ARZ-DB	Drugs and active ingredients data bank
BAUFO	Building research projects
BEI	British Education Index — British educational journals
BIBLIO-DATA	Books and serials published in the Federal Republic of Germany
BID	Bibliography on data processing and law
BIIPAM	Engineering and related subjects
BIOSIS PREVIEWS	All aspects of bio-sciences in particular Biology
BIPA	Banque d'Information Politique et d'Actualité: French political chronicle, speeches, press-cuttings
BUL-L	Documentation on linguistics (German)
CAB	Commonwealth Agricultural Bureaux: agricultural sciences and related subjects
CAB ABSTRACTS/ ANIMALS	Animal and veterinary sciences and nutrition
CANCERLINE	Consists of CANCERLIT, CANCERPROJ and CLINPROT
CANCERLIT	Cancer Literature abstracts
CANCERNET	International documentation on cancer & oncology
CANCERPROJ	Cancer Projects: selected current projects in progress
CA REGISTRY NAME FILE	Comprehensive file of chemical compounds
CASEARCH	Pure and applied chemistry including thesaurus

CAS NAMES	Chemical compound names
CBAC	Chemical Biological Activities
CEE	Case-law of the European Communities' Court of Justice
CETIM	Centre Technique des Industries Mécaniques: mechanical engineering
CHEMABS	As CASEARCH
CHEMLINE	Dictionary of chemical substances with CAS Registry numbers on TOXLINE
CIS-BIT	Centre International d'Informations de Sécurité et d'Hygiène du Travail: work safety and health
CISI-AFO	Financial and stock exchange data of French quoted companies
CISI-BIR	Information on environmental research
CISI-BRUIT	Acoustic characteristics of building material
CISI-ELECNUC	Characteristics of nuclear power stations world-wide
CISI-MEDIAM	Readership data on French medical media
CISI-MEDIAP	Readership data on French publicity media
CISI-OFCE	French companies and external trade
CISI-PI	OECD main economic indicators
CISI-SCE	OECD external trade statistics
CISI-TRANSINOVE	Transferable technology
CIVILE	Case-law of the civil section of the Rome Supreme Court of Appeal
CLINPROT	Clinical Protocols: investigations of anti-cancer agents
COMPENDEX	Computerised Engineering Index: all branches of engineering
CONFERENCE PROCEEDINGS INDEX	Conference proceedings received by British Library
CONFERENCE PAPERS INDEX	Scientific and technical papers presented at conferences etc.
CONSTA	Case-law of Italian State Council
CORTEC	Case-law of Italian Audit Office
COSTIT	Case-law of Italian Constitutional Court
DAFSA	Company ownership
DKF	Documentation on transportation vehicles and automobiles
DKI	Plastics, rubber, fibres
DOMA	Mechanical and production engineering
DOTTR	Summaries of legal doctrine from the legal documentation institute of the CNR, Florence
DRE	Information on electro-technology

DZF	Optical, photographic, biomedical, precision engineering
EABS	Euroabstracts: study reports and publication of results of research financed by the CEC, the European Coal and Steel Community, and Euratom
ECDIN	Data bank on pollution-causing chemical substances
EDB	Energy Information Data Base
EDF-DOC	Electricité de France: electrical engineering
ELECOMPS	Electronic Components — factual data
ELSPECS	Electronic component specification and approvals
ENDOC	Environmental centres in Community
ENERGYLINE	Energy and energy-related subjects
ENEX	Register of experts on environment
ENREP	Current environment research projects in Community
ENSDF	Evaluated Nuclear Structures Data File, including decay data for all isotopes
ENVIROLINE	Environment-related issues
EPIC	Programmes for calculation of physical properties of chemical compounds
ERGODATA	Biometric data bank
EUROCOPI	Data bank on data processing programmes in physics, chemistry, engineering etc.
EURODICAUTOM	Multilingual terminology data bank
EUROFILE	Inventory of data bases and banks available in Europe
EXCERPTA MEDICA/ EM BASE	Bio-medical sciences literature
FRANCE ACTUALITE	Articles from the French Press
FRANCIS	Current information in social and human sciences
FSTA	Food Science and Technology Abstracts
GEODE	International bibliography on earth sciences
GEODIM	Geophysical bibliography on the Alps
HEALTH	Health planning and administration
IALINE	Industrial processing of agricultural products
IBIS	Data on production and distribution companies in 130 countries
IDIS FILES/ SOCIAL MEDICINE	Social and industrial medicine and public health
INIS	International Nuclear Information System
INKA-ASTRO	Astronomy and astrophysics
INKA-CONF	Conference announcements in energy, nuclear science, aeronautics, astronautics, space research, physics, mathematics and astronomy

INKA-CORP	Corporations and affiliations in same fields as above
INKA-DATACOMP	·Data compilations in energy and physics
INKA-HEP	High-energy physics data base
INKA-MATH	Mathematics and related subjects data base
INKA-MATHDI	Mathematical didactics data base
INKA-NUCLEAR	Nuclear science data base
INKA-PHYS	Physics and related fields data base
INKA-PLASMA	Plasma physics and technology data base
INKA-SPACE	Conference papers on aeronautics, astronautics and space research
INKA-SURVAC	Surface and vacuum physics data base
INPADOC-IFS	Patents: INPADOC Family File data base
INPADOC-IPG	Patents: INPADOC Patent Gazette
INPI	Patents: register of INPI (F)
INSPEC	Physics, electronics, computing, mathematics
INSPEC INFORMATION	A subset of INSPEC for training purposes
IPA	International Pharmaceuticals Abstracts
ISDS	International Serials Data Service
ISMEC	Information Service in Mechanical Engineering
ITIS	Business data for 90 countries
KOMPASS	Commercial information about 55000 french companies
LEDA	Earthnet satellite imagery
LEXR	Italian legislation: regional
LEXS	Italian legislation: national
LC MARC	Books and serials catalogued by US Library of Congress
LIT-KRAN	Hospital management, organisation and economics
MEDLARS	All fields of medical literature
MEDLINE	(MEDLARS on-line) As MEDLARS
MERLIN-GERIN I	Business and management
MERLIN-GERIN II	Electronics and electricity
MeSH	Medical Subject Headings: controlled vocabulary for MEDLINE or MEDLARS
MERITO	Case-law of Italian tribunals
METADEX	Metallurgy and related areas of science and technology
NAR	Nutrition Abstracts and Review
NASA	All aspects of aerospace and related fields

NORIANE	Documentation on standards
NPL-SGTE	Thermodynamics
NTIS	US Government-sponsored research, development and engineering reports
OCEANIC	All aspects of ocean studies
ORLIS	Documentation or urban and regional planning
PA	Psychological Abstracts: behavioural issues concerning humans and animals
PASCAL	General coverage of science and technology
PATENT REGISTER	European published patent applications and patents
PENALE	Case-law of criminal section of the Rome Supreme Court of Appeal
PHARMACEUTICAL NEWS INDEX	Important new developments in pharmaceutical, cosmetic and medical fields
PLURIDATA	Chemical data bank
POLLUTION	Pollution and related subjects and issues
RAPRA	Technical, commercial and research aspects of rubber and plastics
RBUPC	Register of Research in British Universities, Polytechnics and Colleges: projects in physical, biological and social sciences
REBI	Bibliographic file on Italy of the Rome Supreme Court of Appeal
REBIS	Bibliographic file on other countries of the Rome Supreme Court of Appeal
RESEDA	Agricultural economics
RINGDOC	Chemical, medical & pharmaceutical information
RIV	Abstracts from law periodicals by the Rome Supreme Court of Appeal
RSWB	Townplanning
RTECS	Registry of Toxic Effects of Chemical Substances
SANI	Register of Italian industrial, commercial and other companies
SANP	National defaulters file in Italy
SAOE	Information on Italian export/import companies
SATELDATA	Satellite technology; Performance and launchdata
SCISEARCH	All natural sciences and techniques
SDILINE	Selective Dissemination of Information on MEDLINE
SDIM	Documentation on metallurgy and metals
SDOI	Italian foreign supply and demand file
SDON	Italian supply and demand file
SGB	Finance and economics

SIBB	Official acts on joint-stock companies in Italy
SIBV	Italian financial market and stock exchange
SOCIAL SCISEARCH	Social and behavioural sciences
SPACECOMPS	Electronic components for spacecraft
SUSIS	Sports and Sport Sciences
TELEDOC	Information on telecommunications, electronics etc.
THERMODATA	Thermodynamic values of elements, components and alloys in minerals
TITLEX	Titles of Italian decrees in force from 1860 to today
TIT 1	Other Italian decrees, 1860-1939
TIT2	Other Italian decrees, 1939 to today
TITUS	Documentation on textiles
TOXBACK	Back files of TOXLINE
TOXLINE	Documentation on toxicology and related subjects
TRIBUT	Case-law of the Italian Central Commission on taxes
UK MARC	Monograph literature Legally Deposited in the UK
URBAMET	Town planning
WORLD PATENT LATEST	Current information from WPI
WPI	World Patents Index: Patents in all fields
ZDE	Electro technical engineering, data processing, control engineering

HOST ADDRESSES
December 1979

HOST ADDRESSES

The following is a list of the names and addresses of the hosts who will offer their services through Euronet DIANE.

ARDIC-CIDA **ARDIC-CIDA** 25 rue Jussieu, 75005 PARIS Telephone +33 1 6332370

BLAISE **BLAISE MARKETING** 7 Rathbone Street, LONDON W1P 2AL UK Telephone +44 1 6361544

CATED **ITBTP** 9 rue La Pérouse, 75784 PARIS Cedex 16 France Telephone +33 1 7208800

CED **Centro Elettronico** di Documentazione Giuridica Palazzo di Giustizia, Via Ulpiano 8, 00193 ROMA Italy Telephone +39 6 6568851

CERVED **CERVED Spa** Corso Stati Uniti 14, 35100 PADOVA Italy Telephone +39 49 760733

CILEA **CILEA** Via R. Sanzio 4, 20090 SEGRATE/MILANO Italy Telephone 39 2 2132541

CISI **Compagnie Internationale de Services en Informatique** 35 Boulevard Brune, 75680 PARIS cedex 14'France Telephone +33 1 5392510

CTI **Ministère des Affaires Economiques** Centre de Traitement de l'Information Rue J.A. de Mot 30, 1040 BRUXELLES Belgium Telephone +32 2 2336737

Data-centralen **I/S Datacentralen** Retortvej 6-8, 2500 VALBY Denmark Telephone +45 1 468122

DIMDI **DIMDI** Weisshausstrasse 27, Postfach 420580, D-5000 KÖLN 41 Federal Republic of Germany Telephone +49 221 442081

ECHO **European Commission Host Organisation** Commission of the European Communities, DG XIII, Bâtiment Jean Monnet, BP 1907, LUXEMBOURG Telephone +352 43011

EPO **European Patents Office** DG I, BP 5818 Patentlaan 2, 2280 HV RIJSWIJK (ZH) Netherlands Telephone +31 70 906789

ERGODATA **Laboratoire de biométrie humaine** Ecole de médecine, 45 rue des Saint-Peres 75270 Paris 6eme France Telephone +33 1 2603720 ext. 4265

FIZ-Technik **Fachinformationszentrum Technik e.v.** Postfach 700430, D-6000 FRANKFURT aM Federal Republic of Germany Telephone +49 611 8306300 or 8306304

GID **GID** Herriotstrasse 5, Sektion für Technik, Postfach 710370, D-6000 FRANKFURT aM Federal Republic of Germany Telephone +49 611 66871

INFOLINE **INFOLINE** Brettenham House, Lancaster Place, LONDON WC2E 7EN UK Telephone +44 1 8361876

INKA **Fachinformationszentrum Energie, Physik, Mathematik** 7514 EGGENSTEIN-LEOPOLDSHAFEN 2, Federal Republic of Germany Telephone +49 7247 824507

EURONET: The Packet Switching Data Transmission Network for the European Community

Packets. *In a packet switching network, information is carried in the form of packets. Packets Assemblers-Disassemblers (PAD) are located in each packet switching exchange to enable communication by "TTY compatible" terminals.*

Packet switching. *In the Euronet network, there will be four packet-switching exchanges (or PSE); their functions are:*
— *to send packets towards their destination by the most effective route available at the time (the switching operation);*
— *to monitor the packets en route, so as to ensure correct transmission.*

Advantages for Euronet. *The main advantages of packet-switching are:*
— *more efficient use of available lines, since packets for different addresses can be interleaved;*
— *a wide range of terminals compatible with the network;*
— *high quality of service, through automatic correction of transmission errors, and alternative routes through the network;*
— *low, flat-rate (independent of distance) tariffs.*

EURONET AT OPENING DATE

EurOnet

DIANE

IRS	**Information Retrieval Service** ESRIN, Via Galileo Galilei, 00044 FRASCATI Italy Telephone +39 6 9422401
ITF	**Institut Textile de France** 35 rue des Abondances, 92110 BOULOGNE-SUR-SEINE France Telephone +33 1 8251890
JRC	**Joint Research Centre of the CEC**, Ispra Establishment, 21020 ISPRA (Varese), Italy. Telephone +39 332 780131
SPIDEL	**Société Pour l'Informatique** 98 Boulevard Victor Hugo, 92115 CLICHY France Telephone +33 1 731 11 91
Télésystèmes-Questel	**Télésystèmes** 40 rue du Cherche Midi, 75006 PARIS France Telephone +33 1 5443813
Thermodata	**Thermodata B.U.S.** Domaine Universitaire, BP No. 22, 38402 SAINT MARTIN D'HERES France Telephone +33 76 427690

THE COMMON COMMAND LANGUAGE

Many of the on-line information retrieval systems, available through the DIANE facility, use different sets of commands. The potential user is therefore faced with the possibility of having to learn several search languages.

A study carried out for the Commission of the European Communities has devised a COMMON COMMAND LANGUAGE which allows users to search on different retrieval systems using one language.

This set has been accepted as a formal guideline for use by DIANE hosts; it is already under implementation on DIMDI, ECHO, FIZ-TECHNIK, INKA, IRS and will be offered as an option. Many other DIANE hosts will offer it in the next future.

The advantages of being able to search a number of systems with the same commands are:

— *All systems can be searched with equal ease*
— *New systems joining DIANE are more immediately accessible*
— *Users experienced in one or two systems can more easily search for information in related disciplines, on other hosts*
— *Users do not have to learn a new language every time they wish to search new systems*
— *The use of standard commands does not interfere with the provision of specialised search facilities on any system.*

The Standard Command Language is not meant to replace existing sophisticated search languages, but as an alternative to help users who want, and need, to search on a number of different systems.

The Common Command Language has its own syntax and offers the following main commands.

Command	Function
BASE	to identify the data base to be searched
STOP	to end a session or part of it
FIND	to enter a search statement
DISPLAY	to display a list of search terms
SAVE	to save search statement for later use
SHOW	to display or type records on-line
PRINT	to print records remotely
DEFINE	to override default parameters
DELETE	to delete statements or requests
MORE	to display more data
BACK	to display previous information
HELP	to obtain guidance on-line
NEWS	to obtain latest information on system
INFO	to give general information on aspects of service (with specific sub-commands)
OWN	to allow use of original commands

It makes provision for various search options which are not always implemented on all systems.

TERMINALS

Euronet has been designed to accommodate as wide a variety of terminals as possible. Virtually all teletype-compatible terminals are usable for dial-up access; a wider range of terminals can be connected by leased line.

Types

— *Terminals working in asynchronous mode. These are basically the simple varieties of printer or VDU terminal. As long as they conform to the ESP 20 protocol (or CCITT X 28 recommendation) they can be operated with Euronet; most existing terminals on the market belong to this group (often described as "teletype-compatible").*

— *Terminals working in synchronous mode. These are broadly known as "intelligent" terminals. As long as they conform to the CCITT X 25 recommendation, they can be connected to Euronet.*

Speeds and connection possibilities

Asynchronous terminals can be connected either by dialing through the national public telephone network, or by a leased line connection.

Speeds catered for are:

dial-up	110 to 300 bits/s
	1200/75 bits/s and in some countries 1200 bits/s full duplex
leased line	up to 1200 bits/s

synchronous terminals must be connected by leased line. Speeds between 2,400 and 9,600 bits/s are possible.

For more information, please consult the Euronet representative of your national telecommunications administration, or your equipment manufacturer.

Author and Subject Index

Academic institutions, training in, 110
Accession number, 46
Acoustic coupler, 22, 26
Adjacency/positional/proximity/relational operator, 67
Advantages of online searching, 3, 72, 101
AFDAC, 111
Aids in teaching, 23, 115
American Library Association, 111
American Society for Information Science, 111
Analysis of search topic, 80 (*see also* Appendix 1)
Appendix 1, 123
Appendix 2, 128
Appendix 3, 138
Appendix 4, 145
Appendix 5, 152
Appendix 6, 173
Appendix 7, 188
ARIANE, 22
ASIDIC, 111
Association Française de Documentation Automatique en Chemie, 111
Atherton, P., 4, 108
Ausinet, 9
Author dictionary, 62
Author searching, 62, 87

BASIS, 8, 9
Batch search service, 2
Battelle Automated Search Information System, 8, 9
Baud rate, 25
Belgium, 111
Bias in databases, 81
Bibliographic Retrieval Service, 2, 8, 9
Biosis, 80, 87, 110
Biosystematic codes, 83

Blaise, 2, 8, 9, 22, 36, 117 (*see also* Appendix 2)
Blaise Newsletter, 42
BNIST, 111
Boolean/logic operators, 32, 65, 66, 81
Bourne, C.P., 120
British Computer Society, 111
British Library, 8
British Library Automated Information Service, 2, 8, 9, 22, 36, 117 (*see also* Appendix 2)
British Library Research and Development Department, 110
Broadening searches, 90 (*see also* Appendix 1)
BRS, 2, 8, 9
Bunch, S.R., 26
Buntrock, R.E., 94

CAB input form 47−51
CA Registry number, 93
Canadian Association for Information Science, 111
Canadian Online Enquiry, 8
Can/Ole, 8
Careers, effect on, of online searching 103, 107
Carriage return key, 29
Caruso, E., 120
Cassette recorder, 23, 24, 114, 115
Chaining/stacking/stringing search terms and commands, 35, 90
Changing files/databases, 39
Charging for a search service, 106
Check list for searching, 75 (*see also* Appendix 1)
Check tags, 84
Chemical dictionary file, 93

Chemical nomenclature, 92
Chemical Society, 8
Chemline, 93
Chemname, 93
Choice of files/databases, 79 (*see also* Appendix 1)
Choice of systems, 80 (*see also* Appendix 1)
Chronolog, 42
Circuits busy, 30
Citation searching, 78, 88
Citroen, C.L., 94
Classification codes, 42, 83, 84
Codes, in searching, 62, 83
Collinge, B., 19
Combining search terms, 31, 65, 80, 82
Command language, specific training in, 113
Command/search language, 28, 57
Common command language, 28, 71, 100 (*see also* Appendix 7)
Commonwealth Agricultural Bureaux (CAB), 110
    sample record, 44
    sample record input to database, 48–51
Comparison, of online with manual searching, 3
Comparison of searchers, 96
Competition, 10
Compound terms/phrases, 54, 65, 69, 86, 87
Computer-assisted instruction, 117
Concepts in the search query, 80
Connection to system, 29
Contracts, 104
Controlled terms, 83
Cooper, M.D., 108
Cost, 12, 18, 96, 104
Courses, 41, 103
    design, 112
Cross file/multifile/searching, 71, 91
CRT (cathode ray tube) terminals, 23
Cuadra, C.A., 4, 19
Current awareness, 40, 70

Daisy-wheel printer, 25
Daniels, L., 94
Databanks, 10, 11
Database, 42
Database(s)
    availability on various systems, (*see* Appendices 2–7)
    document – specific, 12
    guides to, 104 (*see also* Appendices 2–7)
    multidisciplinary, 12
    number of, 9, 11
    points to watch, 18
    producers of, training by, 110
    size of, 12
    specific, training in, 113
    structure of, 43
    subjects covered, 11 (*see also* Appendices 2–7)
Date ranging, 88
Default field, 64, 86

Default file, 31
Default option, 61
Deleting sets/search statements, 39
Demonstration searches, 114
Department of Industry, 8
Derwent Publications Limited, 8
Deutsches Institut für Medizinische Dokumentation und Information, 2, 22
Dewey, 83
Dialog, 7, 9, 28, 32, 117 (*see also* Appendix 5)
Dialtech, 138
Dialtech Newsletter, 42
Dictionary, 47, 53, 56, 58
    mixed, 52, 61
    term selection from, 60, 84, 88
Dictionary file, 46
DIMDI, 2, 22
Directly searchable term, 46
Disadvantages of online searching, 4
Document descriptions, 13
Document ordering, 41
Document record, 43
    examples of, 13, 14, 15, 16, 44, 82
Document-specific databases, 11
Dolan, D.R., 100
Dougherty, R.M., 108
Dunning, A.J., 26
Duplex, 25, 29

Edit commands, 70
Editor, 8
Education and training, 109–120
Eisenberg, L.J., 120
Elhill, 8, 9, 28, 36
Elias, A., 108
Embedded strings, 68
Engineering Index Inc., 110
Error correction, 36
Esanet, 22
ESA-IRS, 2, 7, 9, 22, 85 (*see also* Appendix 3)
Euronet, 2, 9, 22, 72, 100, 111 (*see also* Appendix 7)
Euronet Diane News, 42
European Space Agency, 2, 7, 9, 22, 85 (*see also* Appendix 3)
EUSIDIC, 111
Eusidic Database Guide, 10
Expand command, 33
Explain command, 36
Explosion facility, 83

Ferguson, D.G., 108
Field, 43, 53
Field descriptor/field identifier, 45, 56, 61, 63
Field integrity, 53
Field searching, 61

File structure, 45
File/database changing, 39
Films, training, 118
Fixed-print formats, 17
Floppy disc, 24
Fluency of searching, 96
Foreign languages, training aids in, 111
Format of queries, 62
Format of terms, 83
Formats of document records, 17
FOSSILS, 117
France, 111
Frequency lists, 42
Friendliness of systems, 6
Full duplex, 25
Full text inversion, 53

Generic searching, 86
Go list, 55
Growth of online searching, 2, 6
Guide to databanks, 10, 11
Guide to databases, 10, 11

Half duplex, 25
Hall, J.L., 4, 19, 94
Hardware, 20
Harley, A.J., 19
Harter, S.P., 120
Hawkins, D.T., 4, 94
Help command, 36
Henry, M., 74
Hierarchical terms, 38, 84
Highly posted terms, 88
High-speed transmission, 23
History/log of search, 39, 71
Hits/postings, 47, 57
Holmes, P.L., 100
Hoover, R.E., 19
Host down, 30
Host operators, 7 (*see also* Appendices 2–7)
Houghton, B., 4
Hyphens, 87

Impact printer, 24
Implicit concepts, 81
Index Medicus, 2, 7
Index term file, 46
Index terms, 83
Indexing rules, 87
Infoline, 8, 9 (*see also* Appendix 4)
Information Bank, 8
INSPEC, 8, 82, 83, 89
Institute of Electrical Engineers, 8, 110
Institute of Information Scientists, 111
Institute of Scientific Information, 32, 78,
    88, 110
Intact field, 62
Intelligent terminal, 24, 117
Inter-library loans, effect on, of online
    searching, 107
Intermediary, 72, 75, 123

Intermediary (*cont.*)
    intellectual tasks, 98
    management tasks, 98
    qualities required, 99
    role of, 95
Internal truncation, 59
International organisations, training by, 111
International Packet Switching Service, 21,
    29
International textile information database,
    9
Inversion, 55
Inverted file, 46, 53, 59, 67, 87
IPSS, 21, 29
ISI, 32, 78, 88, 110

Johnson, S.M., 4
Journals, 42

Keenan, S.K., 108
Kent, A., 4, 119
Key term file, 46
Keyboard training, 113

Lancaster, F.W., 4, 27, 56
Leased line, 23
Library Association, 111
Library schools, 110
Limit command, 88
Limiting searches, 69
Lipow, A.G., 108
Local Cataloguing Service, 8
Locas, 8
Lockheed, 2, 7, 9 (*see also* Appendix 5)
Log/history of search, 39, 71
Logging on, 29
Logic/Boolean operators, 32, 65, 66, 81
Lynch, M.F., 56

MacCafferty, M., 119
McCarn, D.B., 5, 19
Maina, W.E., 120
Maintenance of equipment, 25
Major term, 54, 55, 64, 85
Management role, 101
Manuals, 42, 78, 103 (*see also* Appendix 1)
Mapping databases, 100
Marc, 8
Marc search fields on Blaise, 63
Markey, K., 120
Masking, 59
Matched phrases, 55
Mediatron, 115
Medical Literature Analysis and Retrieval
    System, 7, 83
MEDLARS, 7, 83
Medlars Technical Bulletin, 42
MEDLARS thesaurus, 83–84
Medlearn, 117
Medline, 38, 42, 80, 84, 117
Mellordata, 115

Mesh headings, 55, 83
Message sending, 38
Microcomputer systems, 117
Microfiche search aids, 42
Mixed dictionary, 52, 61
Modem, 26
Modern Language Association, search fields on Lockheed, 63
Moghdam, D., 120
Moureau, M.L., 108
Multidisciplinary databases, 12
Multifile searching, 71

Narrowing searches, 69, 82, 90 (*see also* Appendix 1)
NASIC, 41
National Library of Medicine, 2, 7, 9
National organisations, training by, 111
Natural language, 86
Netherlands, 111
Network, 2, 21
New York Times, 8, 9
News command, 38
Newsletters, 42, 78
NLM, 2, 7, 9
Node 21
Noise from terminals, 25
Nomenclature, chemical, 92
North East Academic Science Information Centre, USA, 41
Norway, 111
NOT logic, 66
Numeric fields, 69
Nutt, J., 120

Occurrence value, 56
Offline printing, 21, 23, 35, 92
Off-peak periods, 90
Online, 42, 78
Online Information Centre, 104, 111
Online printing, 34, 92
Online Review, 42, 78
Ontap, 117
Oppenheim, C., 94
ORBIT, 7, 9, 28, 31, 117 (*see also* Appendix 6)
Oulton, A.J., 108
Overnight search, 8

Packet switching, 21
Padin, M.E., 94
Parentheses, 66
Parity, 25, 29
Parking, 31
Passwords, 29, 30
Phrase searching, 54, 65, 69, 86, 87
Portable terminal, 24
Ports busy, 30
Positional/proximity/relational/adjacency operator, 67
Post, Telephone and Telegraph, 21

Postings/hits, 47, 57
Pratt, G., 120
Preco-ordination, 84, 86
Predicasts Product Codes, 83
Predicasts thesaurus, 84
Pricing strategy, 8
Print, speed of, 18
Print formats, 17, 92 (*see also* Appendix 1)
Print terminals, 23
Printed indexes, 7
Printers, 24
    daisy-wheel, 25
Printing results, 34, 92 (*see also* Appendix 1)
Product names, chemical, 92
Professional societies, training by, 111
Promoting online searching, 101
Proximity/relational/adjacency/positional operator, 67
Proximity searching, 69
PTT, 21
Publicity, 102
Punctuation, 62
Pure dictionary, 52

Quest, 9, 28
Question number/set number/statement number, 57

Radwin, M.S., 27
Ranging, 69
Recon, 7
Recorded searches, 115
Record number, 46
Record structure, 43, 44, 45
Reference interview, 78
Registry number, 93
Related terms, 61
Relational/adjacency/positional/proximity operator, 67
Response time, 90
Retrospective coverage, 9, 12
Royal Institute of Technology, Sweden, 110
Running a search service, 105

Sampling results, 92
Save search/search save/storesearch, 40, 70, 86, 90, 91
Scannet, 22
Scisearch, 32, 38
SDC, 2, 7, 9, 31, 82 (*see also* Appendix 6)
SDC News, 42
SDI, 70
Search aids, 42, 78 (*see also* Appendix 1)
Search codes, 62
Search/command language, 28, 57
Search facilities, 35, 57
Search-fields, examples of, 63
Search history, 39, 71
Search plan, 89
Search preparation, 72, 75 (*see also* Appendix 1)
Search process, 3, 91

Search request, 78
Search save/storesearch/save search, 40, 70, 86, 90, 91
Search statement, formulation, 80
Search strategy, 72, 75 (*see also* Appendix 1)
Search term selection, 31, 82, 88 (*see also* Appendix 1)
Search topic, analysis of, 80 (*see also* Appendix 1)
Security, 70
Selecting from dictionary, 60, 85, 88
Self-instructional packages, 117
Senlowitz, L., 19
Sequential file, 45, 68
Sequential/string searching, 68
Service contract, 25
Set number/statement number/question number, 57
Setting up a service, 104
Short Term Experimental Information Network, 97
Signing on, 29
Size of databases, 12
Size of document record, 13
Somerville, A.N., 94
Sorting, 92
Speed of printing, 18
Speed of terminals, 24
Spelling, variations in, 87
Spelling errors, 60
Stacking/stringing/chaining search terms and commands, 35, 90
Stairs, 8, 9, 28
Statement number/question number/ set number, 57
STEIN, 97
Stem limit, 59
Stems, 87, 88
Stewart, A., 27
Stockey, E., 120
Stop list, 53, 87
Stop word, 53, 67, 89
Storesearch/save search/search save, 40, 70, 86, 90, 91
Strategy in searching, 72 (*see also* Appendix 1)
String/sequential searching, 68
Stringing/chaining/stacking search terms and commands, 35, 90
Structuring of information, 43
Subject coverage, 9
Subject-specific databases, 11
Suitability of online, 79 (*see also* Appendix 1)
Summit, R.K., 19
Suppliers of online search services, 7, 9 (*see also* Appendices 2–7)
Sweden, 110
Synonyms, 87
System Development Corporation, 2, 7, 9, 31, 82 (*see also* Appendix 6)
Systems operators, 7 (*see also* Appendices 2–7)
training by, 112

Tape recorder, 24
Teaching aids, 115
Tedd, L.A., 100, 120
Telecommunications charges, 106
Telecommunications network, 2, 21
Telenet, 2, 21
Telephone, 20, 22
Teletypewriter, 1
Terminal identifier, 29, 30
Terminals, 105
noise, 25
portable, 24
selection of, 23
speed of, 24
Terminology, chemical, 92
Thermal printer, 24
Thesaurus, 38, 42, 55, 61, 78, 83
Time limit, 79
Timesharing, 21
Timing information, 41
TITUS, 9
Tomberg, A., 19, 26
Training, 103, 109
Training films, 118
Tree command, 38
Truncation, 3, 58, 59, 68, 87, 88
Tutorials, 117
Tymnet, 2, 21, 30

UKCIS, 111
UK Online Information Centre, 23, 104, 111
UMIST, 97
Uncontrolled terms, 83, 86
UNISIST, 111
United Kingdom Chemical Information Service, 111
University of California at San Diego, 110
University of London, 115
University of Manchester Institute of Science and Technology, 97
University of Pittsburgh, 117
Update, 69
Update frequency, 19
User friendliness, 6
User groups, 104
training by, 112
User-defined formats, 17

Van Camp, A., 100
Variable formats, 17
VDU (visual display unit) terminals, 23
Vickery, A., 120
Videotape, in training, 114, 115, 118

Wanger, J., 94, 100
Watson, P.G., 5, 120
Weighting of search terms, 85
Williams, M.E., 4, 5, 19, 100, 119
Williams, P.W., 100
Word addressing, 53, 67
Word position, 67

UNIVERSITY OF STRATHCLYDE
Architecture & Building Science
Information Room